Thriving Sustainably on Planet Earth

How do we thrive sustainably on planet Earth? This is an urgent question to which this book provides a range of fresh responses. From diverse disciplinary perspectives, academics provide compelling visions for education that disrupt but also open up and inspire new pedagogic opportunities. Responding to these visions, teachers, teaching assistants and school leaders offer practical reflections, describing the ways they are living out these new ideas in their classrooms and schools. Bridging the gap between theory and practice, the book invites us to consider what education can and ought to look like in a world beset by challenges. Despite the seriousness of the manifestos, there is optimism and purpose in each chapter, as well as a desire to raise the voices of children and young people: our compassionate citizens of the future. This title is also available as Open Access on Cambridge Core.

JAMES BIDDULPH, MBE, is CEO of Avanti Schools Trust. He was the founding headteacher of the University of Cambridge Primary School and is an award-winning teacher, school leader and author with more than two decades of experience working in primary education.

EMILY SHUCKBURGH, CBE, is Director of Cambridge Zero, the University of Cambridge's major climate change initiative, and Professor of Environmental Data Science at the Department of Computer Science and Technology, University of Cambridge. She is co-author with HM King Charles III and Tony Juniper of the *Ladybird Book on Climate Change* (2017).

HARRY PEARSE is Research Director at the Centre for Deliberation (National Centre for Social Research). Formerly a Research Associate at and founding member of the Centre for the Future of Democracy at the University of Cambridge, he has published on democratic theory and seventeenth-century natural philosophy in both academic and media outlets.

EDUCATION VISIONS

Series Editors
James Biddulph (Homerton College, Independent Scholar)
Emily Shuckburgh (University of Cambridge)

Education Visions is a bold and timely series that reimagines the future of education in a world shaped by global crises – from the climate emergency to deepening social inequalities. Co-edited by Dr James Biddulph and Professor Emily Shuckburgh, the series connects visionary academic thinking with practical classroom application, bridging the gap between theory and everyday educational practice. Each volume centres around a pressing theme, such as climate change, sustainability, equity or digital transformation, and presents a collection of 'manifestos for change' by leading international thinkers. These are linked to practitioner chapters, where diverse educators from across primary and secondary settings offer grounded, creative and hopeful responses, transforming abstract theoretical ideas into actionable strategies. Designed to be accessible, dynamic and reflective of diverse voices, Education Visions enables educators to engage with fresh perspectives, challenge assumptions and co-create more sustainable, equitable and inspiring futures for learners.

Thriving Sustainably on Planet Earth

Inspiring Innovation in Children's Education

Edited by

JAMES BIDDULPH
Homerton College, Independent Scholar

EMILY SHUCKBURGH
University of Cambridge

HARRY PEARSE
National Centre for Social Research

Shaftesbury Road, Cambridge CB2 8EA, United Kingdom

One Liberty Plaza, 20th Floor, New York, NY 10006, USA

477 Williamstown Road, Port Melbourne, VIC 3207, Australia

314–321, 3rd Floor, Plot 3, Splendor Forum, Jasola District Centre, New Delhi – 110025, India

103 Penang Road, #05–06/07, Visioncrest Commercial, Singapore 238467

Cambridge University Press is part of Cambridge University Press & Assessment, a department of the University of Cambridge.

We share the University's mission to contribute to society through the pursuit of education, learning and research at the highest international levels of excellence.

www.cambridge.org
Information on this title: www.cambridge.org/9781009309035

DOI: 10.1017/9781009309042

© Cambridge University Press & Assessment 2026

This publication is in copyright. Subject to statutory exception and to the provisions of relevant collective licensing agreements, with the exception of the Creative Commons version the link for which is provided below, no reproduction of any part may take place without the written permission of Cambridge University Press & Assessment.

An online version of this work is published at doi.org/10.1017/9781009309042 under a Creative Commons Open Access license CC-BY-NC 4.0 which permits re-use, distribution and reproduction in any medium for non-commercial purposes providing appropriate credit to the original work is given and any changes made are indicated. To view a copy of this license visit https://creativecommons.org/licenses/by-nc/4.0

When citing this work, please include a reference to the DOI 10.1017/9781009309042

First published 2026

Cover image: Photo by John Sanders, University of Cambridge Primary School

A catalogue record for this publication is available from the British Library

A Cataloging-in-Publication data record for this book is available from the Library of Congress

ISBN 978-1-009-30903-5 Hardback
ISBN 978-1-009-30901-1 Paperback

Cambridge University Press & Assessment has no responsibility for the persistence or accuracy of URLs for external or third-party internet websites referred to in this publication and does not guarantee that any content on such websites is, or will remain, accurate or appropriate.

For EU product safety concerns, contact us at Calle de José Abascal, 56, 1°, 28003 Madrid, Spain, or email eugpsr@cambridge.org

Contents

List of Figures	*page* vii
List of Tables	ix
List of Contributors	x
Foreword ALISON PEACOCK	xiii
Acknowledgment	xvii

	Introduction: Problems and Possibilities JAMES BIDDULPH, HARRY PEARSE AND EMILY SHUCKBURGH	1
1	Manifesto 1: What Role Can Education Play in Addressing the Interlinked Climate and Environmental Crises? AMY MUNRO-FAURE, EMILY SHUCKBURGH AND BHASKAR VIRA	21
2	Practitioners' Response to Manifesto 1: Sustainability Education JENNA WATSON AND ORLANDO GARCIACANO	38
3	Manifesto 2: Weaving a Hopeful Future – Voice, Agency and Practical Wisdom as Threads of Change JULIA FLUTTER	48
4	Practitioner's Response to Manifesto 2: Promoting Children's Voices KIRSTIN MACVICAR	62
5	Manifesto 3: Suffrage and Political Equality – Where Do Children Fit? HARRY PEARSE	73

6	Practitioners' Response to Manifesto 3: Democratic Education ELISE KINNEAR AND ALIABBAS DHANJI	88
7	Manifesto 4: A (Post-Human) Transdisciplinary Manifesto for Future-Making Education PAMELA BURNARD	98
8	Practitioners' Response to Manifesto 4: Adopting a Transdisciplinary Approach LIAM CONNOLLY, AINO UKKONEN AND CONSTANTINOS XENOFONTOS	110
9	Manifesto 5: The Biology of Stress – Implications for Education and Lifelong Health SARAH TEMPLE AND ISABELLE BUTCHER	126
10	Practitioners' Response to Manifesto 5: Implementing an Understanding of the Biology of Stress AIMEE DURNING AND ELENA NATALE	145
11	Manifesto 6: Science and Spirituality – Cultivating Meaning and Purpose in Education AKHANDADHI DAS	160
12	Practitioner's Response to Manifesto 6: Integrating Philosophical Thinking and Practices in Education ANNABEL SHARMAN	175
13	Manifesto 7: A Two-Way Education for Climate Justice BENARD ISIKO, ANNA BARFORD, MOLLEN NYIRANEZA, ANTHONY MUGEERE AND PAUL MAGIMBI	184
14	Practitioner's Response to Manifesto 7: Educating Differently about Sustainability LUKE ROLLS	198
	Afterword: Empowering Education for a Changing World JAMES BIDDULPH, HARRY PEARSE AND EMILY SHUCKBURGH	209
	Index	215

Figures

0.1	Schools play a central role in empowering children and creating opportunities for them in the development and implementation of sustainability policies	page 8
0.2	A framework for thinking about empowering sustainability education	16
1.1	Pani Pahar is a research programme on water and water scarcity in Indian mountain areas	32
1.2	Artwork from children at Fawcett Primary School Cambridge, inspired by the *Ladybird Book on Climate Change*	34
2.1	Our ecological areas on the Early Years and Main School site provide a meaningful space to observe living things grow and change	41
2.2	Some of the students behind the 'Authors of Our Future' initiative who gathered donations of sanitary products for young mothers in prison and designed early stimulation training for these women	46
3.1	Influences on teacher's praxis and decision-making without *phronēsis*	55
3.2	Teacher's praxis and decision-making led by *phronēsis*	56
3.3	Threads for discussion	59
7.1	A rhizomatic of transdisciplinary practice	103
7.2	A manifesto poem for re-visioning transdisciplinary future-making education	108
8.1	The selburose	116
8.2	Geometric transformations	117
8.3	One petal leaf and a Scratch code that produces the one leaf	118
8.4	The selburose drawn by having a function drawing each leaf	119
8.5	Repeating the selburose five times	120

8.6	Tote bag	121
9.1	Center on the Developing Child (2021) model of positive, tolerable and toxic stress	128
9.2	EHCAP's adaptation of Dan Siegel's metaphor 'the river of well-being'	133
9.3	Interplay between the Center on the Developing Child's three principles and healthy development and educational achievement when a child is engaged with adult caregivers who are responsive and economically stable	137
11.1	The three functions which compose human awareness and identity	169
12.1	Question from two of our children in Year 1	181
13.1	Recent climate change–related disruptions in Uganda	187
13.2	Young people's observations of changes to droughts during the past five years, by region	188
13.3	Perceptions of the main causes of environmental change, by highest level of education	190
13.4	Most trusted information source, by highest level of education	192
13.5	Pupils with a 'talking compound'	194
13.6	Climate change lesson at a teacher training college, led by Benard Isiko	195
14.1	Curriculum design model	201

Tables

1.1 Examples of solutions and skills with the potential to deliver a climate-resilient net zero future	*page* 33
9.1 Emotion-responsive phrases compared with emotion-dismissive or -disapproving phrases	129
11.1 Three functions at work in speech	170
14.1 Definitions of three forms of curriculum knowledge	202
14.2 Lesson plan structure	205

Contributors

Anna Barford, Cambridge Institute for Sustainability Leadership and Murray Edwards College, University of Cambridge

James Biddulph, Avanti Schools Trust, UK

Pamela Burnard, Faculty of Education, University of Cambridge

Isabelle Butcher, Department of Psychiatry, University of Oxford

Liam Connolly, University of Cambridge Primary School

Akhandadhi das, Science and Philosophy Initiative, UK

Aliabbas Dhanji, University of Cambridge Primary School

Aimee Durning, University of Cambridge Primary School

Julia Flutter, Faculty of Education, University of Cambridge

Orlando Garciacano, Instituto Tecnológico Autónomo de México and El Colegio Británico (The Edron Academy), Mexico City

Benard Isiko, Restless Development, Ntinda, Kampala, Uganda

Elise Kinnear, University of Cambridge Primary School

Kirstin MacVicar, University of Cambridge Primary School

Paul Magimbi, School of Social Sciences, Makerere University, Kampala, Uganda

Anthony Mugeere, School of Social Sciences, Makerere University and Advocates Coalition for Development and Environment (ACODE), Kampala, Uganda

Amy Munro-Faure, Cambridge Zero, University of Cambridge

Elena Natale, University of Cambridge alumnus

List of Contributors

Mollen Nyiraneza, School of Social Sciences, Makerere University, Kampala, Uganda

Harry Pearse, Centre for Deliberation (National Centre for Social Research), UK

Luke Rolls, British School in Tokyo

Annabel Sharman, University of Cambridge Primary School

Emily Shuckburgh, Cambridge Zero, University of Cambridge

Sarah Temple, EHCAP Ltd

Aino Ukkonen, Faculty of Education and International Studies, Oslo Metropolitan University

Bhaskar Vira, University of Cambridge

Jenna Watson, El Colegio Británico (The Edron Academy), Mexico City

Constantinos Xenofontos, Faculty of Social Sciences, Oslo Metropolitan University, Norway

Foreword

The purpose of education has long been a point of discussion for parents, politicians, educators and society more generally. The diversity of responses and the passion with which ideas and beliefs are presented have grown, especially since the invention of social media. Everyone has an opinion about education – and so they should: it is the most important consideration of any society – the value given to children, their childhoods and the pathways to adulthood that lead to a flourishing life. But what does it mean to flourish? What does it mean to achieve and become educated? And what is the purpose of school?

The teaching profession holds the key to the evolution of schooling and to considering answers to these questions. To this purpose, the Chartered College of Teaching, an international, professional body designed to empower teachers and teaching assistants by providing them with support, challenges and access to research, was founded in the UK. We encourage the development of practice through reflective collaboration, providing learning pathways to new ideas and opportunities. Increasingly, the role of the College is to stimulate and lead professional enquiry into practice that supports teachers (and those who work with them), not only to support them in their thinking about what they do and how they do it but also to reflect on why they do it.

To truly reimagine the purpose of education, educators must believe that *all* children can be educated and can flourish within the classroom. Inclusion is vital. We know that there are many changes (and challenges) ahead. For our teaching profession, the art is to continue to teach as well as we can, whilst providing space for children to imagine and to dream – and also providing those spaces for the educators who enable learning to happen. A reimagining of education raises the following aspects:

- To support the development and flourishing of children beyond the family

- To introduce new areas of study and to show the interconnectedness of all human knowledge
- To provide role models and offer spiritual guidance, moral guidance, and leadership

A future focus for education policy should be to develop a forward-looking workforce, including teachers, leaders, teaching assistants and those who engage with children in schools, which is ready to embrace change and for whom challenge is part of the exciting journey. This journey arises when supported by high-quality professional development, within cultures of learning enabled by leaders and when given the professional autonomy and responsibility to do what is right for the children and young people in their care.

When the College published the academic journal *Impact*, the purpose was to bridge academic research and evidence with practitioners' understandings as experienced in schools. It was to give a meaningful resource to help busy teachers to rethink and build evidence into their practice. This inspiring series, called Education Visions, of which this book is the first, goes an additional step in seeking new visions for education and bringing diverse ideas together. In the dialogue between academic manifesto chapters and the practitioner wisdom chapters, the reader can see the grappling with ideas, the articulation of practical ideas and the passion to explore new ideas.

The authors demonstrate a compassionate response to consider new ideas for children and young people. In a world that seems increasingly fractured, we need compassionate teachers, teaching assistants and leaders more than ever. Educators must focus more on what it means to flourish as a human. We need to bring that dialogue into our educational spaces. Language is thought, and developing language builds cognition. We need thinking classrooms full of debate, decision-making and social interaction – where children explore what it means to be an educated, compassionate person. And because of this, we need the same in our staffrooms: places of debate, autonomy to make decisions and celebratory social interaction.

In this book, the variegated ideas contribute to a kaleidoscope of possibility thinking about how our children and young people *could be* as they journey through their lives. How do we reduce the impacts of stress in our classrooms? How can spiritual questioning bring children and young people closer to a sense of awe and wonder? Where are the voices of children represented in our schools? How do we move away from seeing separate entities in siloed thinking and towards a more interconnected approach? Can democracy be strengthened because children have a direct, early experience of it? And can sustainability education move beyond making posters about endangered species? All these questions are raised in the eclectic mix presented herein – in a unique dialogue between academic and practitioner.

With the advent of artificial intelligence, schools face a crossroads. Either technology will replicate much of the traditional work of the teacher, reducing her role to that of supervisor, or, in the hands of skilled educators, technology will provide powerful tools (say, video and virtual reality) capable of inspiring discovery and enhanced understanding of our world. If knowledge is freely and instantly available to everyone, it will cease to be the purpose of formal education. Instead, it might focus on interpreting and interrogating the veracity of 'facts'. Humans will need to become skilled, critical consumers of information. Teachers will need to embrace interdisciplinarity, work in cross-curricular teams and focus on the characteristics that make us human – our capacity for empathy, kindness, curiosity and humour.

The biggest threat to schools and the teaching profession is that lesson content is becoming increasingly automated, at the same time as children's learning is becoming measured by machines. We might end up in a situation in which lessons are centrally planned by leaders who never enter the classroom, with teachers simply required to deliver them. Teachers will not need to think anymore. It is possible that the role of the teacher could be reduced to being a guard – ensuring safety and compliance and not much else. In some regions of the world – where centralised instruction delivered by a combination of machine and supervisor is cheaper than employing a qualified professional teacher – this is a familiar scenario. In response, the teaching profession must be adaptable; learning how to utilise new technologies, while also advocating for the benefits of group learning through interaction, shared perspectives and the building of collaborative solutions.

Increasingly, I believe, society will look to the teaching profession to provide moral and spiritual guidance, not only to children but also to families. And that is why this book is a good contribution: it says that academics have ideas, school educators have ideas, and with the diversity of ideas come new pathways to enable flourishing children – and an education that fosters a more wholesome, happier society, perhaps?

As we look to the world of future employment, we need to focus on the values of humanity and on addressing the deep concerns about our environment. We can't stem the tide of 'progress'. However, I was interested to read recently that some supermarkets are removing automated tills in favour of tills manned by humans who can talk to customers, some of whom may not have other social outlets. Maybe the work of the future will value imagination and compassion much more. Our societies have many ills: inequity, loneliness, poverty, greed, consumerism, selfishness, attention deficits and an increasing need for instant gratification. We need to help teachers do more to build recognition of the power of humane ways of engaging with one another. Recently, I visited an intergenerational nursery housed in sheltered accommodation for the elderly. I accompanied a small group, including several adults with dementia and their carers, for a story-based activity. The joy on the faces of both the children and the adults as the children arrived was wonderful to witness. More could be done to provide intergenerational learning spaces. Both examples are about people thinking differently. Doing, differently.

Biddulph, Pearse and Shuckburgh, the co-editors, rightly say that this collection of visions is incomplete. Everyone has an opinion about education, and so everyone should. It is for each educator, and indeed anyone interested in education and the future of the world, to read each chapter within the context of their own community and school; to consider, question, doubt, find possibilities and opportunities in what they read. Reject what the authors say, by all means. Create a better idea, build on the ideas, open up your communities to new visions. Engage in the ideas. It is through this knowledgeable engagement that the future is held in safe hands. A trusted, knowledgeable profession would be much better placed to deal with accountability pressures of governments and parents and to support governments in making the right decisions about education that is truly aimed at helping *everyone* to flourish. We need society to recognise the importance of education and the fact that teachers are essential agents of change. The Chartered College of Teaching stands ready to support, inspire and nurture our amazing educators, with love.

Dame Alison Peacock
CEO, The Chartered College of Teaching

Acknowledgment

This book would not have come to fruition in the way it has without the exceptional support of Orlando Timmerman, who acted as sub-editor. His insight, care, and meticulous attention to detail have shaped the manuscript at every stage, and we are deeply grateful for his invaluable contribution.

Funding from Cambridge Zero made it possible for this book to be published Open Access, making the digital version freely available for anyone to read and reuse under a Creative Commons licence.

Introduction
Problems and Possibilities

JAMES BIDDULPH, HARRY PEARSE AND EMILY SHUCKBURGH

How teachers are supported, inspired and nurtured has long been a focus of academics, school leaders and politicians. In a world of increasingly restricted resources, both financial and material, it becomes imperative to consider new ways to ignite new thinking about the purpose of education as well as the role of educators. We hear about children being the future, that our future is in their hands, that we need to prepare children with twenty-first-century skills but beyond the rhetoric, practice, professional learning opportunities and systems seem glacial in their ability to adapt and flex to the needs of the era. If the jobs that today's children and young people will have in the future, are not yet invented and with climate anxiety on the rise, how are teachers and school leaders preparing themselves to inspire and nurture those in their care? Though this is not political statement, since the turn of the century, politicians, academics, business leaders and educators have been repeating a similar mantra – children are not ready for a world in which climate change and other sustainability challenges will impact their lives, livelihoods and ways of living. This book aims to provide a catalyst for discussions in staff rooms, classrooms, lecture rooms and any other space in which the questions about the *purpose of education now* are evoked.

Before framing the purpose of this book, let us introduce ourselves. James is an experienced school leader and has a doctorate in the study of the diversities of creative learning. He is the founding Headteacher of the University of Cambridge Primary School, a research-informed government school in the UK. He is now the CEO of Avanti Schools Trust, a multi-academy trust that runs primary and secondary schools in the UK. Emily is a professor of climate science, a leading voice in the international discourse about climate change and founding director of Cambridge Zero, the major transdisciplinary climate initiative at the University of Cambridge. And Harry is an historian and political theorist who co-launched Cambridge's Centre for the Future of Democracy. This could be the beginning of a bad joke: a teacher, a scientist and an historian ... But the diversity of our disciplinary interests reflects the approach of this Education Vision book – to bring together a range of voices with different perspectives from diverse subject areas to talk about the big challenges of the day.

The book is structured with two different types of chapters: manifesto chapters and teacher response chapters. The manifestos in this book are written by different authors and derive from different disciplines. They're obviously not party political – they certainly don't offer comprehensive policy prescriptions or precise governance strategies – nor do they share ideological commitments or even the same views on the role or purpose of education.

Each manifesto has its own distinct structure and orientation. Some are empirical, others theoretical. Some are declarative, others are more discursive. Most rest in part on personal reflections, a few are framed from a more distant perspective. The rhythm and emphases of their arguments differ. They are diverse, and deliberately so.

What they have in common, however, is an expansive view of the role and potential of children (in schools, in society, in politics), and the capacity for educational reform. In that sense, they're all, in a certain way, optimistic. The pictures they paint of current educational conditions or worldly predicaments are sometimes bleak. But they all accept that change is possible and that children – as either agents or participants – must be placed at the heart of it.

The first manifesto sets out the challenges children will face over their lifetimes, in particular challenges arising as consequences of climate change and the destruction of nature within the context of growing social inequalities. Subsequent manifestos are focused on the response of children to these threats, though they are applicable more broadly. How can we enable children to have a greater voice in their future, and where do children fit in our democratic decision-making structures? How can our pedogeological structures respond to provide the holistic view, spanning sciences and arts, that is required to reimagine our relationship with the world? How can we support children to thrive – on one hand by drawing in practical terms on an understanding of the biology of stress and on the other more prosaically by enabling them to consider the purpose of life? Finally, how can we better connect our knowledge and experiences globally to inform and empower children around the world, and through education support a journey to a sustainable future that is also fair and just?

In different ways, each manifesto registers scepticism about prevailing disciplinary norms and the effects these norms have on the way children are perceived, understood and treated. Each also proposes a new mode of operation or way of thinking, designed to both reorient a field of research and do greater justice to the dignity, importance and power of young people. All the manifestos in this collection make a call to action.

Readers are encouraged to question these claims and reflect on the differences and similarities – in structure, tone and content – between the manifestos. The collection is intentionally eclectic. And while we hope all of them resonate and persuade, we don't expect every manifesto to land with every reader. They should all, in their own way, be stimulating and provocative, but it's readers' responsibility to adjudicate their strengths and weaknesses and draw conclusions about what's useful or needed. Conventional manifestos put prescriptiveness front and centre. By contrast, we want the relationship between author(s) and reader to be dialogic and democratic.

Following each chapter, practising teachers, school leaders and teaching assistant write responses, to suggest ways in which the manifesto ideas/ideals could manifest in the context of classrooms and schools. At the end of each practitioner chapter, there are provocations to invite the reader to contribute their own thinking for their own contexts. The reader will note that each chapter looks different. We offered authors the freedom to respond freely, allowing for diversity of positioning, presentation and purpose. We included some stylistic 'hooks' especially at the end of the practitioner wisdom chapters, the 'Over to You' sections, to invite the reader to join us in the dialogue. This is not a book with answers. It is a book that aims to provoke new thinking and to ask for more, better, bolder questioning about how we work as educators in schools. In the remaining part of this chapter, we position the reason why a book like this has relevance and why its questions will have longevity in our collective endeavour to contribute new ideas to the mix.

0.1 Climate Matters: To Children

The idea for this book came from the school where James was Executive Headteacher, which Emily's children attend and where

Harry has conducted research about democracy. It started with the adults listening to the children:

Vignette of Despair

Gemma turned the TV off. Sir David Attenborough, the famous British natural scientist, had taken her on a journey to the furthest corners of the planet and warned of the dangers to penguins, polar bears, snow leopards and many other animals. Gemma turned to her mum and said, 'There is no point in living, just no point.' Her mum looked horrified and frightened. How could her nine-year-old daughter be so pessimistic about life? How had her childhood become so caught up in worry about the future that she felt there was no longer any point? Gemma went on to explain that she wasn't speaking about herself as an individual, rather the whole of humanity: she didn't understand the point of humanity if the outcome of our collective actions is simply destruction.

Vignette of Values

Tom is autistic. He visits his headteacher's office daily. Sometimes he talks. Sometimes he sits eating crackers and then leaves. Today he spoke.

'You see, the problem is the adults need to do more to teach us about life. We need to know about being kind and doing stuff for other people. You know what I mean, like, on the way to school, this parent in front of me said to his son, "just push past everyone else", but you see that is not compassionate because everyone is trying to get to school on time. That dad should have thought about everyone not just his son and pushing past. You know what I mean? We need the adults to show us more gratitude – I mean how to be grateful for what we have in life, for this school, for the teachers, for the stuff we have, isn't it? Otherwise, everyone will be selfish and not think about the community ... and then the world will die.'

Vignette for Action

Alistair and Aisha came to class with a bag of coins. They had raised £12.80. 'We made a stall outside Al's house and we made lemonade and sold it. We wanted to raise money to help protect animals.'

These three vignettes give an example of the ways children engage in a world that they see is increasingly fractured. More than ever, children have access to information, misinformation and populist/influencer accounts of realities that, instead of providing knowledge, have left them confused and worried. Dame Rachel de Souza, the UK children's commissioner, has sought evidence and possible responses to influence government policy; to explain to politicians that climate change matters to children and that therefore it must matter to adults, and

Introduction 5

especially to those who work in schools. What follows in this chapter are three starting points to consider how we approach climate change and living sustainably on a planet with finite resources.

0.2 Developing Knowledge and Understanding of Climate Change and Sustainability for Education

It is evident that our current model of society is unsustainable. We use more resources than our planet can deliver. We are at the brink of a human-induced mass extinction of species. Our polluting and destructive ways threaten our own lives. The inequalities in global society are extreme and compound the environmental threats to the human and natural world. Social cohesion is strained and being further stressed by climate change threatening basic provisions. The very sense of individual purpose and meaning is, for many people, waning.

Feelings of anxiety and despair abound, especially among young people. Drawing on the work of tens of thousands of experts, the Intergovernmental Panel on Climate Change has concluded that there is a 'rapidly closing window of opportunity to secure a liveable and sustainable future for all' (IPCC, 2023). If that is a shocking statement to read as an adult, pause and imagine for a moment what is means to a child today.

But if we have arrived at such a dysfunctional, dystopian place in our history, what place does education have in helping to shape a productive response? How can we better prepare young people around the world for the future? How can we build the foundations to support more sustainable and just societies? How can we empower learners to take informed decisions and take personal and collective action to change society and care for the planet?

This book attempts to offer some preliminary thoughts to these important questions as well as invite more questions in the contexts the reader finds themselves. A starting point is to understand what it is we are wanting to achieve through children's education in the context of climate change and sustainability.

Firstly, we can ensure children have an awareness of the challenges that are likely to be defining features of their lives. The three C's of climate, conservation, community are not the traditional components of educational curricula, and they transcend traditional disciplines. However, it is vital to develop knowledge and a holistic understanding of these topics to properly equip children to comprehend the challenges that are facing the world today. The environmentalist Mary Colwell has argued for the need to reconnect young people in the UK with the natural world around them through education, 'not just because it's fascinating, not just because it's got benefits for mental health, but because we'll need these young people to create a world we can all live in' (Colwell, 2021). This dialogue must happen in an inclusive way that respects cultural diversity – too often some groups of society are perceived to be the unique custodians of these issues. For example people of colour in the UK face systemic barriers in accessing and thriving in green spaces (Pettinato, 2023). A transdisciplinary approach is required that not only encompasses scientific facts of environmental change, but addresses the social, economic and behavioural facets of climate justice and action-based solutions, and contextualises this in learner's real-life experience and aspirations (UNESCO, 2020).

Secondly, we can ensure children develop the knowledge, skills, values and attitudes to respond to these challenges over their lifetimes. This relates to the UN's Sustainable Development Goals which include a target that by 2030 all learners acquire the knowledge and skills needed to promote sustainable development. In part it means encouraging learners to discuss and explore alternative values to those of highly consumer-driven societies, recognising young people are an important consumer group and that the way their consumption patterns and behaviours evolve will greatly influence the sustainability trajectories of their countries (UNESCO, 2020). It means responding to the opportunities and risks brought about by technological advances and understanding what role technology can play in supporting sustainable futures. It also means identifying the vocational training required to underpin the employment of the future, and the inspiration and competencies for them to lead the change. Showcasing potential green careers is an essential element of this. A summer intern working with Emily at Cambridge Zero produced a series of films to 'raise awareness of the great diversity of green jobs that are currently available, as well as those that will be available in future … thereby empowering young people to pursue a career that has a positive impact on the planet' (Prosser, 2021). More broadly, and reflecting one of the vignette's above, it means giving children a values-based framework to enable them to construct a new, fairer and more sustainable society.

Finally, we can ensure children are supported emotionally and have the confidence to undertake transformative action or influence societal change towards a more sustainable world. It is important to recognise the real anxiety of many children and young people about their future, and to provide them with the tools to cope. Studies in the UK indicate that while there is little generational difference in terms of belief in climate change and its impacts, younger generations have stronger negative emotions of fear, guilt and outrage. Responding to that means giving children a sense of agency today, enabling them to meaningfully participate in actions and decisions that will impact their future. Doing so will not only fulfil our duty to respect and to support children (who often have ingenious solutions to sustainability challenges), it is also the right and just thing to do – a first step in tackling inter-generational inequity (Poortinga, Demski and Steentjes, 2023).

A creative project to embed a sense of agency that was delivered at James' school in collaboration with Cambridge Zero. Children created artworks in five categories – poles and oceans, endangered animals, trees and plants, people, and words/phrases associated with climate change – which were adhered to the faces of cardboard cubes. The cubes could be moved around and rotated, representing our ability to enact change, and mirrors were incorporated to highlight how we can all be agents of change – the children and those enjoying their work (see Figure 0.1). The project had powerful symbolism and provided an opportunity for rich discussions among the children. It also highlights the importance of a fourth C as a key component of educational offerings: creativity. This is an essential enabler of the sort of innovative thinking required to imagine and realise a sustainable future.

A coherent and effective strategy for educating children on climate change and sustainability needs to sit within a reimagined lifelong learning framework and a broader context of supporting active and compassionate citizenship. The objective should be not only to support the accomplishments of individuals, but also to contribute to the collective prosperity of the world we inhabit. Measurements of the quality of such an educational offering will need to be developed – which may focus more on learning content and its contribution to sustainability, and less on the achievement of specific learning outcomes.

Schools have a central place themselves within communities. The learnings that are conveyed to students in educational establishments, can rapidly diffuse through family networks and other community

Figure 0.1 Schools play a central role in empowering children and creating opportunities for them in the development and implementation of sustainability policies.

pathways, dissemination which can be proactively supported through engagement activities that embrace local contexts. Schools can also ensure sustainability-related learning content and its pedagogies are reinforced by the way their own facilities are managed and how decisions are made within their institution, including empowering children and creating opportunities for them to take an active role in the development and implementation of sustainability policies.

0.3 Developing Democratic Spaces for Children in Education

Since Greta Thunberg and Fridays for Future movement, children have played a more visible role in protest politics. However, because children are excluded from formal democratic activities, like voting, their voice and agency carry less political weight. So, notwithstanding their profile in public campaigns, children's concerns and interests are more likely to be overlooked in political discourse and decision-making.

The vignettes of despair and value, discussed above, give a taste of children's predicament. They show that, although children have political preferences (about climate change), and moral priorities (about community), their relative disempowerment means their interests and concerns are liable to be ignored in favour of adult preferences. This exposes a major error in one of the common assumptions about the place and role of children in democratic life. It's argued that children don't need more democratic rights because their interests and preferences are already represented by their parents or family, their teachers and maybe even by politicians. However, as these vignettes reveal, adults don't always or necessarily understand or cater for children's preferences, and, as a consequence, children are often inadequately represented.

Harry encountered similar viewpoints while conducting research into children's attitudes to democracy, voting and representation – hosted in the University of Cambridge Primary School (Pearse, 2023b). As a group, children don't share the same concerns or priorities; they're not a homogenised constituency – much in the same way that adults aren't. Many of the children involved in the research were engaged in politics, or at least curious about the prospect of voting. Others, however, were not. And some, in fact, were already disillusioned with democratic process and actors. And yet, despite this range of opinion, most of the children were sceptical about existing processes or mechanisms of child representation. They understood that, in certain respects, parents and teachers were able and willing to act in children's interests, but also largely agreed that the people best placed to understand the interests, beliefs or conundrums of children are children themselves. They acknowledged that children have political perspectives, and ethical viewpoints or intuitions, which are sometimes unfamiliar to other cohorts; and that their perspectives and intuitions not being adequately considered or heeded by adults or the democratic institutions.

To some extent, this helps explain children's increasing involvement in grassroots political protest. Many children recognise that democratic politics is failing to reflect or represent their interests, and that the best way to channel and communicate one's priorities is often to do so oneself, rather than leave it to others.

Of course, the same calculation does not, and cannot, apply in more formal political settings. Children aren't allowed to stand for parliament and represent other children, for much the same reasons they're not allowed to become surgeons or lawyers or police officers – jobs that rightly require qualifications that children inevitably lack. However, just because descriptive representation is off the table, it doesn't mean a more general form of political representation should be as well. In fact, the latter is increasingly urgent, for without representation, children will remain excluded from political discourse and processes, and their preferences and perspectives will continue to be overlooked or marginalised. As the UK Children's Commissioners (2020) put it, as children's 'right to be heard and involved in decision-making processes ... is being denied ... the UK government does not prioritise children's rights or voices in policy or legislative processes'.

Climate change is probably the issue that best illustrates the disjuncture between children's political concerns and concrete political action. We know that young people and children are acutely anxious about climate collapse (Hickman et al., 2021). And yet, despite their concerns, adult-run politics has failed to take adequate preventative or mitigatory action. The UK Children's Commissioners cite England's initial COVID-19 response measures as further evidence that children's political interests are frequently deprioritised – in this case, relative to commercial retail interests or the safety of the elderly. As a backdrop to these policy failures, electoral outcomes are increasingly skewing by age (see Brexit and the election of Donald Trump), with young people routinely losing out to the old (see the fate of Jeremy Corbyn's Labour Party in 2017) (Runciman, 2018, pp. 163–164). Children – who can't vote – are in an even worse position than younger voting demographics. And still, in the long run – after every electoral decision, or constitutional change, or period of existential policy inaction – children will inevitably face the lion's share of the consequences (measured temporally).

The justifications for the marginalisation of children are weak, and in the interests of fairness and justice, children require a more significant political voice. Children are not lesser citizens than adults. They have as much moral value and integrity, and they're as familiar with, and as shaped by, their personal experience, as their adult peers. In many important ways, children and adults are equals (Pearse, 2023a). And yet, politically, they're jarringly unequal, and children have considerably less scope to express and prosecute their beliefs and perspectives.

This arrangement is propped up by another common but erroneous assumption that children are incapable of 'properly' participating; that they lack the qualities – competence, rationality, wisdom – that equip a person for democratic life. Unhelpfully, the definition of these qualities, and what they entail, is unknown, or not agreed upon. Furthermore, a voting age threshold justified by virtually any definition of competence or wisdom wouldn't just stop children from voting; it'd also disqualify most adults from democratic participation. Democracies have mostly dispensed with the idea that political rights are only to be gifted to those with particular characteristics – be it wealth, or maleness, or whiteness, or the right religion (Olsson, 2008, pp. 57–59). Universal suffrage ought to mean that every citizen is entitled to a democratic life, irrespective of intelligence, identity or resources. Age (as a vague proxy for competence) is the only remaining exclusion. And this too – at least in its current form (excluding all those under eighteen) – is likely to be overcome eventually.

What it might mean, or what it could look like, to better integrate young children into democracy is uncertain. Extending the franchise is the most radical option, but there are other ways of ensuring children have a voice in democratic politics. They could be included in deliberative exercises – either with adults, or just with other children – or allowed to contribute to decision-making in the institutions they're most closely involved in, like schools (Pearse, 2022).

0.4 Developing Spaces for Enquiry in Education

Being an educator in the twenty-first century has become an increasingly complex role. Educating children to be healthy, engaged and active citizens in a world that is fraught with complex political, economic and social issues is vital and incredibly difficult. Governments, parents and society expect more from schools and the people (the teachers, teaching assistants and school leaders) who work within them. Being an educator requires more than the delivery of (often myopic) government edicts and strategies. The act of teaching necessitates new thinking, an invigorated and empowered professionalism, and a view that teaching is an intellectualised profession; doing more of the same will not support better social mobility and outcomes for children.

What really matters in education? Though the question is continually asked, the answers are often evasive. In many ways, the COVID-19 pandemic emphasised that if one thing can be relied upon, it's that things change. However, we also know that state education is very slow to do so. And here lies the crux of our dilemma as educators: how can we better respond to the fast-paced changes in the world, in technology, in social and cultural norms, to massed migration? If climate change matters to the world and to people, how does it matter within education systems and within schools? In the post-pandemic context, the questions about how we educate our children and young people have become more urgent with our answers more critical.

The world is in crisis. The future for our children, grandchildren and great grandchildren is uncertain. There are at least three existential uncertainties: the survival of planet Earth, the unravelling of cohesive communities, and the risks to individuals' sense of purpose and meaning. The forces for change are held back by technocratic and unimaginative responses to these challenges. Our education systems are no longer fit to reimagine, reinvent and reinvigorate our response-*ability* (the ability/capability to respond) to the challenges that will arise. The world – and the education systems we create – require a revolution of the social imagination through education, leading us to a tomorrow of active and compassionate citizenship.

Schools are important social places. Whilst there is a centralised attempt to standardise schools, in reality, they are diversely experienced intercultural spaces. They adapt and change as society evolves around them. In recent times, there has been an increase in massed migration across the globe, and unprecedented levels of interaction among diverse populations. We live in times of massed uncertainty with a perceived sense of the rise in xenophobia (and associated social phobias like Islamophobia, homophobia) in response to the challenges of cultural diversities.

Within this context, in recent years, there is a growing call for the teaching profession to be 'research-informed'; for example the current UK Government has invited schools to apply to be 'research schools' to disseminate meta-research, or 'big data' evidence, about what works in schools. However, teachers' engagement with research, and their use of research in their own classrooms has not yet become the norm. This is because such large-scale research does not always translate into the nuanced dialects/contexts/realities characteristic of our range of schools and classrooms. Teachers need resources that explicitly demonstrate, with real examples, how the use of research can be applied in classroom and school contexts. Teachers need to reframe their roles as teaching-researchers, as intellectuals who research their practice – people who ask questions about their practice, who problematise, who seek new opportunities and who 'tinker' with existing conventions, building not only research-informed but also research-generating practices.

Research-informed practice could be nurtured in three key aspects: by developing an ethic of trust, by acknowledging that phronēsis (or practical wisdom) arises when teachers bridge their practitioner wisdom with academic research and by giving opportunities for teachers to identify what things matter in their classrooms (see the Foreword). There have been examples of these aspects in James' school.

Schools are busy places. What goes on in schools is much more complex than the delivery of a curriculum. The principle of developing research-informed practitioners and practice is evident in the mission of the Chartered College of Teaching, which was established in the UK as a professional body for teachers and teaching assistants. A sense of teacher and children agency and *ethic of trust* became a cultural norm at the University of Cambridge Primary School. As the following vignette demonstrates, one of James' colleagues was able to inspire change in strategies to support inclusive practice – this was a result of a culture of trust within the school.

Box 0.1 Reflections from a Headteacher

In our first year, I noticed one of my new teaching assistant colleagues. She was passionate and believed in the power of reading to effect change. I gave Aimee a copy of the 'Maximising the Impact of Teaching Assistant' research. This research analysed the impact of teaching assistants (TAs) on outcomes for children. Although the Education Endowment Foundation suggested that they have little impact on students' outcomes, we know that TAs add value to the life of a school.

On Monday morning, Aimee was sitting outside my office and said, 'You need to deploy the TAs differently.' She explained the negative results of one-to-one support and instead spoke of scaffolding up, not differentiating down. I said, 'Go on then. Make the changes.' What arose was a TA community that developed a researcher mindset – each week they pose problems, and together they discuss possible solutions, drawing from research into speech and language, for example.

Professional development in schools is another way to support the notion of teachers not as researchers but as teachers with researcher mindsets. A lesson study approach (Rolls and Seleznyov, 2020) can be beneficial. This involves identifying problems and using academic expertise to shine different knowledge on the matter, which in turn supports teachers' planning. Following a period of shared planning, the academic expert and practitioners observe and model lessons which are then discussed and analysed. Bridging these different forms of knowledge creates a cultural shift where teachers were actively engaging in research and new ideas, and are creating ways to use and develop these within their classrooms. There is explicit recognition of practitioner wisdom sitting alongside academic knowledge.

The third aspect in developing research mindsets is for teachers to *identify things that matter* for the children in their care. For example the curriculum design in James' school gives primacy to oracy and dialogue – based on the practical reflection that children who speak and ask questions seem to do academically and socially better than those who do not. It drew inspiration from social sciences and built on the concept – to Professor Robin Alexander's work on culture and dialogue and his collation of research for the Cambridge Primary Review (Alexander, 2010). The University of Cambridge Primary School was fortunate to work with Professor Sue Gathercole, whose research about working memory helped frame how teachers should give instructions so that the roughly 30 per cent of people with poor working memory do not miss out on key learning. The school also has an ongoing relationship with Professor Usha Goswami and is participating in a project about music, rhyme and rhythm and their impact on language development from a neuroscience perspective. This research has provided new insights into practical issues faced in classrooms, and as such, teachers have found it meaningful and are willing to engage with it.

0.5 A Draft Framework for Thinking about Sustainability Education

We uphold the view that siloed thinking about climate change will not help us find innovative and meaningful mitigations and solutions.

We are of the view that, as well as academic knowledge about the climate, science and technology, there is a need to support children and young people in developing *possibilities thinking* mindsets, where creativities and critical thinking are vital and not peripheral to the education experience. Moreover, as well as the scientific knowledge, other domains of learning, for example philosophy, religion, ethics, arts, languages, politics, psychology and sociology, must be included in the possibilities thinking. What happens when theologians and climate scientists grapple with the issues? What will arise if musicians work with sociologists to make sense of the complexities and nuances of sustainability? What happens if we think in a transdisciplinary way? Moreover, where are the democratic voicings in our schools and examples of innovation (see also Biddulph and Baldacchino, 2023; Biddulph, Rolls and Flutter, 2023)?

If we maintain a post-human theoretical perspective, which states that humans are *a part of* the ecosystem and not in a privileged position *apart from* or above the system, then we start thinking differently about how the world is ordered and our place, privilege and power within it. Figure 0.2 presents a new framework for thinking about ways to reimagine education.

The framework presents three broad forms of intelligences – human, environmental and artificial. It provokes questions about how humans interact with AI and the environment. In this worldview, what does human intelligence offer? And how does this compare to the intelligence of the environment, to wisdom traditions and qualities of intuition and spirituality? How can artificial intelligence contribute? As well as these intelligences, there are new knowledges about democracy and community, about children's co-agency and pedagogic ways to raise children's voices and new meaningful knowledge about climate change. The interconnected relationships are messy with multiple pathways and opportunities. This view of sustainability education is articulated through dialogue between educators, between children and between educators and children – co-authoring and co-creating new routes towards a sustainable education. It is education enacting in terms of possibilities, creativities and as the social imagination.

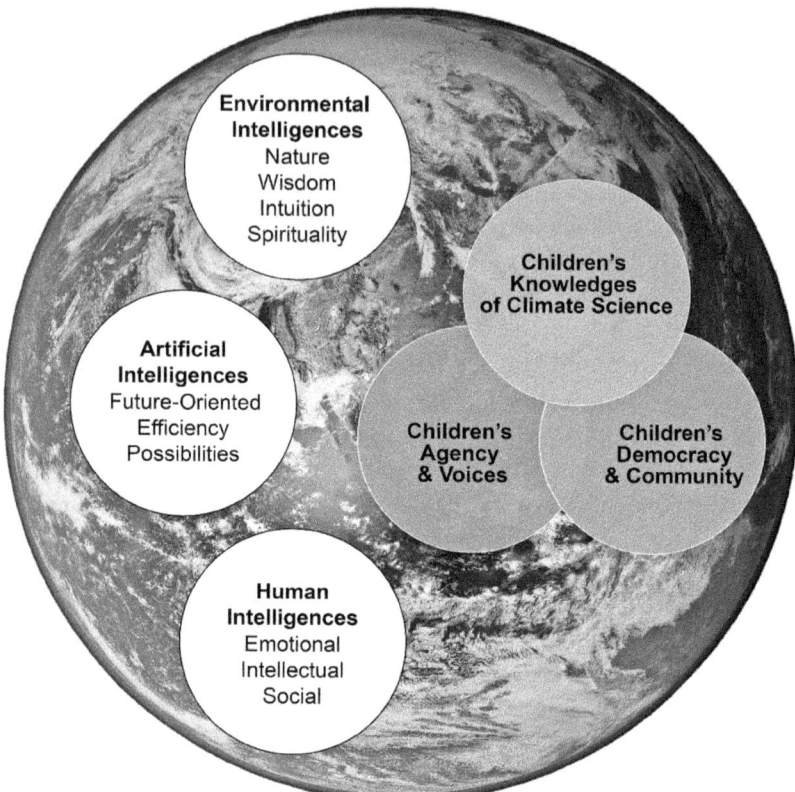

Figure 0.2 A framework for thinking about empowering sustainability education.

0.6 A Purposefully Eclectic Book

It has been a very difficult book to bring together. Our intention was to forge a bridge between academic research and the ideas, insights and wisdom of primary school teachers. However, trying to connect case studies from across the globe, ensuring a rich and diverse response to the environmental challenges we all face, has been almost impossible. And yet, this book and the books that follow attempt to bring 'possibilities and creativities thinking' (Burnard and Loughrey, 2023) into the DNA of our education systems, schools and classrooms, as well as the mindsets of those people who work with our children and young people.

Possibilities and creativities thinking is the imaginative and action-oriented process driving us from *what is* to *what could be*. It is more than the use of the imagination. Considering the challenges or problems with which we are faced, possibilities thinking offers a theoretical way of bridging current ideas with exploring the diversity of new ideas. Creativities thinking involves transdisciplinary and intercultural ways of approaching problems. This involves dialogue, appreciation of diverse ideas, welcoming cultural differences, responding to problems with the use of the arts, allowing for uncertainty to exist and remain, and brought about in social contexts (Burnard and Loughrey, 2023). Both concepts are a response to Maxine Greene's (2000) call to educators to think more imaginatively – to reimagine society as it could be, to remember our duty to build our social imagination, and to develop the capacity to (re)invent visions of society. Possibilities and creativities thinking is most promising when considered as a collaborative participatory endeavour. It is intercultural and situated in social actions. It is positive, hopeful and passionate, and it represents a firm belief in the potential of human creativity and the collective human spirit.

So, why has it been difficult to build new global collaborations to discuss the uncertainties of thriving on planet Earth? How do we address the dominance of white hegemonic thinking, and the fact that climate change discourse is rooted primarily in the Global North? Why has it been difficult to find case global studies, or engender trans- and intercultural dialogue about our planet?

In part, the reasons for these problems stem from the systematic rigidity of our governance and education systems – our silos of knowledge and research disciplines, and the ways we organise societies. Rather than building bridges, society has constructed barriers between people, places and politics. In a recent professional journal entry, a reflective diary that some school leaders keep, James noted some of the problems of his and his fellow editors' white, educated, privileged positioning, bringing to the fore the challenges experienced in collating the collection of Education Visions.

Box 0.2 James' Journal Entry for August 2023

This book seems an enormous task. Reminds me of my doctoral thesis, exploring diversities, trying to make sense of who I was and how I was to engage with people who, in the context in which I was working, were seen as the 'other'. Through the process, I was reminded to ask questions about how I located myself, how much I revealed about myself, to reconcile my different roles and positions. As Helene Cixous (1994, p. xv) explains,

> Like all those whose vital substance is cut from the same fabric as writing, I am constantly impelled to ask myself the questions engendered by this structure which is at once single and double: questions of the ethical, politico-cultural, aesthetic, destinal value of this constitution; questions of the necessity of writing for myself and for others; of the usefulness, the strangeness of forever being here and elsewhere, ever here as elsewhere, elsewhere as here, I and the other, I as the other, etc.

It has been difficult to find contacts across the world, to weave into the fabric of our possibilities thinking the threads of sub-Saharan Africa, or first peoples' wisdom, or of island states, or countries in the Middle East, or from experts in countries for whom raised sea levels will obliterate life. And yet, the book started with the intention to weave this rich diverse human capacity to invent new visions. As McLaren (in hooks, 1994, p. 31) says, we must guard against seeing diversity as somehow a harmonious, 'ensemble of benign cultural spheres' but instead to acknowledge that, 'when we try to make culture [diversities] an undisturbed space of harmony and agreement where social relations exist within cultural forms of uninterrupted accords, we subscribe to a *form of social amnesia* in which we forget that *all knowledge is forged* in *histories* that are played out in the *field of social antagonisms*'.

Who am I (we) in presenting possibilities without 'whitewashing' the issues? How do we make sense of the nuances, in the inflections of accents, languages, ways of thinking, knowledges and practices? How do we invite more dialogue? How do we embrace the uncertainties that arise with the niggling feeling that we need to hear more voices?

Many examples in this book are drawn from experiences at the University of Cambridge Primary School (UCPS), in the UK – partly for the practical reason that James, the concept editor of Education Visions, works there and partly because the school's raison d'être is to be global and a conduit for partnerships. The school is a state-funded school with no additional resources from the University of Cambridge. It opened in

2015 and serves a diverse community, including disadvantaged families and a much higher than average intake of children with special educational needs and disabilities, with some families from academics working at the University of Cambridge as well as those representing the local community. UCPS currently has more than 600 pupils, from nursery to Year 6 (age three to eleven). It is the first university training school for primary education in the UK and partners with colleagues at the University to collaborate in research projects and provide initial teacher education to trainee teachers. The hope is that in subsequent books, greater diversities will be presented. As such, we want to make it clear from the outset that this book is necessarily incomplete. Its completion comes when the reader brings together people in their own countries, homes, schools, education communities and other social spaces to discuss the issues raised. Its completion comes when the readers challenge the visions and our collected responses. Its completion comes when new ideas are offered.

References

Alexander, R. (2010) *Children, their world, their education: final report and recommendations of the Cambridge Primary Review*. Oxon: Routledge.

Biddulph, J. and Baldacchino, J. (2023) 'Wilful strangers in a possible democracy', in Biddulph, J., Rolls, L. and Flutter, J. (eds.) *Unlocking research: unleashing children's voices in new democratic education*. Abingdon: Routledge, pp. 43–62.

Biddulph, J., Rolls, L. and Flutter, J. (eds.) (2023) *Unlocking research: unleashing children's voices in new democratic education*. Abingdon: Routledge.

Burnard, P. and Loughrey, M. (2023) *Unlocking research: sculpting new creativities in primary education*. Abingdon: Routledge.

Cixous, H. (1994) 'Preface', in Sellers, S. (ed.) *The Helene Cixous*. Abingdon: Routledge.

Colwell, M. (2021) *GCSE natural history*. Available at: https://teach.ocr.org.uk/naturalhistory.

Greene, M. (2000) *Releasing the imagination: essays on education, the arts and social change*. San Francisco: Jossey-Bass.

Hickman, C. *et al.* (2021) 'Climate anxiety in children and young people and their beliefs about government responses to climate change: a global survey', *The Lancet Planetary Health*, 5(12), 863–873. https://doi.org/10.1016/s2542-5196(21)00278-3.

hooks, b. (1994) *Teaching to transgress: education as the practice of freedom*. London: Routledge.

IPCC (2023) *Synthesis report of the IPCC sixth assessment report (AR6) summary for policymakers*. Available at: www.ipcc.ch/report/ar6/syr/downloads/report/IPCC_AR6_SYR_SPM.pdf.

Olsson, S. (2008) 'Children's suffrage: a critique of the importance of voters' knowledge for the well-being of democracy',*International Journal of Children's Rights*, 16(1), 55–76. https://doi.org/10.1163/092755608x267120.

Pearse, H. (2022) 'Refurbishing democracy: more direct, more deliberative, and younger', *Perspectives on Public Management and Governance*, 5(1), 11–15. https://doi.org/10.1093/ppmgov/gvab029.

Pearse, H. (2023a) 'Children, voting, and the meaning of universal suffrage', *Political Studies Review*, 22(4), 821–838. https://doi.org/10.1177/14789299231195454.

Pearse, H. (2023b) *Do children want the vote? lessons from a primary school*. Available at: www.bennettinstitute.cam.ac.uk/wp-content/uploads/2023/03/Do-children-want-the-vote.pdf.

Pettinato, D. (2023) *People of colour in 'green spaces': key barriers and the role of academia*. Available at: https://renewbiodiversity.org.uk/people-of-colour-in-green-spaces-key-barriers-and-the-role-of-academia/.

Poortinga, W., Demski, C. and Steentjes, K. (2023) 'Generational differences in climate-related beliefs, risk perceptions and emotions in the UK', *Communications Earth and Environment*, 4(1), 229. https://doi.org/10.1038/s43247-023-00870-x.

Prosser (2021) *Careers to solve the climate crisis*. Cambridge: Cambridge Zero. Available at: www.zero.cam.ac.uk/green-careers.

Rolls, L. and Seleznyov, S. (2020) 'Easily lost in translation: introducing Japanese lesson study in a UK school', in *Unlocking research: reimagining professional development in schools*. Abingdon: Routledge, pp. 50–64.

Runciman, D. (2018) *How democracy ends*. London: Profile Books.

UK Children's Commissioners (2020) *Report of the Children's Commissioners of the United Kingdom of Great Britain and Northern Ireland to the United Nations Committee on the Rights of the Child*. Available at: www.cypcs.org.uk/wpcypcs/wp-content/uploads/2020/12/crc-report-2020.pdf.

UNESCO (2020) *Education for sustainable development: a roadmap*. Paris: UNESCO. https://doi.org/10.54675/YFRE1448.

1 Manifesto 1

What Role Can Education Play in Addressing the Interlinked Climate and Environmental Crises?

AMY MUNRO-FAURE, EMILY SHUCKBURGH AND BHASKAR VIRA

The alarm bells are deafening, and the evidence is irrefutable: greenhouse gas emissions from fossil-fuel burning and deforestation are choking our planet and putting billions of people at immediate risk. ... The solutions are clear. Inclusive and green economies, prosperity, cleaner air- and better health are possible for all if we respond to this crisis with solidarity and courage.

António Guterres, 9 August 2021, in the secretary-general's statement on the IPCC (2021) Working Group 1 *Report on the Physical Science Basis of the Sixth Assessment*

1.1 Introduction

A child born in the world today can expect to live until the end of the century – global life expectancy at birth is now around seventy-three years (UN Department of Economic and Social Affairs, 2022). What will that child's life be like from infancy and adolescence to adulthood and old age? What opportunities will be available to them and what challenges will they have to navigate? What role can education play in providing the knowledge and skills to enable them to thrive? This manifesto argues for the critical role of education in cultivating informed and capable planetary citizens who can critically analyse complex issues and drive change by advocating for, developing and deploying just and sustainable solutions.

It is clear that the future lives of all children will be profoundly affected by human-induced environmental change, including climate breakdown; species extinction; pollution of the air, soil, freshwater and oceans; and resource depletion. Sadly, it makes a difference where a child is born – some are at greater risk than others. Nearly half of the world's children (1 billion) live in countries that are at extremely high risk from the impacts of climate change. Other societal inequalities are intertwined. Today, the disparity between the country with the highest and the country with lowest life expectancy at birth is more than thirty years; and within countries, income and wealth inequalities have risen nearly everywhere since the 1980s (Chancel *et al.*, 2022). In a global population of 8 billion, around three-quarters of a billion people faced hunger in 2022, double that number did not have enough water to meet their everyday needs and conflict left more than 100 million displaced from their homes.

The Lancet Countdown on Health and Climate (Watts *et al.*, 2019) has traced the possible impact of fossil fuel use and climate change through the life of a child born today. Infants can be permanently affected by undernutrition resulting from crop failures and are at risk from extreme heat; children are very susceptible to diarrhoeal diseases propagated by flooding and are especially vulnerable to dengue fever as mosquitos encroach into new regions. Through adolescence and beyond, air pollution causes an accumulation of damage to the heart and lungs, which today results in 7 million premature deaths globally each year. Families and livelihoods are put at direct risk from extreme weather and sea level rise, and indirect risk through the knock-on impacts on food, freshwater, disease, habitation and critical infrastructure. The elderly are particularly vulnerable to deadly heatwaves, which are increasing in frequency and severity. Climate change will have widespread social implications with some areas of the planet becoming unliveable. Thus, today's children will experience a world which looks dramatically different to the present. This raises questions such as how do we prepare young people for such a future, and how can we train them to design novel solutions to mitigate these problems and to adapt to a changing environment in resilient and creative ways?

1.2 Unsustainable Consumption

We currently use more resources and burn more fossil fuels than the Earth's systems are able to regenerate and adsorb the emissions from. In the past fifty years, the human population has doubled, the global economy has grown nearly four-fold and global trade has grown ten-fold, together driving up the demand for energy and materials. The term the *Anthropocene* is sometimes used to describe our current epoch. This gives us a frame of reference to say that there has been a profound change in the way in which we, as humans, are impacting the fragile planet that we happen to inhabit. The Intergovernmental Panel on Climate Change (IPCC, 2023) put things in stark terms in its most recent report, stating that there is a 'rapidly closing window of opportunity to secure a liveable and sustainable future for all'. That is a startling phrase and one that immediately leads to questions as to what a sustainable future for all means in the context of debates around justice and injustice.

The challenge of controlling the global consumption of resources is often referred to as the 'Tragedy of the Commons'. This idea, based on a parable of over-grazing of livestock on common land, describes a scenario where there is some shared resource which individuals can benefit from using but where the costs of using it accrue to a group. The simplistic description indicates the challenge could be overcome through regulation and enforcement to constrain individual excesses. Yet the challenge is not simply one of overcoming self-interest – issues such as equity, justice and good governance are equally important. In recognition of this, the United Nations Framework Convention on Climate Change has since its inception in 1992 enshrined the principle of 'common but differentiated responsibility'.

1.3 The Climate Crisis

Human-induced climate change is driving extreme weather and climate events in all regions of the world, including deadly heatwaves, wildfires, floods and droughts (IPCC, 2023). In 2023, the annual average global temperature was 1.45°C higher than it was in the latter half of the nineteenth century, which is often termed the 'pre-industrial' era.

Society in many parts of the world has been transformed through industrialisation but this has generated greenhouse gas emissions, largely by burning fossil fuels, deforestation, intensive farming and industrial processes. Greenhouse gases such as carbon dioxide (CO_2), methane and nitrous oxide act to trap heat from the sun in the atmosphere. As greenhouse gas concentrations rise, so do global temperatures, leading to sea level rise, ice loss and extreme weather, with increasingly devasting consequences. Today's levels of CO_2 are around

420 ppm, having increased by 50 per cent since the start of the industrial revolution. This is far outside natural variability which has seen CO_2 slowly oscillate between about 180 and 280 ppm as the Earth has in the past moved in and out of ice ages over hundreds of thousands of years. Methane and nitrous oxide have also seen huge, abnormal increases as the world has industrialised (over 150 per cent and nearly 25 per cent increases, respectively).

One prominent sign of warming has been the dramatic melting of ice. In the last decade, ice mass loss from Greenland has doubled in comparison to the previous decade, and in Antarctica it has tripled, leading to an acceleration of sea level rise. At the end of the summer melt season each year, Arctic sea ice now covers a little over half the area it did at the start of the satellite record in 1979, while Antarctic sea ice reached its lowest extent in the satellite record in 2023. Glaciers around the world are retreating rapidly, with those in Switzerland losing 10 per cent of their remaining volume in just two years from 2021 to 2023. In the ocean, marine heatwaves have increased in frequency and intensity, and the waters are becoming more acidic as carbon dioxide dissolves in the seas, with major implications for marine life.

Climate-related risks to health, livelihoods, food security, water supply, human security and economic growth are projected to increase with global warming of 1.5°C and even more so above that. There exist many potential tipping points in the climate that could lead to catastrophic change, including collapse of ice sheets in Antarctica and Greenland, changes in ocean circulation, release of frozen methane from the Arctic and the rapid dieback of the Amazon rainforest. The destabilisation of areas of the Antarctic polar ice sheet and/or the irreversible loss of the Greenland ice sheet could cause a rise of several metres in sea level on time scales ranging from centuries to millennia. These instabilities could be triggered by around 1.5°–2°C of sustained global warming. A large fraction of warm-water corals may be lost at 1.5°C of warming and nearly all at 2°C. This is highly consequential as over half a billion people rely on them for their livelihoods (e.g. fishing, tourism) and over a quarter of marine species for part of their life cycle. Overall, two to three times more plants and animals are anticipated to suffer severe habitat loss at 2°C versus 1.5°C of warming. Increases in heat and humidity mean that, increasingly, the threshold of human physiological survival could be passed in some locations: regions at greatest risk include India and the Indus River Valley (population

2.2 billion), eastern China (population 1.0 billion) and sub-Saharan Africa (population 0.8 billion); at 3°C of global warming, parts of North and South America risk passing survival thresholds.

This is a devastating picture of the future. Mitigating the dangerous effects of climate change requires deep, rapid and sustained emissions reductions and bringing CO_2 emissions to net zero that will be challenging to achieve. Yet there is hope – the IPCC has highlighted that feasible, effective and low-cost nature-based, social and technical solutions are already available. But they need to be deployed at a grand scale, while maintaining a pipeline of new innovations. That requires the right finance and policy support, but it also requires people who have the relevant technical, managerial and vocational skills. In other words, it requires the right support from our educational system.

In parallel to the development and implementation of mitigation solutions, we need to understand the weather extremes that are already impacting communities and build resilience to them – for example through early warning systems or flood defensive measures. Skills training associated with adapting to climate change has its own set of priorities and will likely be very different in different places. In small island developing states, for example, adaptation education may include strategically preparing young people for migration; in other countries it may include supporting young people to be compassionate towards climate migrants.

1.4 The Ecological Crisis

Today we face an ecological crisis that is inextricably linked to the climate crisis. Exploitative human activities mean we are currently experiencing a sixth mass extinction which is taking place more rapidly than the extinction that wiped out the dinosaurs 66 million years ago. Previous mass extinctions – generally defined to be periods when over three-quarters of species on Earth have been lost in 2 million years or less – were caused by extreme temperature changes, rising or falling sea levels and catastrophic, one-off events such as huge volcanic eruptions or an asteroid hitting Earth.

Today the largest single driver of biodiversity loss is habitat destruction by people through changes in land and sea use, including by cutting down rainforests to provide land for agriculture and urbanisation. The space left for nature is increasingly small, and biodiversity loss is further exacerbated by direct exploitation of organisms, pollution, invasion of alien species and climate change. Outside of a few special places, such as Antarctica, there are few places of 'wilderness' left. This has led to criticism that television nature documentaries sometimes portray a world that for the most part no longer exists. However, humans and nature have co-existed for thousands of years, and there have long been very few completely pristine locations. Instead, problems for biodiversity have arisen in recent times, not simply through the presence of humans but through our destructive actions on a grand scale (e.g. Thurstan, Brockington and Roberts, 2010).

The global rate of species extinction is already at least tens to hundreds of times higher than the average rate over the past 10 million years, and it is accelerating. Meanwhile the World Wildlife Federation's Living Planet Index (Almond et al., 2022), which tracks the abundance of vertebrate organisms (everything from fish to elephants to birds to frogs), has shown that global wildlife populations have plummeted by two-thirds since 1970. These losses are not distributed evenly – some regions experience more loss than others and particular sets of organisms have challenges that make them especially vulnerable. For example global amphibian populations are collapsing due to reductions in freshwater, which is needed for reproduction, plus the emergence of multiple disease threats.

Reflecting on this picture of extinction and habitat degradation, one might ask: how or in what way does this matter for humanity? Beyond the implicit value of these organisms, and the fondness we may hold for them, what is their functional value? People are fundamentally linked to, and a part of, ecological systems and we rely on them one way or another for the majority of our needs – they provide vital 'ecosystem services'. The Intergovernmental Science-Policy Platform on Biodiversity and Ecosystem Services (Brondizio et al., 2019) notes, 'Nature is essential for human existence and good quality of life. Most of nature's contributions are not fully replaceable, and some are irreplaceable.'

Pollination is an example of an ecosystem service upon which humanity relies. Pollinators contribute to the agricultural yield for an estimated 35 per cent of global food production and are directly responsible for up to 40 per cent of the world's supply of some micronutrients, such as vitamin A. Yet there is growing evidence of wild pollinator population declines due to changes in land management, climate change and agrochemical use (Dicks *et al.*, 2021). There are a vast number of other ecosystem services, ranging from flood prevention to the regulation of air quality, climate and freshwater quantity and location; the formation, protection and decontamination of soils and sediments; and the regulation of ocean acidification and energy – not to mention the many medical innovations humanity has taken from the natural world and the effects that nature has on people's psychological well-being. Ecosystem services are fundamental to human existence and well-being but are themselves dependent on the organisms and ecology, which we are losing at scale.

Education is essential for people to understand the critical importance of these systems and our reliance on them, and to develop the skills required to halt and reverse the damage.

1.5 The Planetary Crisis

In 2015, the United Nations adopted a set of Sustainable Development Goals to be achieved by 2030. These included ambitions to realise human rights of all, eradicate poverty, end world hunger and ensure access to clean energy, clean water and sanitation for all. The 2024 update demonstrates that the majority of the goals are not on track and more than one-third are stalled or regressing (UN, 2024). This isn't only a climate crisis or an ecological crisis – it is a planetary crisis directly impacting human well-being that is connected to a broad set of planetary injustices.

The global food system faces explicit threats from a changing climate, meaning weather-sensitive food production centres may need to shift. This provides additional challenges in that pollinators may not be able to shift their range as fast as the arable crops they pollinate, leading to potential further system breakdown. The current meat consumption of Western culture remains aspirational at a global scale. This is a challenge, as animal agriculture is far less efficient than arable – each gram of protein produced using animal agriculture requires a far greater input of land, resources and energy – essentially because animals use energy to move around, breathe and reproduce. Also, some common livestock animals, such as cows and sheep, produce high volumes of methane, a highly warming greenhouse gas. The heavy use of fertilisers drives emissions of nitrous oxide, another greenhouse gas, while intensive farming practices can lead to a loss of pollinators and soil microbe diversity, both of which are essential for the continued good functioning of the food system. Climate, environmental and societal dimensions are intertwined.

Usable fresh water represents only 1 per cent of all water on the planet, with the majority either in the oceans or frozen as ice. We get fresh water from rivers, lakes, groundwater and rain, and this water supply is dependent on the water cycle. In the water cycle, water evaporates from multiple sources, including the oceans and evapotranspiration from plants, and turns into water vapour. Water vapour then rises and cools to form clouds, and the water eventually falls back to Earth in the form of rain. Increasing temperatures due to climate change are increasing the rates of evaporation and precipitation, but these changes are not evenly distributed around the world with implications for water supplies. Melted snow and glacial ice from the Himalayas and other mountains feed the Indus, Ganges and Brahmaputra river systems, providing water for communities, agriculture, industry and hydropower stretching from India to China and beyond. The region provides water to 2 billion people, but climate change is threatening the supplies.

Climate change, biodiversity loss and environmental damage can also directly impact human health. Higher temperatures are leading to the geographic spread of some diseases, for example as new locations become viable for the mosquitos that carry diseases such as malaria and dengue. The effects of severe weather incidents can also have impacts on human health, for example drought leading to famine and malnutrition, flooding leading to poor sanitation and increased spread of disease, high variation in summer temperatures leading to heat stress induced mortality and storms leading to injuries, fatalities and mental health issues. Air pollution increases the risk of asthma and cardiovascular disease. Environmental degradation can lead to forced migration and can exacerbate tensions leading to civil conflict. As we continue to encroach on habitats for agriculture and housing, there is also an increased likelihood of zoonotic disease, where diseases in animal reservoirs are transmitted to humans.

Overall, we are already seeing devastating effects arising from our overuse of the world's resources, from our emissions of greenhouse gases and through habitat destruction, which severely impacts the ecosystems that provide us with the essential resources that humans need for life. When these effects are coupled with a set of global economic constraints that prioritise continued overextraction and resource use, and interact with underlying social inequalities, the challenges we face are severe.

The Dasgupta Review (2021) on the economics of biodiversity highlighted a paradox which is about how we measure human prosperity. Compared to being alive in 1750, being alive today, for most people, is better. Average incomes have gone up, and the likelihood that you might live in absolute poverty is significantly reduced. Life expectancy is much better; mortality rates have dropped. As a human, perhaps we're living in the best of times. But from a planetary perspective, we're living in a pretty terrible time. Extinction rates are up, ecosystem services are declining and global temperatures are increasing. The framework of planetary boundaries suggests that a number of the constraints that we have around human existence in terms of the planet's ability to sustain us are being breached. So what's going on here? On one hand, measured prosperity, especially gross domestic product, tells us that everything is great. And all the other indices say that the world is actually in serious crisis. That begs the question, Are we measuring the wrong thing?

1.6 An Unequal World

Different people in different parts of the planet are experiencing these changes in very different ways. This justice perspective is easily hidden in an aggregated description of the challenges. Why does inequality matter? Human-induced greenhouse gas emissions are not caused by "people" in general, but by specific human activities by specific people or groups of people.' This is something Indian scholars Anil Argarwal and Sunita Narain (1991) discussed thirty years ago in their book *Global Warming in an Unequal World*. There is a similar narrative for biodiversity. The decline of the biosphere creates enhanced inequality with a circular relationship where enhanced inequality is contributing to further declines in the biosphere.

The numbers demonstrate this inequality clearly. Today, one-tenth of the global population is responsible for close to half of all carbon emissions, and the top 1 per cent emits about 50 per cent more than the entire bottom half of the population. The top six emitters by country in 2022 covered 67 per cent of global emissions: China 31 per cent, the US

14 per cent, India 8 per cent, the EU 7 per cent, Russia 4 per cent and Japan 3 per cent. Per capita emissions in Europe (6.3 tonnes/person) are more than half those of the US (14.9 tonnes/person) but now less than China (8.0 tonnes/person), which has seen a rapid increase in recent years. Within country inequalities are great: the top 10 per cent in the US emit 3.5 times the average, and in China the top 10 per cent emit 4.5 times the average. In India the top 10 per cent emit four times the average, with a similar per capita emissions to the European average. Talking about emissions in an undifferentiated way is not really drawing adequate attention to the different consumption patterns of different people. This question of extreme inequality matters – the overconsumption of the rich is constraining the space for the legitimate consumption needs of the poor.

In addition to the inequality between people and between nations there is also, obviously, an intergenerational inequality. As we think about the role of education, it is really important to see how the consumption actions of the present high-consuming generation are constraining the space available for future generations. The remaining 'carbon budget' can be considered to be the total future emissions that give a 50 per cent likelihood of limiting warming to 1.5°C. For someone born in 2024, the carbon budget available to them, assuming it was equally shared, would be one-fifth that of a parent born in 1994. We tend to think about human prosperity as future generations being better off than ourselves, and yet this a context in which we are constraining the space for the youth of today.

1.7 The Role of Education

On the basis of the foregoing assessment of the state of the world and the challenges of the coming decades, what role can education play in supporting an appropriate response that ensures the planet remains survivable and society thrives?

Perhaps the most important thing that is needed is engagement with a positive vision of what is possible. Of course, many young people today have an acute understanding of the climate and environmental crises we face, how they have come about, the danger of inaction, and in broad terms what can be done to address the threat. But action at scale requires widespread awareness of and engagement with the issues which can in turn drive governments and markets to change the way in which they devise policy and conduct business to ensure sustainability is at the heart. It also requires a common belief that we *can* catalyse the change that is needed for a resilient and sustainable future. If an example is needed that it is possible, the rapid decrease in the cost and useability of solar power is a clear illustration of how policy and innovation can drive meaningful change.

The citizen's voice is becoming more and more visible, in particular, the voice of young people. But how do we create space for informed citizens to be part of the dialogue rather than for that dialogue to be dominated by experts sitting in conferences convened well outside of everyday discourse? One interesting approach that has been attempted in the UK is a Citizens Assembly, where a group of people come together and deliberate with each other. In the face of evidence that is presented to them, as you might have in a criminal trial, they are expected to come up with a reasoned judgement about the next step forward. And how can we, especially in the Minority World, ensure we are open to the rich knowledge that already exists across the globe? We don't need to educate people in Bangladesh about the impact of climate change – they are experiencing it on an everyday, visceral level. But as we mentioned earlier, people like Anil Argarwal and Sunita Narain have provided profound insight for decades – how can we embrace this, rather than us rediscovering and misappropriating or re-appropriating the language and the knowledge which already exist?

Context-specific education which enables and empowers young people to gain the knowledge and skills they need to be resilient to the climate crisis is essential. One such example, Pani Pahar, described in detail in Chapter 14 (see also Figure 1.1), started as a research programme on water and water scarcity in Indian mountain areas and developed through collaboration with educators in India into a free resource across three stages of the school curriculum in relation to climate, water, justice, equity and activism. In a further example, Cambridge Climate Quest is a climate literacy programme, launched in India in 2024, which aims to help young learners aged fourteen to sixteen in their journey of climate awareness, literacy and action. The focus of the programme is to develop youth awareness of climate-related issues and to facilitate climate action at a grassroots level.

The solutions that have the potential to deliver a climate-resilient net zero future, and the skills and training required to support this vary

Figure 1.1 Pani Pahar is a research programme on water and water scarcity in Indian mountain areas. Source: Toby Smith.

between countries and sectors of the economy. Several examples relevant to the UK are provided in Table 1.1.

We need to reinforce the notion that every action counts. The challenges posed by climate breakdown and the destruction of nature are global and can therefore appear overwhelming – too great in scale for individual action to make a difference. Yet, while governmental response is required at an international level, much of the impact will ultimately come from a multitude of actions by individuals at a local level. This manifests in multiple ways; for example, in the UK, subsidies that supported the uptake of solar energy were enacted at a national scale, but the experience of having solar panels on a roof or in a field and the economic changes that the owner of the roof or field may experience are experienced locally. Similarly, whilst local projects can feel as if they are meaningless in the context of the whole challenge, they can in fact serve as meaningful and tangible beacons for change that can be replicated again and again.

This sense that individual actions matter is highlighted in the *Ladybird Book on Climate Change* (HRH The Prince of Wales *et al.*, 2023): 'Everyone must work towards stopping climate change and

Table 1.1 *Examples of solutions and skills with the potential to deliver a climate-resilient net zero future*

Sector	Example responses	Example sustainability skills/training needs
Energy	Rapid transition to renewable energy sources including wind and solar; intelligent control systems	Energy system engineers; smart technology innovators
Buildings and infrastructure	Home insulation, heat pumps, zero-carbon concrete and steel, sustainable and resilient urban planning	Plumbers; architects
Transport	Support for walking, cycling and public transport; zero-carbon shipping and aviation	City planners; aeroengineers
Industry, business and finance	Emissions reductions from industrial processes, factories and facilities, operations and supply chains; circular economy implementation	Investors; executives
Farming and land use	Changing farming practices, land use planning, tackling deforestation, nature-based solutions	Farmers; policymakers

protecting and restoring nature. On our own and together, young and old, we can all help. Every day we can decide to do things that cut the amount of carbon dioxide we put into the atmosphere. Every day we can take positive steps to keep the natural world healthy. We have had a bad effect on the natural world for too long, and we need to stop now and instead work towards a better future' (see Figure 1.2).

As a global society, we need people who have a variety of different skills, including a capacity for innovation, who can collaborate to respond to the challenges we face and to turn them into opportunities. This applies across business, finance, agriculture, policymaking and more, and it must encompass both technology and ideas. Market mechanisms have been developed to address disparities in consumption, for example through trading of carbon credits, but it has been

Figure 1.2 Artwork from children at Fawcett Primary School Cambridge, inspired by page 42 from the *Ladybird Book on Climate Change*.

argued that this can create an instrumental attitude towards nature and undermine a spirit of shared sacrifice. Radical new thinking is required to set a value framework for decision-making in a sustainable and equitable world. Human history is full of examples where we've done that: the debates around universal suffrage, the abolition of slavery, child labour and gender equality were not driven by cost benefit analysis. They were driven by a value framework that enables us to say this is the right thing to do.

In response to these challenges, we point to the importance of six key underpinning concepts, which could be supported through education:

1) *Active citizenship*. The voices of citizens need to be part of the decision-making framework. Education has a role in supporting people's ability to make critical judgements and their ability to have a value-based framework which enables them to act in the face of knowledge. A values-led education would give people the tools and the ability to act when they are confronted by the realities and injustices that that trigger the need to act. In this way people

around the world can be empowered to be responsible and informed citizens who can actively participate in the debate.

2) *Creativity and resilience.* We need people who can devise novel solutions to the challenges we face, and who can confront traditional orthodoxies and provide fresh approaches and frameworks. Young people need to have had the opportunity to develop their imagination and the technical skills which will enable them to turn innovative concepts into reality. Resilience is also key – the challenges we face are potentially devastating and existential in nature. This provides an emotional challenge as well as a practical one – we are going to need people who can be courageous in the face of adversity.

3) *Knowledge and understanding.* People need to have a clear understanding of the sustainability threats we face to enable them to be informed democratic citizens. Curricula need to be clear on the evidence base for the next decades' challenges and the current thinking on how they might be addressed. People must acquire the relevant knowledge and skills to support future solutions, whether that is the knowledge required to support greener lifestyles (e.g. through dietary choices) or to install and use new technologies (e.g. heat pumps in homes) or practical skills required for new green jobs.

4) *Listening and compassion.* Widespread systemic change is required, varying according to geography and the socio-cultural factors at play in any one place. Understanding the impacts of policies required to enact this change on diverse groups of people will require radical listening. The existential nature of the environmental crises routinely inspires anxiety and fear for the future. We need people who can provide compassionate reassurance and empathy in challenging conditions.

5) *Systems thinking and interdisciplinarity.* The challenges we face are systemic and require holistic thinking that identifies root causes and solutions that address many different problems simultaneously. Whilst certain disciplines, like engineering, have very clear applications in this context, identifying robust and effective solutions will require adopting multiple disciplinary lenses. For example the social sciences can enhance understanding of how a new public transit system might be used, and the arts and humanities can help us understand our fundamental relationship with the environment.

6) *Local action with global impact.* Tackling the planetary emergency is going to require the global aggregation of many local actions. Everyone experiences the world at the local level, so policy changes enacted on a global scale are also experienced locally. This provides an important opportunity to develop a sense of individual agency and practical experience of instigating change. For example persuading a local authority or parish council to enact a policy change is excellent preparation for motivating change at larger scale.

The challenge that faces us as a global society is enormous, but it is not impossible. The responsibility to solve the interlinked environmental crises doesn't and shouldn't fall only on young people; however, they are the ones who will be most affected. Everyone can make a difference by helping to protect and preserve the natural world upon which we depend for our own survival. Educators have an opportunity to inspire and support young people with the understanding, confidence and optimism they will need to be active citizens, with the knowledge and skills to help design solutions and with the creativity and compassion needed to navigate a world that is changing rapidly and unequally.

References

Almond, R.E.A. *et al.* (eds.) (2022) *Living planet report 2022 – building a nature positive society.* WWF. Available at: https://wwfint.awsassets.panda.org/downloads/embargo_13_10_2022_lpr_2022_full_report_single_page_1.pdf.

Argarwal, A. and Narain, S. (1991) *Global warming in an unequal world.* New Delhi: Centre for Science and Environment. Available at: https://cdn.cseindia.org/userfiles/GlobalWarming%20Book.pdf.

Brondizio, E.S. *et al.* (eds.) (2019) *Global assessment report on biodiversity and ecosystem services of the Intergovernmental Science-Policy Platform on Biodiversity and Ecosystem Services.* Bonn: IPBES Secretariat. https://doi.org/10.5281/zenodo.3831673.

Chancel, L. *et al.* (2022) *World inequality report 2022.* World Inequality Lab. Available at: https://wir2022.wid.world/.

Dasgupta, P. (2021) *The economics of biodiversity: the Dasgupta review.* London: HM Treasury. Available at: www.gov.uk/government/publications/final-report-the-economics-of-biodiversity-the-dasgupta-review.

Dicks, L.V. *et al.* (2021) 'A global-scale expert assessment of drivers and risks associated with pollinator decline', *Nature Ecology and Evolution*, 5(10), 1453–1461. https://doi.org/10.1038/s41559-021-01534-9.

HRH The Prince of Wales *et al.* (2023) *Climate change (a ladybird expert book)*. London: Penguin.

IPCC (2021) *Secretary-General's statement on the IPCC Working Group 1 report on the physical science basis of the sixth assessment*. Available at: www.un.org/sg/en/content/sg/statement/2021-08-09/secretary-generals-statement-the-ipcc-working-group-1-report-the-physical-science-basis-of-the-sixth-assessment.

IPCC (2023) *Synthesis report of the IPCC sixth assessment report (AR6) summary for policymakers*. Available at: https://doi.org/10.59327/IPCC/AR6-9789291691647.001.

Thurstan, R., Brockington, S. and Roberts, C. (2010) 'The effects of 118 years of industrial fishing on UK bottom trawl fisheries', *Nature Communications*, 1(2). https://doi.org/10.1038/ncomms1013.

UN (2024) *The sustainable development goals report 2024*. Available at: https://unstats.un.org/sdgs/report/2024/.

UN Department of Economic and Social Affairs (2022) *World population prospects 2022: summary of results*. Available at: www.un.org/development/desa/pd/sites/www.un.org.development.desa.pd/files/wpp2022_summary_of_results.pdf.

Watts, N. *et al.* (2019) 'The 2019 report of the Lancet countdown on health and climate change: ensuring that the health of a child born today is not defined by a changing climate', *The Lancet*, 394(10211), 1836–1878. https://doi.org/10.1016/S0140-6736(19)32596-6.

2 Practitioners' Response to Manifesto 1
Sustainability Education

JENNA WATSON AND ORLANDO GARCIACANO

2.1 Introduction

The manifesto calls on educators to inspire and support young people with the skills they will need to respond to the pressing climate and environmental crises and to navigate a world that is changing rapidly and unequally. Whilst the importance of sustainability education is easily recognised in principle, it can be challenging to integrate it within a curriculum dominated by traditional disciplines. In this response, Watson and Garciacano draw on their experiences from a school in Mexico City, providing practical examples and underpinning concepts that illustrate how sustainability education can be embedded in the curriculum and school culture as part an approach that empowers individuals to become active and informed agents of change.

2.2 The Educational Panorama in Terms of Sustainability Education

So often in education, we talk of preparing children for jobs that haven't been created yet or equipping them with the skills to address tomorrow's challenges. But, as clearly put forward by Amy Munro-Faure, Emily Shuckburgh and Bhaskar Vira (Chapter 1), the time to act is now. What is required is an education that allows children to develop an understanding and awareness of the interlinked climate and environmental crises occurring at this very moment, and to be able to take meaningful action, however small, through what they are presently taught in school.

Schools are incredibly relevant to sustainable efforts on a local and in some cases a global scale; this is due to their ability to reach a broad cross-section of a community and beyond that individual their family and other significant individuals in their lives. To bring about real change in terms of providing a rich, environmentally responsive education, all actors in a school need to work together, identifying relevant issues and opportunities. However, there are significant challenges faced across all types of organisations, including schools, which are that understanding, adoption and monitoring currently depend on a few individuals taking the initiative. This means that, often, actions linked with environmental issues and climate change are approached through isolated efforts and philanthropy and not seen as a lengthy process which must be embedded in the curriculum and the culture of the school from the earliest stages of a child's life in a school all the way to their graduation day.

Therefore, it is very important that all members of the school community, including students, parents, administrative and academic staff, suppliers and the wider community, be actively involved in sustainable initiatives and have sufficient information and motivation. There are some fantastic examples of programmes, such as the Harmony approach (Harmony Project, 2024), which places the principles of nature at the heart of curriculum design, or schools such as the Green School (2024) in Bali, which is doing pioneering work in developing educational approaches that drive forward the importance of educating learners about the reality of the environmental and climate crises we're facing. However, for the most part, education, like many other systems, is slow to change, and there is not yet a critical mass or a significant coordinated approach towards teaching for a sustainable future. As Scoffham and Rawlinson (2022, p. 12) echoed, 'Sustainability, the most urgent issue of our time, is hardly mentioned in the formal curricula of most "developed" nations.'

Unfortunately, in many schools, it is a 'business as usual' approach, focusing on maintaining 'high academic standards'. And because of this, there is not sufficient time or space to meaningfully address issues related to the crises that we face. This may stem from a lack of understanding and knowledge, or simply from apathy – if one is not directly affected or cannot see the impact of their choices, why change? This mindset is dangerous and wastes the potential of education to address climate and environmental issues. Moreover, as Dunne and

Martin (2021, p. 82) argued, education for sustainability need not 'run counter to the drive for high standards of attainment'.

It is clear we can no longer avoid creating informed and relevant learning opportunities for young people. This is particularly true in Mexico City, where we are directly impacted by both the climate and environmental crises. In what follows, we speak about the ways we are working to address these challenges. We use the six underpinning concepts put forward in Chapter 1 to structure our examples and explore potential next steps for us as an institution.

2.3 The Mexican Context (Environmental and Climate Crises)

Nowhere on Earth will be exempt from the interlinked climate and environmental crises. In Mexico, geography and human actions have created a unique challenge in which multiple, compacting issues require a significant, coordinated approach. Mexico has ratified the Paris Agreement and has worked to incorporate the Aichi Biodiversity targets into a national strategy. It was also the first of the large oil-producing countries to adopt climate change legislation with the General Climate Change Law in 2012 (Government of Mexico City, 2019). However, when one takes a deeper look at Mexico's progress statistics, cross-checked against the Sustainable Development Goals (SDGs), there are multiple areas, such as the efficient use of natural resources, sustainable uses of forests and the protection of threatened species, in which Mexico has made no progress, or is even moving backwards.

Across Mexico, challenges such as deforestation, water insecurity and droughts and a projected 40–70 per cent decline in workable farmland, alongside vulnerability to natural disasters, such as earthquakes and hurricanes, makes for a precarious climate and environmental context (Climate Reality Project, 2018). Acknowledging these significant and worrying national challenges, we now look to Mexico's capital – Mexico City.

2.4 The School Context: What Are We Doing and Where Are We Going?

The capital of Mexico has its own unique geography with multiple microclimates, and, built on reclaimed swamp land, it is vulnerable to all of the aforementioned climate-related issues. Our school is situated

Practitioners' Response to Manifesto 1 41

in the south of Mexico City; the area is hilly and forested, full of coniferous trees and homes built on steep inclines. Locally, there are severe issues with water scarcity, droughts and habitat destruction, and on our own grounds – built on a former landfill site – we experience severe soil erosion and an ecological area built on a former landfill site. Our school is an all-through school, providing education for children from the age of eighteen months to eighteen years, which means we have a unique opportunity to actively support and contribute to our children's development as compassionate citizens who have a positive impact on the world around them.

To illustrate some of the ways the school has attempted to address climate and environmental challenges (see Figure 2.1 as an illustration of the spaces created to enable this learning to become explicit), we will utilise the underpinning concepts put forward by Munro-Faure, Shuckburgh and Vira: active citizenship, creativity and resilience, knowledge and understanding, listening and compassion, systems thinking and interdisciplinarity and local action with global impact. All of these activities and practices relate to active citizenship, and many invoke or apply to several of the other five concepts; there is

Figure 2.1 Our ecological areas on the Early Years and Main School site provide a meaningful space to observe living things grow and change. Source: Orlando Garciacano.

significant crossover. It is also important to state that, together, these separate actions have culminated in the launch of an internal Centre for Sustainability, our attempt at creating a coordinated effort both within and beyond our community.

1) *Fostering creativity and resilience.* As an educational institution, much of the work we do to support children's holistic development focuses on developing resilience and creativity. However, such skills must be put into, and used in, context. Here are some examples of how we foster creativity and resilience as a school:

    - *Arts-themed projects.* Spanning at least one week or longer, these projects use art as a medium to address a particular theme. Our upcoming project utilises a text: 'La Tierra es Mi Amiga' (The Earth is My Friend) each level of the school from early years to Year 6 (eighteen months to eleven years) are working to create an image of themselves in nature, with the youngest identifying what they love and appreciate about nature and the older children considering specific ecosystems and learning about these through the research process conducted whilst creating their unique artwork.
    - *Themed days and weeks.* Our yearly calendar is planned carefully to provide meaningful events to draw awareness to, and develop understanding of, a range of issues that affect our community and our world. For example each year we hold an Earth Week. This event is conducted with the support of parent volunteers from the schools' Ecological Committee and involves experts within and beyond our community. This year, our focus is water scarcity. Each year group will participate in a range of different activities; one example is finding ways to wash a baby doll with a limited amount of water to challenge children to think creatively about the ways in which we use the resources we have.

2) *Developing knowledge and understanding.* It is essential children have a deep and informed understanding of climate change, biodiversity loss and wider sustainability challenges. As an all-through school, we have a unique opportunity to carefully plan how we can support children as they acquire and explore concepts in an age-appropriate way, while exposing them to the 'big ideas' they need to understand. We do this in the following ways:

- *Curriculum design.* In early years and primary, we operate using a topic-based approach to learning, and each topic has been designed to have a specific sustainability focus. For example a topic in nursery; children learn about toys and the importance of sharing toys with others when we no longer want them, developing the early foundations for understanding circular economies. Year 1 has a topic named 'What a Wonderful World', which focuses on animals and plants. Throughout this topic, children develop and grow their own rooftop garden, learning about the challenges of caring for plants, the threats they face from insects, disease, overexposure to sun and heat, and a lack of water. At primary level, children in Year 3 learn about the impact of humans on marine life, in particular the Deep Horizon Oil Spill in 2010 and the significant damage that human activity can have on marine ecosystems.
- *Reaching out.* Whilst each topic has a sustainability focus, we complement this by reaching out to experts to add deeper meaning to the learning and further develop children's knowledge and understanding of the real-world implications of these topics. One of our reception topics, 'To Infinity and Beyond', focuses on space and new technologies, and children have the opportunity to speak to an expert who works for NASA to find out about space beyond the role of the astronaut.

3) *Creating space for listening and compassion.* The importance of authentic listening, perspective-taking and compassion cannot be underestimated in these challenging times. It is important to equip children with these attributes so as not to end up in conflicts, finger-pointing and blaming one another for the situations we find ourselves in. Moreover, as argued by Munro-Faure, Shuckburgh and Vira, it is critical that we 'listen to one another as we collectively search for solutions'. We approach this in the following ways:

- *Philosophy for children and debating.* In our early years and primary sections we utilise the Philosophy for Children programme. This is not only powerful for developing children's abilities to express their ideas in a second language, it also encourages children to think deeply about their own ideas and those of others. Understanding that there is not always one answer to a problem or one perspective on a topic or issue.

This practice is further developed in secondary through debating exercises, where children can analyse and weigh up different arguments and perspectives. A strong emphasis is placed on listening – to develop deep understanding and consideration of the ideas of others. Children are given the opportunity to approach topics beyond their basic themes, and deal with bigger concepts – for example they might engage with the fact that countries pollute, but also try to understand ideas of power, political influence, culture, and economics, and the ways their coalescence contributes to pollution. As we collectively search for solutions, children need to have the capacity to consider the validity and strengths in the perspectives of others.

- *High-quality texts for empathy.* An area that we have been investing time and staff training on has been the ways in which we use key learning texts, selected not only for their academic potential but also for the emotional skills they might foster in their readers. Each topic in kinder and primary features a range of texts which allow the children to connect with the feelings and perspectives of the characters.

4) *Harnessing the potential for systems thinking and interdisciplinarity.* In our early years and primary sections, the use of a topic-based approach to learning allows for a range of opportunities for interdisciplinary learning, and at a secondary level participatory and collaborative programmes further facilitate this:

- *Inquiry-focused learning.* Each topic in early years and primary has an inquiry focus which allows children to engage with 'big ideas' and see connections between them. For example, in Year 1, when learning about 'Adventurers and Explorers', children ask the question, 'How do we show respect for the places we visit?' developing the concept of responsibility and respect when visiting new places and knowing new people. This guides the children to plan their own adventure respectfully, considering the impact of leaving behind waste or taking away something from its natural habitat.
- *Cross-department projects.* At a secondary level, there are increased opportunities for collaboration across disciplines. For example a recent project shared between the Arts and Science Departments resulted in children designing plant pots and

growing plants. From an arts perspective, children learnt about the history of pottery, and where different ceramic materials are sourced and how to work with them. On the science side, students learnt about composite materials and components, as well as physical and chemical properties.

5) *Supporting local action with global impact.* We situate our school firmly in the local community and the issues that affect us.
   - *Global social leaders.* This is a voluntary programme that empowers students to develop their own social enterprise. With guided support, students consider all aspects of their project, including its alignment with the SDGs and how to reach out to external partners and organisations and plan for impact. Students' participation in this programme was life changing, not just for them but for the individuals touched by their projects and the adults involved in supporting them. Some examples of initiatives set up by students through this programme were: an early stimulation education programme[1] for mothers in prisons, enabling them to support their children (who are allowed to remain with their mothers until the age of three); another drew inspiration from Akira Miyawaki's methodology (Lewis, 2022) of urban forest to create a plant nursery in our school (see Figure 2.2).
   - *Local action projects and connecting with local organisations.* In both an organised and organic way, school-based action and interaction with local organisations is supported by senior leadership from all quarters of the school community – students, parents and staff. For example, within our school community, students run an enterprise selling locally produced, sustainably farmed honey, and parents run a weekly recycling programme in conjunction with local organisations.

Whilst we are proud of and celebrate each of these different activities, and hope they will be useful ideas for other educators looking for ways they can develop their schools' approaches to climate and environmental education, we are aware that many of these actions are isolated and require a coordinated, strategic approach. As a result, we have been working to develop our own Centre for Sustainability Education.

[1] https://www.globalsocialleaders.com/authors-of-our-future-2/

Figure 2.2 Some of the students behind the 'Authors of Our Future' initiative who gathered donations of sanitary products for young mothers in prison and designed early stimulation training for these women. Source: Orlando Garciacano.

The purpose of the Centre is to unify the efforts made across the school, ensuring that climate and environmentally responsive themes are the golden threads that weave their way throughout everything we do as an organisation. The purpose of this initiative is to reach across and beyond, maximising education's multiplying effect to touch the lives of and empower our students, our parents, our local communities, staff and external partners, and ultimately generate research and resources for other schools and organisations to use themselves. Echoing the words of Munro-Faure, Shuckburgh and Vira, we are taking to heart the idea that 'every action counts'. We hope that, through our work, we can offer a 'meaningful and tangible [beacon] for change that can be replicated again and again'.

Over to You

Much of what we describe herein is about space making. Spaces are important for children. School is often a space of safety, of care and of freedom as well as a space that becomes the opposite. In terms of the themes we present, the following questions could guide the reader in their own space for new thinking to bring about better climate and environment science learning and action:

- How is space created in your context? How do you know the experiences of the children who enter the space?
- How do you connect learning in school with experiences at home? On the street? In the children's diverse lived experiences?
- How do teachers learn about climate and environmental science?

References

Climate Reality Project (2018) *How is climate change affecting Mexico?* Available at: www.climaterealityproject.org/blog/how-climate-change-affecting-mexico.

Dunne, R. and Martin, E. (2021) 'Learning to learn from nature: how principles of harmony in the natural world can guide curriculum design', in Biddulph, J. and Flutter, J. (eds.) *Inspiring primary curriculum design*. Oxon: Routledge, pp. 81–96.

Government of Mexico City (2019) *Innovation and rights; a program to enhance sustainable development in Mexico City*. Available at: https://sdgs.un.org/sites/default/files/2021-04/Mexico%20City%20VLR.pdf.

Green School (2024) *Green School, Bali, Indonesia*. Available at: www.greenschool.org/bali/.

Harmony Project (2024) *Putting sustainability and nature at the heart of learning*. Available at: www.theharmonyproject.org.uk/.

Lewis, H. (2022) *Mini-forest revolution: using the Miyawaki method to rapidly rewild the world*. White River Junction: Chelsea Green.

Scoffham, S. and Rawlinson, S. (2022) *Sustainability education: a classroom guide*. London: Bloomsbury Academic.

3 Manifesto 2

Weaving a Hopeful Future – Voice, Agency and Practical Wisdom as Threads of Change

JULIA FLUTTER

3.1 Introduction

When the late Professor Jean Rudduck and I began researching the notion of student voice in education in the early 1990s, a search for the keywords 'pupil voice' and 'student voice' would only have retrieved works on vocal cords and speech disorders. Now, thirty years later, a similar keyword search in the British Education Index or Google yields tens of thousands of references to research, practice and policy on initiatives that involve the participation of children and young people. This proliferation of interest in consulting young people and involving them directly in matters concerning their lives and their futures has been widely noted. However, the growth of the student voice movement has not been without challenge and controversy. Some feel it is going too far when children and young people are invited to comment or give their views on matters that are traditionally associated with adult domains, or when children campaign in ways perceived to undermine adult authority. We have also seen a reaction against the tokenism that can arise when children's voices are used as mere decoration or to tick a box politically. If we are not listening to children and young people with a sincere regard and respect for their views, perspectives and capacities, then student voice efforts risk doing more harm than good.

Adults often applaud children and young people, like Greta Thunberg, Luisa Neubauer and Xiuhtezcatl Martinez, who speak on public platforms about profound and serious issues. However, the contributions of these individuals, although widely celebrated and highly influential, are rarely acted upon directly by policymakers. There is a problematic assumption that the action of voicing itself – being given the opportunity to express oneself – is what matters, whilst the need for adults to listen seriously and act is less significant. The voices of children and young people warrant recognition, but recognition should also (sometimes) give rise to action in terms of policy and practice. In this manifesto, I argue that the time has come to expand the notion of student voice to encompass another largely neglected idea – Aristotle's notion of practical wisdom (*phronēsis*) – in order to achieve transformative change in education. I will return to this idea later, but first we need to understand why the principles of student voice and agency have not yet been implemented in full.

Student voice emerged as an idea in the late twentieth century and gradually took root, becoming a worldwide movement of change in education (Rudduck and McIntyre, 2007). The movement has its origins in earlier studies in the 1970s which explored students' perspectives on teaching and learning. And the idea of student voice was given impetus by Article 12 of the United Nations Convention on the Rights of the Child (UNCRC) (United Nations, 1989). Consulting students and giving them opportunities to take an active role in the decisions that affect their lives and education keyed in with the UNCRC's aims. Still, the notion of student voice has been interpreted in different ways in different countries. Some, including the UK and Canada, have focused on student voice as a tool for school improvement initiatives, whilst others, such as Denmark and Sweden, have used it as a way to enhance democratic education. There have also been groundbreaking projects like the Design for Change programme, founded by Indian educator, Kiran bir Sethi, which seek to inspire children and young people to design and lead social change projects within their communities (Biddulph, Rolls and Flutter, 2022). While many of these efforts have had a positive impact on children and young people's opportunities for active participation, there is little evidence they led to sustained changes in policy. Concerns have also been raised that short-term initiatives sometimes fail to engage all students, leaving some marginalised and silenced, which can increase students' sense of alienation, leading to cynicism and disaffection. Furthermore, in cases where students are consulted but their views not taken into consideration in the final decision-making, the result can be a loss of trust in democratic processes and adult authority. In addition, not all educators have welcomed the rise of student voice principles, and some teacher unions have objected to student involvement in school decision-making processes. In recent years, it has been argued that teacher agency has been undermined by prescriptive policymaking, and this has led to concern that student voices are being heard whilst teachers' are being silenced. It seems fair to ask the question, How can educators nurture agency in young learners if they do not possess it themselves? As the Cambridge Primary Review warned, 'Pupils will not learn to think for themselves if their teachers are expected merely to do as they are told' (Alexander, 2010, p. 496).

The fallout of a pandemic, as well as ongoing global economic, social, political and environmental issues, have focused our minds: without a significant shift in our policies and practices, education will become anathema to the lives of our children and young people. Transformation is needed to reimagine an education which is dynamic and young person centred.

So, in a nutshell, our problem is that focusing on developing children and young people's agency and voice has not led to transformative change in education. In fact, at times, our efforts have resulted in the opposite. Though we were not wrong to set out on this journey, we have reached something of a cul-de-sac. However, having come this far, I believe we should look to practical wisdom to help us uncover a more hopeful way forward.

In this manifesto I argue that by weaving voice, agency and practical wisdom together as threads of change, we can foster collaborative capacities for values-led action and decision-making in our schools and in the world at large. By equipping future generations with the capacity for practical wisdom, we can empower them to make better decisions, act as responsible stewards of the planet and become effective problem solvers capable of addressing complex social issues.

3.2 What Is Practical Wisdom, and Is It Needed?

Writing two and a half thousand years ago, in a time and society very different to our own, the philosopher Aristotle spoke of practical wisdom as being an 'intellectual virtue' – a way of being and a way of thinking – that enables a person to lead a flourishing life. Philosopher Stephen Kemmis (2012, p. 156) offers this modern take on what practical wisdom is and entails:

[Practical wisdom] is a quality of mind and character and action – the quality that consists in being open to experience *and* being committed to acting with wisdom and prudence *for the good*. The person who has this virtue has become informed by experience and history and thus has a capacity to think *critically* about a given situation ... and then to think *practically* about what *should be done* under the circumstances that pertain here and now, in the light of what has gone before, and in the knowledge that *one must act*.

Practical wisdom is about deciding what is right under the circumstances – deciding what is the best action to take in the here and now. It is a deliberative process that draws on knowledge, values and experience, and it provides an essential foundation for voice, agency and action. Practical wisdom involves balancing different types of knowledge, ethics, reasoning and skill to reach a judgement that informs action. Before we can express our voices and show agency, we must possess the courage of our convictions and know that what we say and what we are striving for are right. The Jubilee Centre for Character and Virtues at the University of Birmingham in the UK has been looking at practical wisdom (*phronēsis*), and their team has sought to understand its development in adolescents. The Centre's researchers describe *phronēsis* as a meta-virtue which plays 'a fundamental role in bridging the "gap" between knowing the good and doing the good' (Kristjánnson and Pollard, 2021, p. 6). Individuals acquire practical wisdom by interacting with others. And when it is enacted collectively through dialogue, it becomes informed, critical deliberation that characterises the intellectual freedom of which John Dewey (1960, p. 287) spoke:

Social conditions interact with the preferences of an individual – in a way favorable to actualizing freedom only when they develop intelligence, not abstract knowledge and abstract thought, but power of vision and reflection. For these take effect in making preference, desire, and purpose more flexible, alert, and resolute. Freedom has too long been thought of as an intermediate power operating in a closed and ended world. In its reality, freedom is a resolute will operating in a world in some respects indeterminate, because open and moving toward a new future.

So, although the starting point for practical wisdom lies within the individual, its development and enactment are necessarily social, and integral to expressions of voice and agency. Interestingly, the Great Learning (*Da Xue*) (Chinaknowledge, 2022), one of the Chinese Confucian texts, written in roughly the same time period as Aristotle, expresses a similar interrelationship between personal and societal responsibility and envisions 'great learning' – a notion that embraces knowledge, virtuous character and ethical understanding – as being at the heart of civilised life.

The Great Learning

> The ancients who wished to illustrate illustrious virtue throughout the kingdom,
> first ordered well their own states.
> Wishing to order well their states, they first regulated their families.
> Wishing to regulate their families, they first cultivated their persons.
> Wishing to cultivate their persons, they first rectified their hearts.
> Wishing to rectify their hearts, they first sought to be sincere in their thoughts.
> Wishing to be sincere in their thoughts, they first extended to the utmost their knowledge.
> Such extension of knowledge lay in the investigation of things.
> Things being investigated, knowledge became complete.
> Their knowledge being complete, their thoughts were sincere.
> Their thoughts being sincere, their hearts were then rectified.
> Their hearts being rectified, their persons were cultivated.
> Their persons being cultivated, their families were regulated.
> Their families being regulated, their states were rightly governed.
> Their states being rightly governed, the whole kingdom was made tranquil and happy.
> From the Son of Heaven down to the mass of the people,
> all must consider the cultivation of the person the root of everything besides.
> It cannot be, when the root is neglected, that what should spring from it will be well ordered.

Despite profound technological and social change in the intervening centuries, these ancient philosophical ideas still resonate with the dilemmas of the twenty-first century. These dimensions of practical wisdom and the Great Learning – sincerity, ethics, reason, dialogue, knowledge, trust, reciprocity and respect – are vital to the successful functioning of civilised societies. And yet, unfortunately, we are still – across the world – a long way from their fullest actualisation. Put crudely, in what way are current educational practices preventing problem solvers from addressing social concerns (e.g. climate)? And what exactly will the inculcation of practical wisdom in subsequent generations do for their capacity to think around/through climate disaster? The question is, How can we cultivate practical wisdom through education for a more hopeful future?

3.3 Practical Wisdom: Creating New Educational Spaces

To create educational spaces that foster the development of practical wisdom, we must review and evaluate the conditions of learning. We can start by considering what is being taught and what aims underpin our curricular decision-making. If we aim to induct children and young people into societies that value justice, equity and sustainability, then a curriculum needs to avail students of different types of knowledge, capacities and reasoning. Moving beyond the commonplace and see-sawing 'skills versus knowledge' argument, an emphasis on practical wisdom requires us to offer curricula that seek to balance theoretical knowledge, practical skills, ethical understanding and experiential, intuitive and embodied ways of knowing. As the Cambridge Primary Review proposes, a curriculum needs to build a sense of empowerment, 'to excite, promote and sustain children's agency, empowering them through knowledge, understanding, skill and personal qualities to profit from their present and later learning, to discover and lead rewarding lives, and to manage life and find new meaning in a changing world' (Alexander, 2010, p. 197).

As well as reimagining our educational aims and curricula, we should create educational spaces that foster collaborative learning and reflection. Schools must look for new ways to enable young people and teachers to express their voices and agency together in a spirit of collegiality, reflecting Maxine Greene's (1995) call for school communities that question and seek out possibilities for social justice, equality and transformative change. Voice and agency flourish when students engage in dialogue with their peers, teachers and communities.

It is important to support students' empowerment as leaders of transformative change who can draw on their capacities for practical wisdom to make well-informed, values-based judgements. Our educative efforts must be suffused with values, morality and character so that students and teachers can develop practical wisdom – becoming active members of learning communities in which relationships and dialogue are framed as collaborative, constructive and respectful. Far from being an abstract or cerebral ideal, practical wisdom is about taking action, and schools of the future must enable students and teachers to hone their capacities for practical wisdom, both within and beyond their gates. One example of this approach in action can be found in the Round Square international network of schools, described here by Round Square's chairman, Rod Fraser (Round Square, 2018):

> Created collaboratively with 160 schools involved and a writing team that spanned six continents, the RS Discovery Framework offers a structure for teaching and learning, both inside and beyond the curriculum, that connects the *Spirit* inherent in each of the Round Square <u>IDEALS</u> (International Understanding, Democracy, Environmental Stewardship, Adventure, Leadership and Service) with twelve *Discoveries* that students explore on their learning journey: inquisitiveness, tenacity, courage, compassion, inventiveness, ability to solve problems, self-awareness, sense of responsibility, appreciation for diversity, commitment to sustainability, communication and team-working skills. Within this Framework, Students and Faculty in RS Member Schools are encouraged to discover and develop their own capabilities through a range of experiences, activities, taught lessons, collaborative projects and challenges. One of the many factors that sets the RS Discovery Framework apart is that it is rooted in genuinely global, multi-curricula practical implementation. It describes, rather than dictates; is examples-led, not theoretical; and whilst it was conceived through a gradual meeting-of-minds between Round Square Heads of School over a number of years, it is inspired and empowered by student voice.

3.4 Practical Wisdom as a Foundation for Teacher Professionalism

I suggested earlier that teachers' autonomy as professionals has been under pressure in recent decades as a result of educational policy that is increasingly managerial, marketized and prescriptive. In response to this threat to teacher professionalism, there has been growing interest in *phronēsis* – as a discourse and vision for practice that 'resists a passive acquiescence to the discourses of professional life that are increasingly instrumentalist, technicist, and managerial' (Kinsella and Pitman, 2012, p. 171). Elizabeth Kinsella and Alan Pitman explain:

Manifesto 2

The professional is not simply a technician; rather, the professional is charged with the tasks of making complex interpretive judgements and taking action, as spaces for learning and for professional development. ... Phronēsis is a concept of interest, and of hope, for elaborating current conceptions of professional knowledge and for advancing an approach to practice in the professions that seeks to fill the void in current practices – an approach that is felt as a morally informed guiding force oriented toward a wiser path. (p. 171)

Fostering practical wisdom for the teaching profession means creating new structures for reflection and collaboration within teacher settings and communities, both nationally and globally, so that opportunities for building *phronēsis* are magnified by shared languages, expertise and

The teacher reads an interesting, recent research report which puts forward a new approach that may help in addressing these concerns. The report highlights the positive outcomes of the research but currently no training or detailed guidance on using this new approach is offered for teachers.

The teacher has reservations about the approach promoted in the official guidance as it does not have a clear, theoretical rationale and evidential basis. The research report's evidence seems overwhelmingly positive but the teacher does not feel confident applying its ideas without training and guidance, so the teacher continues to follow the policy recommendations.

Uncertain of what next steps to take in response to the disappointing outcomes, the teacher nevertheless feels obliged to continue implementing the recommendend practices.

A teacher aims to support every student to achieve their full potential but feels concerned that some students are currently not making good progress with aspects of their learning. The teacher is keen to find new strategies to help these students to improve their learning.

The teacher is concerned that new policy guidance will mean introducing a specific approach for tackling these concerns, and compliance with this policy will be checked in school inspections. The evidence from the research report does not seem to align with this official guidance, creating a dilemma for the teacher.

Monitoring and evaluation of the students' progress at the end of term indicate that the approach recommended in policy guidance has not helped the students who are struggling, and they are continuing to fall behind their peers.

Feeling frustrated and isolated, the teacher feels unable to try an alternative strategy to address the problems. The lack of opportunities for professional development and collaboration with other teachers and schools hampers finding new ways forward.

Figure 3.1 Influences on teacher's praxis and decision-making without *phronēsis*.

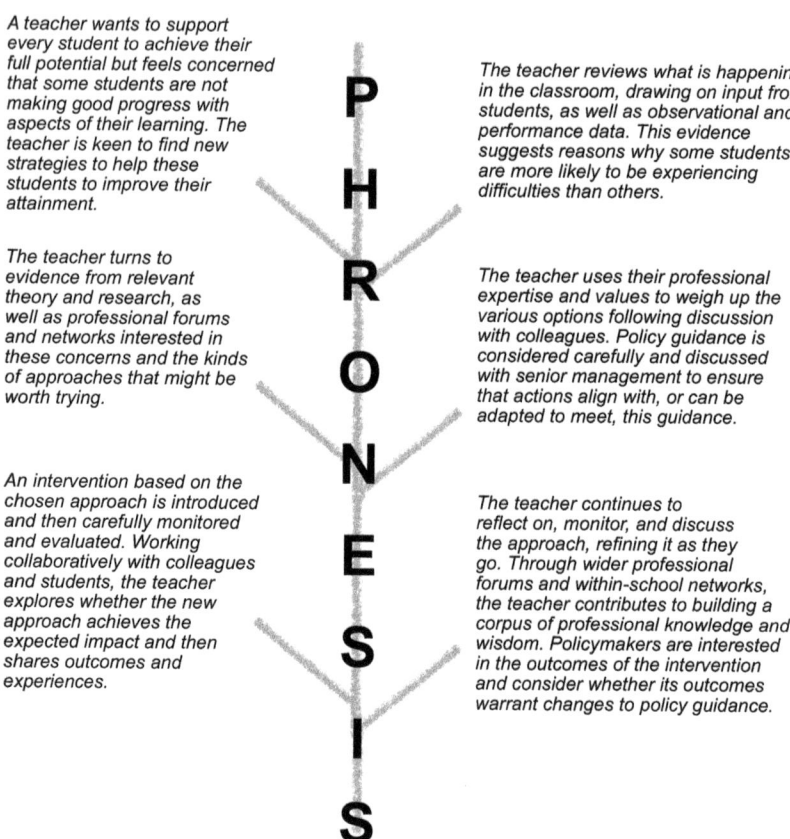

Figure 3.2 Teacher's praxis and decision-making led by *phronēsis*.

visions. What might this look like in practice? Professional bodies, subject associations, initial teacher education institutions, teacher unions, educational networks and forums could become repositories that curate professional knowledge, drawn from accumulated practice experience, relevant theory and rigorous research. There are encouraging steps being taken in this direction already: for example the Chartered College of Teaching in the UK is curating teachers' research through its journal, *Impact*, and its online platform. Similarly, the growth of teacher-led initiatives like ResearchEd suggest that teachers are concerned that their practices are 'evidence-led' and 'research-informed'. However, *phronēsis* requires more than theoretical research evidence to arrive at wise decisions and actions: at its core are the professional values which must shape and determine practice. Figures 3.1 and 3.2 use a fictional scenario to contrast the constraints evident in current practice with the affordances created through a divergent framework of *phronēsis-framed collegial professionalism*. In Figure 3.1 we see the teacher struggling to enact their professional values amidst competing pressures. The teacher's professional knowledge and values are unrecognised and overwritten. Figure 3.2 suggests that a *phronēsis-framed collegial professionalism* would allow practice and decision-making to be driven by teachers' values, informed by an ongoing, collaborative process of critical reflection and collegiality. Such a conceptualisation of teacher professionalism would strengthen teachers' agency and autonomy and help to create an expanding professional knowledge base for initial teacher education and professional development.

3.5 Weaving a Hopeful Future

'We do not inherit the Earth from our ancestors, we borrow it from our children' – this adage attributed to Chief Seattle (also rendered as *Sealth* or *Seathl*, Chief of the Duwamish and Suquamish peoples, Washington, USA) reminds us of our obligation to future generations who will inherit the planet. We want those future generations to make better decisions, to take greater care and act as wiser custodians of this planet than we have been. We cannot proffer solutions to the problems they might face in the future, but perhaps we can arm them with the capacities for practical wisdom that will enable them to be better decision-makers and collaborative problem solvers. As we grapple with worldwide challenges in this third decade of the twenty-first century, the words of American philosopher Richard Bernstein (1983, p. 229) strike a prescient chord, drawing our attention to the urgent need for practical wisdom, community and dialogue:

At a time when the threat of total annihilation no longer seems to be an abstract possibility but the most imminent and real potentiality, it becomes all the more imperative to try again and again to foster and nurture those forms of communal life in which dialogue, conversation, *phronēsis*, practical discourse and judgment are concretely embodied in our everyday practices.

Despite the prevailing sense of urgency and fear, there is hope on the horizon, and it can be heard in the voices of children and young people themselves. We must listen. For the past century, every year, a group of young people have come together to write the Peace and Goodwill Message, which is now translated into 100 different languages and sent out to the children of the world, under the auspices of Urdd Gobaith Cymru, the Welsh National Voluntary Youth Organisation. The Urdd's (2022) message, marking its centenary, is titled 'The Climate Emergency'. I offer this manifesto in the hope that it may inspire you and your students to explore new possibilities for nurturing practical wisdom; I leave its final words to the young people of Wales (Urdd Gobaith Cymru, 2022).

Neges Heddwch ac Ewyllys Da (Peace and Goodwill Message) 2022
The Climate Emergency

The clock is ticking
And our world is on fire.
It's time to wake up.

Floods, fires, starvation, and poverty,
this is our reality.

Migration, conflict and displacement,
is this what our future holds?

Why are we still listening
to the blah, blah, blah of those in power?

Why do we still believe
that we can buy our way out?

It's time to wake up.
It's time to make a change.

We can't carry on like this.
We have the privilege of choice,
to slow down, to lessen our use,
to think,
to stop overconsumption.

Because we won't be the first to suffer.
And so here's our promise
to change the way we live
and to call for a systemic change
for the sake of those in the Global South.
For the sake of a future.

Manifesto 2

We'll begin with ourselves
by making small changes
And putting pressure on corporations and politicians
to make the big changes.

This is our promise.
What's yours?
It's time to wake up.

3.6 Discussion Points: Gathering Threads

The threads shown in Figure 3.3 do not represent a bullet point list of recommendations or mottoes for a wall poster. There are no carefully worded guidelines, blueprints or sets of principles to prescribe or prioritise; rather, I would like you to think of these words as

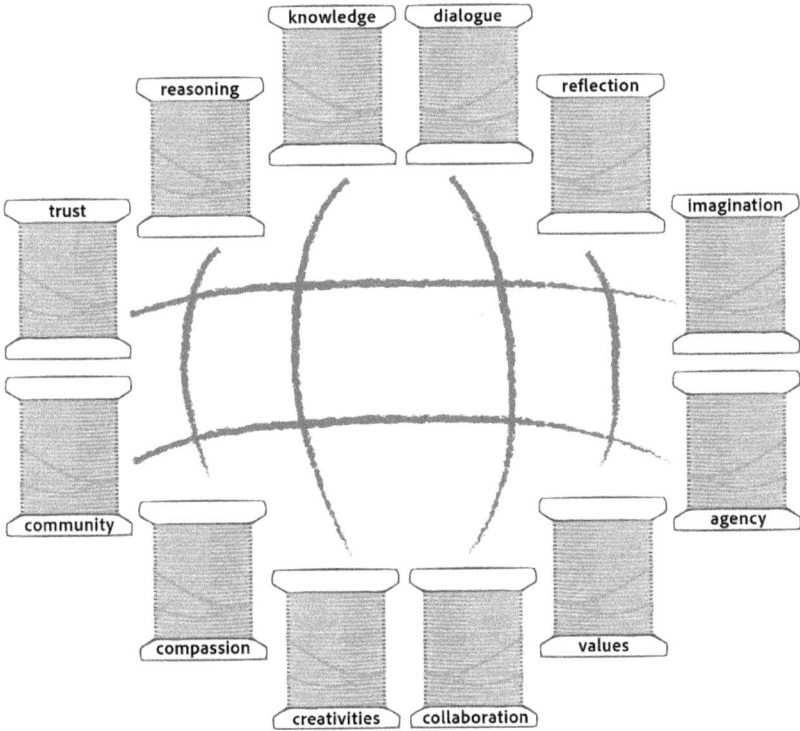

Figure 3.3 Threads for discussion.

threads, to be taken in hand, discussed and woven together into the fabric of the future.

- What do these threads mean? How do you, your colleagues and your students think about each of them? Are some threads particularly important in your setting or community?
- How are these threads woven through your own practice and educational setting right now?
- Are there ways to weave these threads differently to create new patterns of possibility for your students, colleagues and communities?
- What other threads might you and your students, colleagues and communities want to weave in?

References

Alexander, R.J. (ed.) (2010) *Children, their world, their education: final report and recommendations of the Cambridge Primary Review*. London: Routledge.

Bernstein, R.J. (1983) *Beyond objectivism and relativism: science, hermeneutics and praxis*. Philadelphia: University of Pennsylvania Press.

Biddulph, J., Rolls, L. and Flutter, J. (eds.) (2022) *Unleashing children's voices in new democratic education*. Abingdon: Routledge.

Chinaknowledge (2022) *Daxue*. Available at: www.chinaknowledge.de/Literature/Classics/daxue.html.

Dewey, J. (1960) 'Philosophies of freedom', in Bernstein, R. (ed.) *On experience, nature, and freedom*. New York: Liberal Arts, pp. 261–287.

Greene, M. (1995) *Releasing the imagination: essays on education, the arts, and social change*. San Francisco: Jossey-Bass.

Kemmis, S. (2012) 'Phronēsis, experience and the primacy of praxis', in Kinsella, E.A. and Pitman, A. (eds.) *Phronēsis as professional knowledge: practical wisdom in the professions*. Rotterdam: Sense, pp. 147–161.

Kinsella, E. and Pitman, A. (eds.) (2012) *Phronēsis as professional knowledge: practical wisdom in the professions*. Amsterdam: Sense.

Kristjánnson, K. and Pollard, D. (2021) *Phronēsis: using an Aristotelian model as a research tool*. Birmingham: Jubilee Centre, University of Birmingham.

Round Square (2018) *Re-discovering Round Square*. Available at: www.roundsquare.org/articles/rediscovering-round-square/.

Rudduck, J. and McIntyre, D. (2007) *Improving learning: the pupils' agenda*. London: Routledge.

United Nations (1989) *Convention on the rights of the child.* Available at: https://treaties.un.org/doc/Treaties/1990/09/19900902%2003-14%20AM/Ch_IV_11p.pdf.

Urdd Gobaith Cymru (2022) *Peace and goodwill message: the climate emergency.* Available at: www.urdd.cymru/files/4316/4925/7662/English.pdf.

4 Practitioner's Response to Manifesto 2

Promoting Children's Voices

KIRSTIN MACVICAR

4.1 Introduction

The promotion of children's voices has a long history; from the days of John Dewey's democratic education (Dewey, 2000) through the work of Julia Flutter and Jean Rudduck (Rudduck and Flutter, 2000; Flutter and Rudduck, 2004) to present-day efforts to help children articulate their visions for the future of their world. In response to the manifesto about empowering children to release their voices and celebrate the art of the possible, honest reflections are shared about classroom practices in both the UK and India. These are just two examples, and we call on the reader to reflect on their own situations and articulate what it is that allows children to have agency in other contexts too.

Here are some questions provoked by Julia Flutters' manifesto (Chapter 3):

- How do we convey the main points raised in the manifesto to others?
- How do we champion children's voices in adult-dominated domains where age is seen as the defining sign of adequacy?
- How do we ensure that in the process of championing the voices of young people, we do not silence others?
- How can we create classrooms that facilitate collaborations between teachers' and pupils' voices, and how can we ensure that this is replicated in wider society?

4.2 Practitioner Wisdom from Cambridge, UK

You would be hard pushed to find a teacher who does not want to promote the voices of the children with whom they work. Those who work with children, and take the time to listen to them, soon realise their little voices are in fact not so little. These little voices are fundamental if one wants to consider an education system that attends to the whole child, exploring learning in a multifaceted and multidimensional way, with an appreciation for the different skills children bring and acquire, beyond or alongside their academic development. We all have teaching moments that can only be described as magic; I know for me, these have always been centred on the promotion of children voices, whether intentionally promoted or the result of children's sheer determination to be heard! I remember a singing assembly led by our headteacher, Dr James Biddulph. A child came up to him and said, 'Mr Biddulph, I'm not allowed to sing because it's against my culture. ... My dad told me not to sing because we do not sing at home, it is haram.' As a result of this small interaction, the school made a commitment to ensuring children's voices – their ideas, feelings, thoughts, worries, joys and so on – were central to our thinking, planning and educational practices.

Box 4.1 Personal Reflections of a Teacher

After reading the manifesto, I was reflecting on how I incorporated children's voices into my own practices, and the challenges and difficulties I faced in doing so. I am proud of the classroom community I have fostered – one where all children are free to express their ideas, opinions and wants in an environment where they will be heard and respected. However, I have started questioning the authenticity of this process, and asking whose agency is really in play. For despite my influence, it is really the children who are the driving force within this environment. Their ideas on inclusion are often more developed or concrete than my own – offering suggestions for how to include children who are reluctant to speak, or exploring alternatives to verbal engagement, or showing an appreciation for the different facets of participation. It has become apparent to me that the promotion of children's voices is the promotion of all voices, and a vital step towards inclusion inside and beyond the classroom. The specific messages conveyed by young people such as Greta Thunberg are invaluable, but so is what they represent;

> children's voices being expressed and listened to. If harnessed and showcased, representation of this sort will inspire the next generation of voices. In many cases, these voices are already present in our classrooms; they are now just waiting for their 'stage'. This stage does not have to be global, like Greta Thunberg's; in many cases, the promotion of voices on the school stage is a good starting point. Our classrooms are the perfect place to foster these voices – who knows where they will end up?

The chapter provokes interesting questions for educators. Firstly, it raises concerns about the presence of children's voices in otherwise adult domains. Some issues are undoubtably age sensitive. And yet, in most cases, they also touch on ideas or themes that are accessible and suitable for children. How do we, as educators and adults, make these conversations appropriate and accessible for children. Relatedly, how do we then ensure these voices, once expressed, are not only championed but used to make change? Children's voices should not be used in tokenistic ways, and their insights should be combined with, or engaged by, other adult voices. We need to further explore ways of including children in key discussions and ensure their voices are used as catalysts for change.

In order to help answer these questions, a case study from the University of Cambridge Primary School (UCPS) is explored; key pedagogical approaches and their impact on children's voice are outlined, with suggestions for future implementation. Then, a case study from Dhun, India, is explored, presenting an exciting opportunity to rethink school design.

Let's start by exploring a case study illustrating the promotion of children's voices in school decisions through a 'Class Congress'.

Class Congress

Title
Class Congress: An Embedded Curriculum to Release Voices

Context
The curriculum at the UCPS has been specifically designed to incorporate numerous pedagogical approaches that aim to promote pupil voice, creating autonomous learners. The school aims to help learners

develop strong academic foundations and a love of learning. It also strives to cultivate compassionate citizens who are able to respectfully share and discuss their ideas and opinions.

Curriculum Design
At the UCPS, learning is anchored to, and focuses on, five key values – empathy, courage, trust, respect and gratitude – while still ensuring that all curricular demands and government expectations were adhered to. Beyond imparting knowledge, the school aims to harness the natural curiosity and creativity of children to create lifelong learners with the confidence to ask questions and solve problems. The school designed its curriculum around key pedagogical approaches, one of which is 'oracy and dialogue'. Our focus on oracy and dialogue is embedded throughout the school, starting in lesson planning and teaching approaches, and every stage of a child's development. We also include children in debates around what they would like their education to include. The school believes that children must be taught how to actively engage in discussion and debate.

This begins with the integration of 'talk agreements' that are discussed and built on by students, and continues with the introduction of 'talk roles'. A talk agreement is a set of expectations about ways of engaging in a pair or in a group. For example a basic starting point would be that children look at each other when they are talking together, or take turns and don't talk over one another. This ensures that children have an appreciation for the different ways to engage in talk and that they understand its multifaceted nature.

Classroom practices and learning also promote discussion, with children exposed to different conversational formats, such as triads, talk partners, larger-group discussions and whole-class discussions. Children are encouraged to be brave in their ideas. Classrooms and learning spaces are created to facilitate discussion, ensuring children are free to express their ideas in safe spaces, knowing their ideas will be met with respect. In line with this, the teaching staff are also encouraged to talk and debate, knowing their perspectives will be listened to and respected. Even the physical layout of the school creates spaces for children and adults to engage in dialogue; the learning street (the name for the corridor) acts as an extension of each classroom, connecting different form and age groups, and thereby creating spaces where children who ordinarily would not interact can come together, learn and interact. The use of these spaces changes day by day, offering flexibility to our educators and learners, a factor which in itself promotes the importance of pupil voice.

What We Did

In all schools, development is an ongoing process. In 2022, following discussions with children, and after our headteacher, Dr James Biddulph, visited schools in Europe as part of the Erasmus project, the school decided to trial 'Class Congress'. Class Congress is in part a re-envisioned school council, but one that ensures *all* children can have a say. School councils have been commonplace in UK primary schools for decades, but their utility is being questioned, and tweaks are being made to the format. In the typical school council, two people from each class are voted to represent the group, ensuring that the same children, and thus the same voices, are represented. Others are therefore not given the opportunity to develop these skills.

Class Congress was devised as a way to overcome this exclusion and ensure all children are given the space to air their ideas. Class Congress involves weekly sessions between all children and the senior leadership team. As the UCPS is a large school, Class Congresses have been arranged so that each Congress contains one class from each year group. This ensures continuity between each Congress and allows for a range of ideas to be explored. Prior to the Congress, the children in each class decide on two issues or ideas that they want to discuss as a school. Two children are then selected to present the ideas to the Congress. Class teachers are given autonomy over this process, ensuring that all children are given the opportunity over the year. In the Class Congress, all children sit in a circle to promote open discussion and the idea of unity. The representatives from each class then stand up and share their ideas. All ideas are written up on the board, and when all classes have shared their ideas, the children vote for the ideas they want to discuss. All children are then free to stand up and speak, provided certain ground rules are met: only one speaker at a time, speakers must stand when talking and speakers must aim to build on the ideas of previous speakers. It is important that the children are also able to see the impact of their suggestions and discussions, so school leaders ensure that decisions are followed through on, or, when they cannot be taken forward, reasons are given to the children. So far, I am yet to come across an instance when children have failed to comprehend the constraints of the school, showing the value of open communication.

Implications
Overall, the establishment of a Class Congress has been a success, with all children in my class, and the wider school, engaged and excited about getting their say on the running of the school. Although the Class Congress structure is still new, and I am sure it will be reinvented over the years to suit the needs of different cohorts, there are several factors behind its success. Firstly, teachers authentically believe in the idea. The UCPS fosters a community where staff are willing to give things a go, which is essential for getting new ideas off the ground. Teacher autonomy was an essential factor in the success of the project, for empowering teachers means empowering children too. The second factor aiding the smooth implementation of the Class Congress was the fact that the school already had a well-established oracy and dialogue curriculum. Children had already been taught the skills necessary to engage in discussions, and the routines and expectations around talk were embedded into everyday school life. This meant that instead of having to teach these skills, children only needed to be taught to apply them in a new setting, with a few minor tweaks. If Class Congress, or a similar project, was being rolled out in a school without a structured and embedded oracy curriculum, additional modelling of expectations would be required.

The UCPS shows how children's voices can be made central to the development of the curriculum and wider school practices. The case study highlights the importance of explicitly teaching children the skills they need to engage in debates as well as showing the impact that children can have when they know their voices are truly valued. As long as it is revised and developed in line with changing school needs, Class Congress will continue to be a success.

Although thousands of miles away, the aims of the Dhun School for Now in India are similar to those of the UCPS, albeit using different approaches to cultivating and promoting pupil voices.

Dhun School for Now

Title
Project Dhun: An Education That Connects

Context

Project Dhun aims to create a 500-acre neighbourhood in suburban Jaipur, India, combining working, learning and recreation spaces. The Dhun School for Now is a K–12 school (ages five to eighteen) that draws inspiration from nature, and aims to solve future problems through experimental project-based learning. When complete, the school will cater for 420 learners from numerous local communities, fostering intercultural collaborations and knowledge exchanges.

The geographical location of the school has given rise to a new view of learning. The school is surrounded by four separate villages and embraces the knowledge systems and perspectives found in each. It is located near Dhun's regenerated land bank and is thus the perfect place to learn from the natural environment. Although in its infancy, the school has already worked with forty learners; two of whom have been recognised in junior entrepreneur competitions, and five learners have written a book based on their distinct cultural community experiences. The school is clearly developing pupils and promoting their voices. So, how can these practices be embedded into schools worldwide?

Curriculum Design

The school is being developed with pupil voice as central to the curriculum. The school is anchored around three core pillars: Self, Community and Planet. These pillars aim to foster a regenerative and interconnected outlook on education (detailed later), empowering educators and children to find their voice and focus on community engagement. They work in conjunction:

- The pillar of Self focuses on nurturing individual students' agency, autonomy and mastery. It empowers students to become self-directed learners, cultivating a sense of purpose and competence. Children's learning focuses on empowerment, ensuring that pupils understand their skill sets and motivations.
- The pillar of Community emphasises the importance of collaboration, empathy and social responsibility. Students form deep relationships with their peers, teachers and the broader community. They learn to value diversity, to leverage the community's collective wisdom, and contribute positively to the well-being of others. This is achieved through positive staff role modelling, and by ensuring that learning is centred on collaborative projects.

- The pillar of Planet instils in students an appreciation for the environment and a sense of stewardship. It promotes sustainable practices, ecological awareness and a commitment to preserving and regenerating the natural world. Students develop an understanding of the interconnectedness between human actions and the health of the planet. This is achieved by ensuring that all learning is situated and relevant.

Educational Spaces Re-Envisioned?
To pilot these aims, the school set up creative, inclusive spaces for learning, offering opportunities for young minds to learn and develop alongside their peers and educators. The role of the teacher was evolved into the idea of a 'facilitator'. Facilitators act as mentors, encouraging and promoting freedom and experimentation, understanding and nurturing the interest and pathways of learners. The pilot scheme was developed from looking at more than forty schools globally and following some key themes and pedagogical approaches, including the following:

- *Foundational learning*: a focus on the development of fundamental knowledge and skills
- *Nature lab*: learning scientific concepts through immersive experiences in nature, including farming, nature walks and field trips
- *Free play and gymnastics*: fostering bodily intelligence and creativity through unstructured place and gymnastics
- *Space making*: engaging and participating in design processes to shape and optimise learning environments
- *Nook*: enhancing learning through projects and hands-on exploration, as well as critical thinking
- *Studio*: integrating arts into the learning journey and stimulating creativity and expression

Implications
Developing a school from the ground up – like the Dhun School – is a luxury that many of us do not have. However, aspects of the founding principles can be embedded into existing school systems. While not everyone has a 'Nature lab', we do all have access to the natural environment, whatever this might look like. While we do not all have

access to a 'Studio', we all have classrooms that we can use in new or creative ways. The emphasis needs to be placed on how we can adapt our spaces and resources to work for us. This requires creativity, and may mean adapting our preconceived views of education, but the impacts could be invaluable.

Other curricular approaches, such as ensuring that learning is place based and relevant (starting with local knowledge and then extending outward), can be incorporated into any curriculum design. Building flexible learning journeys around individuals is key to building student confidence, voice and agency.

One of the really interesting things about the Dhun School is its focus on individualised learning. This learner-led approach, often referred to a child-led learning, is not a new concept, but it is typically found early in the education system and then pushed out as curricular demands increase. However, as the Dhun School demonstrates, a curriculum centred on children's interests is an important step in fostering pupil voice. Where governmental constraints are in place, it is our role to find ways to ensure child-led learning still has a place in our classrooms. The Dhun School and its pedagogical approaches, offer a possible approach for this.

From these two case studies, we can see that education is increasingly focused on promoting children's voices; children are no longer passive participants in their learning journeys. And, at the same time, both studies show that education practices cannot be 'one size fits all' – there are numerous ways to promote children's voices.

4.3 Reflections on a Manifesto

As educators, it can feel like we have an endless list of tasks to help children for their next adventure. It starts with teaching letters and numbers and moves on to reading and complicated equations. These skills are invaluable. But developing them in isolation is not enough. As educators, we are here to do much more. We are here to help children develop and form their own ideas. We need to ensure they are equipped with the skills and knowledge to make their voices heard – something that starts within education systems.

The importance of children's voices is becoming more apparent. In schools, teachers, teaching assistants and school leaders have the unique opportunity to spend every day with groups of children. Through this, we get to know the characteristics of individuals, their interests, worries and joys; the ways they learn, how they struggle and the things that matter to them. It is this unique social relationship, different from any other, in any other context in which children live their lives, that affords educators with something which we have referred to as practitioner wisdom. And wisdom is strengthened through dialogue and learning with and from one another. The examples are there; it is now our job to learn from each other, combining and adapting practices with our own expertise. Classrooms across the world are bursting with young voices wanting to be heard. No one has better ideas about education than those who are experiencing it, and, having read the preceding manifesto, I believe that education systems should not be designed without consulting those who engage in them. It is our role and responsibility to champion these voices; we know their importance, and it is time to make sure that everyone else does too.

As teachers, we aim to empower the children and young people we work with. We are already hearing their voices in our classrooms and making sure they are given the space to express their ideas. But we need to take this further. We need to ensure their voices are having influence outside of school. This starts by truly valuing their voices and ideas, and ensuring pupils can see the influence their ideas have had. This will look different in different settings, from leading open discussions on current topics to including children in key school decisions; the possibilities are endless.

Over to You

Whether focusing on issues that are directly relevant to them – classroom expectations or their own learning journey – or on large-scale issues, such as climate change, children's views are often insightful. They might present a more innocent view of the world, free from the prejudices we bring as adults. And yet, their voices are also full of new insights that we, as adults, sometimes miss. This makes children the ideal voices for change.

In her manifesto, Julia Flutter describes a vision in which schools include children meaningfully, not tokenistically, in discussions about education, their lives, communities and the world. It is a clarion call to counter myopic views about childhood, children and their education. Children already have a voice; we just need to create systems in which they can be heard and, importantly, acted upon. As we end this practitioner's response, we invite the reader to reflect on the following questions, drawing from their own wisdom and practices, in their own classrooms, schools and social, cultural and educational contexts:

- Where are children heard in your school? Where are they not?
- How can you develop ways in which children can challenge the status quo without classrooms and schools deteriorating into chaos?
- How can we draw on children's nuanced understanding of the world and learn from and with them?

References

Dewey, J. (2000) *Democracy and education*. New York: Free Press.
Flutter, J. and Rudduck, J. (2004) *Consulting pupils: what's in it for schools?* London: Routledge.
Rudduck, J. and Flutter, J. (2000) 'Pupil participation and pupil perspective: "carving a new order of experience"', *Cambridge Journal of Education*, 30(1), 75–89.

5 | Manifesto 3

Suffrage and Political Equality – Where Do Children Fit?

HARRY PEARSE

5.1 Introduction

This manifesto is about who gets included in democracy – that is, who gets to vote and participate in the democratic process – and who doesn't. It proposes a new democratic settlement – one in which ageist assumptions (about children) no longer operate, and children are afforded this same political right as their fellow citizens. This is not a straightforward claim to make. For many, the idea of children voting is conceptually incoherent, and, at present, there is limited political support or momentum for children's suffrage. Consequently, much of this manifesto is concerned with the range of arguments used to police the distinction between democratic inclusion and exclusion, and whether they're sound. Only by reckoning with and rebutting these arguments can the ground be cleared to make a coherent case for children's suffrage. The second half of this manifesto illustrates why the ordinary arguments for franchise rights also – and maybe especially – apply to children.

There was a time when the answer to the question who gets included in democracy was depressingly limited. Before the advent of so-called universal suffrage in the early twentieth century, very few people in democracies were allowed to vote. Various religious groups were excluded, as were men without property, and it's only in the last 100 years or fewer that women have been enfranchised and the voting rights

---

This manifesto is based on a lecture I gave at Eton College on 14 June 2023. For a more thoroughgoing account of some of the same arguments, see Pearse (2023a).

of ethnic minorities properly respected and protected. By contrast, in modern democracies, the question might seem like a non-starter. The franchise is now far more inclusive, and voting populations are considerable. It's true that, in most democracies, prisoners aren't allowed to vote – presumably as punishment for violating the social contract in some way. People who live in a country but aren't citizens can't vote either – being not sufficiently invested in that place's politics and social structures. And yet, relatively speaking, these are fractions of any given population, so hardly significant (or hugely worrying) carve-outs from the franchise.

This is not the case, however, with the only other excluded constituency, children – or those under the age of eighteen. Questions of inclusion are still worth asking because this group is actually pretty massive; even in ageing populations – such as those in England and Wales – children make up 20 per cent of the population (UK Government, 2020). That's one in five people – one in five people who aren't allowed to vote.

In this manifesto, I want to talk about whether or not this is right or justified. What are the arguments for excluding children from the franchise, and are they fair and legitimate? And conversely, what are the arguments of including children, and do they stand up to scrutiny? In 2022–2023, I ran a research project in the University of Cambridge Primary School (UCPS), where I put these and similar questions to six-, eight- and ten-year-olds (Pearse, 2023b). It turns out that young children have a lot to say about democracy, as well as various political issues, and in some cases showed an interest in alternative democratic arrangements. The findings of this research aren't the basis for my view that children should be enfranchised. As I hope to demonstrate, there are independent, and in some cases a priori, reasons why we should think about children as political agents who, like adults, are entitled to vote in elections. Nevertheless, speaking to students at UCPS added colour to these arguments, and left me more optimistic about the scope and prospect of democratic innovation.

In what follows, I'm going to make the argument in favour of children's suffrage in two parts. In the first part, I'll discuss the arguments against children voting, and hopefully show how they're arbitrary or misguided. Then, in the second part, I'll set out the more positive case, and try to show why it's important and right that children participate in democratic politics. And note, by children, I mean anyone under eighteen. Not just sixteen-year-olds, not just six-year-olds; but every single person. (If the prospect of a two-year-old voting sounds faintly ridiculous, don't worry, I agree, and I'll address that reservation at the end; so hold on to that scepticism. For now, however, I just want to stress that when I say children, I don't just mean teenagers; I mean young children as well.)

5.2 The Case against Children Voting, and Why It's Flawed

But I'll start with the arguments against. I think when you ask people 'why aren't children allowed to vote?' they normally answer with one or all the following. The first thing they say is that children are too incompetent to vote responsibly. The second thing is that enfranchising children would distort electoral outcomes and make democratic politics incoherent. And the third is that it'd be nonsensical to grant people voting rights before they acquire other age-related rights – like the rights to buy alcohol and cigarettes, get married, join the army or drive a car.

The issue of competence is, I think, the central question. It's widely assumed – and, on average, it's certainly plausible – that children aren't as competent as adults. They're less knowledgeable, less experienced, and they lack something – reasonableness, wisdom, acuity – that apparently only comes with adulthood. Thus, while adults are equipped for democratic participation, children are not – they lack the ingredients necessary to vote responsibly (Cowley and Denver, 2004).

However, if you want to hold this position, you've got to have an answer to the following question: which capacities, knowledge or skills are *actually* and *specifically* necessary for someone to vote responsibly? Is it the ability to make logical inferences, or reason from abstract principles? Is it knowledge of the different branches of government or the legislative process? How important is it to understand a party's policy platform, and how it differs from others? And should one vote for the common good or in one's self-interest? The problem is that we just don't know – there's no agreement on what someone needs to vote responsibly. And until we collectively decide what's necessary, it's impossible to say adults have it – whatever *it* is – and that children don't.

Still, for argument's sake, let's assume that some sort of competence is required to vote – what might this imply for children? Well, if we assume a minimal competence requirement – say, the ability to loosely compare parties or leaders – many children would presumably qualify. In which case, the grounds for exclusion disappear, and children should be given the vote. By contrast, if we assume a high competence threshold – for example detailed understanding of entire legislative agendas, and the ability to reason from first principles, with an eye on common interests – most children would presumably fall short. However, so too would many adults. According to YouGov (2020), 35 per cent of UK adult voters can't identify their local MP. While, at different times, 59 per cent of Americans haven't been sure which party their state governor belongs to, and only 44 per cent have been able to name a branch of government (Achen and Bartels, 2017).

You can test a version of this proposition yourself. If you're a child, ask your parents or teachers, and if you're an adult, ask anyone, to explain and evaluate the NHS, and Brexit, and macroeconomics, and housing reform, and environment policy, and traffic regulation, or any number of other policy issues. Very few will have mastery of all, or even any, of these issues, let alone piercingly original insights. (Full disclosure: I have absolutely none.)

And yet, in all modern democracies, ignorant and irrational adults – like me – are allowed to vote. We form sketchy judgements – about immigration or labour markets or whatever – and vote accordingly. And rightly so. If we excluded adults for having silly or ill-informed views, the electorate would be a very lonely place indeed. And yet, at the same time, we disqualify children by accusing them of the very same shortcomings. That is, we hold children to a competence standard that we don't apply to adults. This is arbitrary, unfair and something we should reconsider.

That's the first argument against giving children the vote; the idea that children are *uniquely* incompetent – a claim that's either unknowable or not true. The second, related argument is that enfranchising children would lead to policy chaos. Here, the basic idea is that ignorant or disengaged electorates will produce an ignorant or disengaged politics. If we allow inexperienced and irrational children to vote, the outcome of elections and the policy decisions they give rise to, will reflect, and be distorted by, children's ill-conceived and incoherent preferences.

This concern is rooted in a particular view of democracy and the role of elections. It assumes that voting is a mechanism for distilling public opinion, and that the views of the electorate have a powerful influence on the content of law and public policy (Dahl, 1991, p. 126). If this were true – if this was what elections were for – concerns about voter incoherence would be entirely justified. We'd want voters to be reasonable and knowledgeable so that when they vote in elections, their influence on politics was sensible and good.

The problem with this argument, however, and the reason we don't need to be overly concerned about voters' cognitive abilities, is that this is not what elections are all about. Voting in an election is not the same as deciding what happens; voters don't necessarily get their way, and they certainly don't make the law. That's the job – and has always been the job – of politicians and bureaucrats.

It's plausible that, over time, a country's politics will move with the ideological temperament of its citizens – although here we're talking years or decades, not months or news cycles (Caughey and Warshaw, 2018). Democracies aren't unresponsive to their voters' interests and concerns – in fact, the empirical evidence shows they're disproportionately responsive to the concerns of the rich, the white, the educated, and the male (Elsässer, Hense and Schäfer, 2021). Most politicians have it both ways; they pander to voters *and* renege on manifesto commitments. However, the whole point of representative democracy is to put some distance between citizens, who vote in elections, and politicians, who take decisions. It doesn't matter if voters are Einsteins or Zoolanders, because they're not the ones who decide things; politicians are. And this is why democracies have survived – and in some cases, flourished – with ignorant, unreasonable or indifferent electorates (Hannon, 2022).

The point, then, is that allowing children to vote is unlikely to radically distort public policymaking. Democracies might gradually become more responsive to children's needs, which would be no bad thing. But the frivolities of children's lives wouldn't suddenly become policy preoccupations because politicians wouldn't let them.

Nor – I don't think – would we see a major disruption to party politics. If children could vote, their voting options would be limited, just as, in first-past-the-post electoral systems or highly polarised democratic environments, adults' voting options are limited. We'd still have the same political parties, served by the same bureaucracy, and headed by the same (often underwhelming) politicians.

Moreover, even if we assume that children are stupid and irrational – and to a significantly greater degree than adults – what effect would this actually have on the electoral map? There's no reason to assume ignorant children would all vote for one and the same party. On the contrary, their ignorance and irrationality would be distributed across the political spectrum – much as ignorant adult votes are allocated to different people, parties and programmes (Olsson, 2008, p. 67).

The final worry about political disruption is that granting the vote to children would gift an additional de facto vote to parents, who exert considerable influence on their children's preferences. As children are highly impressionable, they're likely to follow their parents' instructions, and parents will thus end up with more political power than other childless adults. But again, I think this concern is misplaced. For one thing, we simply don't know how politically biddable children are. Ballots are private, which gives anyone the freedom to vote as they wish. And as any parent will tell you, children are famed for their disobedience as much as – if not more than – their quiescence.

And yet, to some degree, this also misses the point. Political influence is inevitable. Who reading this has ever had a truly original thought, uninfluenced by environment or other people? Adults are influenced by the newspapers they read, the TV they watch, their work, their friends, their religious groups, their trade unions – and in some cases, still their parents. Children and adults are alike in this regard. Both exist in spheres of influence. And seeing as we don't hold it against adults, we shouldn't really hold it against children.

I've now covered the claims that children are incompetent, and that their votes would mess up public policymaking. The third and final objection to children voting is about the order in which rights and responsibilities – including voting rights – are acquired. In the UK, at present, you can vote at eighteen, which is the same age you can get married and buy cigarettes and alcohol. The age of consent, and the age you can join the army, is sixteen. And incredibly, children in England become criminally responsible at ten years old.

This sequencing works, according to some, because voting is a serious business, and the right to vote should therefore be acquired around the same time – and certainly not before – one acquires the right to do other things of similar weight and consequence, like getting married or joining the army. If you're too young to drink or smoke, surely you're too young to vote? And if you're not deemed fully accountable to a country's laws, presumably you shouldn't have a say over that country's governance?

On the surface, these parallels seem fair and plausible. However, to properly adjudicate their validity, we need to understand why certain rights – be it to drive or marry or drink – are withheld from children in the first place. As freedom is generally thought to be an important quality, and an indispensable feature of any democracy, why is it that adults are free to do some things that children aren't?

Although this sounds like a straightforward question, getting a precise answer isn't easy. For example do adults possess certain qualities – lacking in children – that make them fit for liberty (Uprichard, 2008)? Intuitively, several things come to mind – adults are more reasonable, more experienced, wiser and more knowledgeable than children. And therefore, they're likely to exercise their freedom with greater care. Well, maybe. But like the competency question, the boundary between childhood and adulthood is often blurrier than we think. I've met plenty of children who are reasonable, wise and knowledgeable enough to exercise liberty sensibly. And we've all met adults who are manifestly unsuited to freedom: adults who are frivolous, reckless, thoughtless – and ultimately dangerous.

Nevertheless, in a crude and approximate way, democracies stagger the acquisition of rights to ensure children – whose whole lives are ahead of them – are not unduly or prematurely injured by the misuse of potentially harmful liberties. Adults have the freedom to become alcoholics, or get in car crashes, to get married and divorced, or kill people in battle. But we withhold these rights from children until such a time as they're deemed sensible enough to exercise them, if not with care, then with a greater appreciation of their consequences. We rely on some idea of 'childhood', even though it's a woolly and imperfect category. And we deny children harmful liberties so as not to risk their future freedoms.

This is relatively uncontroversial. There aren't many people who think children – however defined – should be allowed to drive or get married; the risk for harm is simply too great. But while this rationale works well vis-à-vis the right to drink or smoke, or the age of consent, it doesn't apply to voting rights, which aren't obviously dangerous, and which pose no direct threat to children's future well-being (Umbers, 2020, pp. 741–742).

As we've talked about already, the franchise doesn't give someone the power to make a law or decide a course of action. So voting isn't a way for one person to hurt another. Nor is it dangerous for voters themselves – at least not in the same way that smoking endangers smokers, or war endangers soldiers. When someone acquires the right to smoke or get married, they open themselves up to physical or psychological danger. Voting rights, on the other hand, have the inverse effect. Voting is a way to protect yourself – both from the state and your fellow citizens. And it's only when you're enfranchised that your rights and liberties are truly secure – as testified by the twentieth-century experiences of women in the UK and African Americans in the US.

Finally, there's the question of criminal responsibility. It's true that enfranchising children under ten would mean children in the UK could loosely affect the lawmaking process but not themselves be responsible to the law. Perhaps this seems jarring. But remember that the connection between voting rights and criminal responsibility is hardly decisive. People visiting a foreign country are expected to obey the law and are punished if they don't, despite having no say in the law's construction. Allowing children to vote before they can be charged with an adult crime is simply the inverse arrangement. It's hardly beyond the realm of existing practice.

5.3 The Positive Case for Child Enfranchisement

Having been though the flaws in the arguments against children voting, I've hopefully shown that the reasons for excluding children from democracy don't really stack up. In my view, this establishes good theoretical ground to revise, or better yet abandon, our current voting age thresholds. However, in practice, simply noting the unfairness or inconsistency of the status quo is unlikely to bring about reform. For that, we'd also need a standalone case for children's suffrage, and even then, political change is unlikely without a loud and active social movement; which is maybe where you – younger readers – will pick up the baton.

However, with that first condition in mind, in what remains of this manifesto, I'm going to set out the positive case for children voting. There are two, interrelated reasons why children should be given the vote; both gestured at already, but worth drawing out and making explicit. The first is a matter of principle, and the second is a question of political pragmatism.

The principle is that of political equality – the essential democratic attribute. While monarchies and aristocracies allocate political power unequally, democracies share it among members of the political community. Of course, historically, the number of participating members in a democracy was often relatively small – usually confined to male citizens, and only men who had either completed military training or owned a certain amount of property. However, in modern democracies, the demos has become a broader entity, in which virtually every adult citizen has the right to vote. Thus, according to Article 21 of the United Nations' (1948) Universal Declaration of Human Rights, 'The will of the people shall be the basis of the authority of government . . . expressed in periodic and genuine elections which shall be by universal and equal suffrage.'

These universal voting rights are built on, and derive their power from, two interlocking claims about human equality. The first is that everyone is equal in human dignity – that is, we all possess the same moral weight and value, and no person is intrinsically worth more than anyone else. And the second is that we all have unique (though not perfect) access to our own perspectives – in other words, our experiences bear on us in ways that only we appreciate, and shape who we are as people.

Two things then follow from this, politically. First, if we all have equal moral value, no one should be given more authority, or offered greater security, simply because of who they are. We all deserve the same degree of formal respect and protection. And second, if we all have a degree of self-knowledge, we all deserve to formulate our own preferences, and express them publicly if we wish. This, in a nutshell, is what voting is all about. Voting rights are a statement of political equality. They signal that – whoever we are – our opinions have as much weight and influence as anyone else's. And – if we want – they're a means to channel our views and submit them to public scrutiny.

So, the question is, Do children have as much moral value, and are they as privy to their own experiences, as adults? I think the answer is yes. And this means they too are entitled to respect and protection, and an outlet for their views and ideas. In short, they should have the vote. As long as we fail to provide this, 'universal suffrage' is not really universal at all; it's partial suffrage, checked by age, acting as a (not very good) proxy for competence.

A fuller and more faithful understanding of universal suffrage finds support in Article 12 of the United Nations' (1989) Convention on the Rights of the Child, which says that any child 'capable of forming his or her own views [has] the right to express those views in all matters affecting the child'. Which – to me – sounds like the right to vote. Article 13 goes on to say that children's 'right to freedom of expression' should 'only' be restricted if necessary to protect the rights of others, national security and public order and health. As voting rights pose no threat to others nor to the social fabric, allowing children to vote would hardly violate these conditions.

Nevertheless, some people still maintain that voting age thresholds *are* compatible with political equality (Weale, 2007, p. 214; Daniels, 1983). After all, we set the voting age at eighteen, and we assume – all things being well – that every child will eventually pass the age threshold and join the franchise. That is, we all start out as children and end up as adults, and so, over the course of a lifetime, everyone gets to vote, and everyone acquires the right at the same point in their lives. This is what makes the disenfranchisement of children different from the historical disenfranchisement of women or ethnic minorities – the latter constituencies were debarred for life, whereas children are excluded only until they're eighteen.

It's therefore true that the current exclusion of children is less egregious than, say, the historic exclusion of women. However, simply saying that children eventually graduate to adulthood, and thus the franchise, is not a hugely compelling argument. Not least because the same principle could be used to extend the voting age to forty, or justify withdrawing voting rights from everyone over eighty. In both cases, everyone over the course of their lifetimes would be treated the same way and have the same entitlements. And yet, most people recoil from the idea of deferring or withdrawing people's voting rights because establishing unequal franchise rights would create relational inequalities in which some cohorts – in the present moment – have more status and influence, and are shown greater consideration, than others (Bidadanure, 2016). Respect and protection, and the ability to express one's views and perspectives, are things we want now and forever, and therefore political equality isn't something anyone wants to postpone or give up.

A further challenge might be that children don't actually need to vote because their parents or caregivers – people who can vote – understand them, look out for them, and will act on their behalf. This argument has some surface appeal, and it's definitely true that parents are obligated, and well placed, to exercise control over some aspects of their children's lives. At the same time, however, the idea that parents will necessarily act on their children's behalf is simply mistaken. For one thing, it overlooks the fact that some parents are neglectful or indifferent to their children's well-being. But it also wrongly assumes that parents, or adults in general, can comprehensively understand or communicate children's perspectives. It ignores the reality that childhood and adulthood are entirely different experiences. And while adults may remember their own childhoods, times change, and people change too, and it's not obvious that today's adults are capable of speaking to or for the views of today's children. Children have their *own* perspectives, and these perspectives deserve formal representation. And for this, children need the vote.

So, that's the principled argument: children are citizens, and, in the ways that matter, equal to adults, and therefore they should be part of the franchise. However, for many people the equality argument is probably too abstract – a bit divorced from political realities. And that's why the second, pragmatic argument for children's votes is so important. Because this is an argument about the real, concrete costs and benefits of suffrage.

In short, children ought to be enfranchised because, without the vote, their needs and concerns are likely to be overlooked. Remember, it's the politicians, not the voters, who make the law. Citizens may be morally equal, but this doesn't mean they're equally capable of wielding power, or making decisions, or even prosecuting their interests. Consequently, the right to vote doesn't allow citizens to legislate or decide on policy. Instead, voting provides a (loose) guarantee that one's concerns and perspectives will not be systematically overlooked by those other people who *do* decide things – that is, by politicians (Wall, 2021). Representatives aren't beholden to voters, but they're incentivised to look out for them, or respect their interests, because in five years or so, voters will have a say over whether those politicians have a job nor not.

Children are the only citizens who don't have this insurance. They're not allowed to vote, and therefore their views count for less in political discourse, and they're liable to be overlooked in political decision-making. A structural inequality that can lead to exploitation, and even – in the worst cases – persecution (Harris, 1982, p. 50).

This was one of the conclusions reached in a recent report by the UK Children's Commissioners (2020), who warned that 'children's right to be heard and involved in decision-making processes ... is being denied' and therefore 'the UK government does not prioritise children's rights or voices in policy or legislative processes'. As a result, the report argues, England's initial COVID-19 responses 'overlooked children's needs' and instead prioritised the reopening of hospitality and retail. Likewise, the United Nations (2019) recently reported that, in 2018, 30 per cent of UK children were living in poverty, while, across similar timelines, pensioner poverty – a key electoral concern for politicians – had declined by half.

Without the vote, a community's interests are likely to be deprioritised. What's more, there's some evidence that acquiring or expanding voting rights gives rise to socio-political advantages. For example, between 1880 and 1938, franchise expansions in Western Europe had a positive impact on redistribution and the provision of public goods (Abou-Chadi and Orlowski, 2015). Fast-forward to 2011, when various Norwegian municipalities reduced the voting age to sixteen and youth engagement and representation increased, as did the initiatives designed to include young people in local politics (Godli, 2015).

These effects aren't always obvious or immediate, and they can also be hard to anticipate. As an illustration of this, in the late nineteenth and early twentieth centuries, women in the UK were divided on the franchise question. The Suffragettes, obviously, were in favour, but many other women felt detached from politics or believed men were better suited to it (Runciman, 2022). However, the benefits of voting do eventually become apparent. And the fact that no enfranchised group has ever returned or given up the vote says everything about its significance.

5.4 Conclusion

This manifesto makes two interrelated claims. The first is that giving children the vote a requirement of justice, and a way to establish real political equality. The second is that suffrage is a form of political protection – protecting people from neglect or even abuse, and ensuring goods and opportunities are more evenly distributed – that children require. While the upsides of children voting are obvious, the downsides are much overblown. There's no reason to assume politics or policymaking would go berserk or incoherent if children could vote. Nor – if anyone is worried – would enfranchised children be allowed to take up seats in Parliament. There's a difference between electing representatives and having the right to stand as one.

Despite these claims, it's still worth considering the possibility that some – or even most – children aren't really interested in these sorts of questions or arguments. Although, we still know relatively little about what young children think about politics, it's probably safe to assume that many of them don't want the vote, or are happy to wait for it. Of the primary school children I spoke to, roughly half were in favour, half not. Some said they found politics boring, while others said they were put off by its aggression and grubbiness – complaints often made by adults as well.

Importantly, though, none of this changes the basic injustice of children's exclusion. Not caring about politics or not wanting the vote doesn't make not having it any less dangerous – it just makes it less likely that children will campaign for suffrage. On the other hand, many of the children I worked with had lots to say about politics. They were engaged and thoughtful and had distinct political perspectives. And their interests ranged broadly, from climate change, to refugees, to corporate social responsibility. Children are a mixed bag – just as adults are. And while these qualities aren't prerequisites for voting, they make the need for child representation clear and urgent.

Of course, if there were no voting age restrictions, and anyone could do it, one might wonder about the role that two-year-olds would play? Surely, they wouldn't or shouldn't vote, as they probably can't even hold a pen. That's a fair challenge. If you can't hold a pen, it's unlikely you're going to vote. However, all age thresholds are arbitrary. So, if the threshold was two, we'd inevitably find some two-year-olds who could hold a pen, and cared something about politics, but were denied the right to exercise these abilities. The benefit of *not* having a threshold is that anyone who wants to vote – at any age – is able to and isn't excluded. I'm sure most young children wouldn't want to – in much the same way that many adults don't want to either. But having the desire to vote – which implies that one understands what voting means and how elections work, as well as suggesting a basic grasp of the electoral options on offer – should be justification enough for doing so. If a very precocious two-year-old feels up to it, great. If they don't, that's fine too. And the same applies if you're twenty-two or ninety-two.

This manifesto holds that voting is a right of citizenship, not a privilege of competence, and on that basis, we should all be allowed to do it.

References

Abou-Chadi, T. and Orlowski, M. (2015) 'Political institutions and the distributional consequences of suffrage extension', *Political Studies*, 63(1), 55–72. https://doi.org/10.1111/1467-9248.12193.

Achen, C.H. and Bartels, L.M. (2017) *Democracy for realists: why elections do not produce responsive government: with a new afterword by the authors*. Princeton: Princeton University Press.

Bidadanure, J. (2016) 'Making sense of age-group justice: a time for relational equality?', *Politics, Philosophy and Economics*, 15(3), 234–260. https://doi.org/10.1177/1470594X16650542.

Caughey, D. and Warshaw, C. (2018) 'Policy preferences and policy change: dynamic responsiveness in the American states, 1936–2014', *American Political Science Review*, 112(2), 249–266. https://doi.org/10.1017/s0003055417000533.

Cowley, P. and Denver, D. (2004) 'Votes at 16? The case against', *Representation*, 41(1), 57–62. https://doi.org/10.1080/00344890408523289.

Dahl, R.A. (1991) *Democracy and its critics*. New Haven: Yale University Press.

Daniels, N. (1983) 'Justice between age groups: am I my parents' keeper?', *Milbank Memorial Fund Quarterly, Health and Society*, 61(3), 489–522. https://doi.org/10.2307/3349870.

Elsässer, L., Hense, S. and Schäfer, A. (2021) 'Not just money: unequal responsiveness in egalitarian democracies', *Journal of European Public Policy*, 28(12), 1890–1908. https://doi.org/10.1080/13501763.2020.1801804.

Godli, P. (2015) 'Giving 16-year-olds the vote: experiences from Norway', in Tremmel, J. *et al.* (eds.) *Youth quotas and other efficient forms of youth participation in ageing societies*. Cham: Springer, pp. 149–175.

Hannon, M. (2022) 'Are knowledgeable voters better voters?', *Politics, Philosophy and Economics*, 21(1), 29–54. https://doi.org/10.1177/1470594x211065080.

Harris, J. (1982) 'The political status of children', in Graham, K. (ed.) *Contemporary political philosophy: radical studies*. Cambridge: Cambridge University Press, pp. 35–55.

Olsson, S. (2008) 'Children's suffrage: a critique of the importance of voters' knowledge for the well-being of democracy', *International Journal of Children's Rights*, 16, 55–76. https://doi.org/10.1163/092755608X267120.

Pearse, H. (2023a) 'Children, voting, and the meaning of universal suffrage', *Political Studies Review*, 22(4), 821–838. https://doi.org/10.1177/14789299231195454.

Pearse, H. (2023b) *Do children want the vote? Lesson from a primary school*. Cambridge: Centre for the Future of Democracy. Available at: www.bennettinstitute.cam.ac.uk/wp-content/uploads/2023/03/Do-children-want-the-vote.pdf.

Runciman, D. (2022) 'The enfranchisement of women versus the enfranchisement of children', in Wall, J. (ed.) *Exploring children's suffrage: interdisciplinary perspectives on ageless voting*. Basingstoke: Palgrave Macmillan, pp. 91–109.

UK Children's Commissioners (2020) *Report of the Children's Commissioners of the United Kingdom of Great Britain and Northern Ireland to the United Nations Committee on the Rights of the Child*. Available at: www.cypcs.org.uk/wpcypcs/wp-content/uploads/2020/12/crc-report-2020.pdf.

UK Government (2020) *Ethnicity facts and figures*. Available at: www.ethnicity-facts-figures.service.gov.uk/uk-population-by-ethnicity/demographics/age-groups/1.6.

Umbers, L.M. (2020) 'Enfranchising the youth', *Critical Review of International Social and Political Philosophy*, 23(6), 732–755. https://doi.org/10.1080/13698230.2018.1511172.

United Nations (1948) *Universal Declaration of Human Rights*. Available at: www.un.org/en/about-us/universal-declaration-of-human-rights.

United Nations (1989) *Convention on the Rights of the Child*. Available at: www.ohchr.org/en/instruments-mechanisms/instruments/convention-rights-child.

United Nations (2019) *Visit to the United Kingdom of Great Britain and Northern Ireland: Report of the Special Rapporteur on extreme poverty and human rights*. Available at: https://documents-dds-ny.un.org/doc/UNDOC/GEN/G19/112/13/PDF/G1911213.pdf.

Uprichard, E. (2008) Children as 'being and becomings': children, childhood and temporality, *Children and Society*, 22(4), 303–313. https://doi.org/10.1111/j.1099-0860.2007.00110.x.

Wall, J. (2021) *Give children the vote: on democratizing democracy*. London: Bloomsbury.

Weale, A. (2007) *Democracy*. Basingstoke: Palgrave Macmillan.

YouGov (2020) *The YouGov Democracy Study*. Available at: https://yougov.co.uk/topics/politics/articles-reports/2020/12/02/yougov-democracy-study.

6 Practitioners' Response to Manifesto 3
Democratic Education

ELISE KINNEAR AND ALIABBAS DHANJI

6.1 Introduction

In this chapter, Elise and Aliabbas respond to the vision for establishing children's democratic rights – allowing children status as full citizens, entitled to vote in elections – and ask how this vision can be situated in a primary school context. Some of the questions that arose from reading Chapter 5 are, How are our schools democratic? Where are they not? and Do we give authentic opportunities for children to have a say about the workings of their school?

The answer to the latter is that in many ways we do not. Central government sets the direction of state education – making decisions about curricula, setting standards and holding the purse strings. In this context, how can we reflect on what matters to children, and in so doing embrace children's diverse voices in school? The hope is that by experiencing a democratic education, children are more likely to be active citizens when they are allowed to vote. As well as reflecting on their experiences at the University of Cambridge Primary School (UCPS), Elise and Aliabbas explore a case study from a unique school in Germany, where, for decades, democracy has been at the heart of its educational design.

6.2 Practitioner Wisdom from Cambridge, UK: Finding Opportunities for Children's Voices

The UCPS has a guiding principle: to nurture children to become compassionate citizens, curious about the world in which they live, and equipped to participate and engage in society.

We fully support children's right, pursuant to Article 12 of the United Nations Convention on the Rights of the Child (UNCRC) (United Nations, 1989), to participate in politics, have a voice and be heard. In recognition of this, we actively explore ways in which children at our school can have a meaningful voice and a tangible impact on key aspects of their school life. We read Harry Pearse's manifesto at the same time as we were developing two related democratic projects: setting up a school Class Congress as described in Kirstin MacVicar's practitioner's response (Chapter 4) and drafting democracy lesson resources.

After the establishment of the Class Congress, the school hosted a research project, led by Professor David Runciman, Dr Harry Pearse and Ella Bradshaw, on democracy and children's rights. The project – based on a series of workshops with primary school–aged children – sought to understand how children think and feel about their disenfranchisement (Pearse, 2023).

In his thought-provoking chapter, Pearse challenges us to confront the status quo and critically analyse the current age restriction imposed on suffrage in the UK. It is arguable that the voting age of eighteen is only accepted because it is all most of us have ever known (having come into force in 1969); because there is broad parity in voting age thresholds across Western democracies; and because it is assumed that, with the extension of voting rights to women, the great fight for universal suffrage has already been won. Save for recent debates about lowering the voting age to sixteen, as is the case in Scottish and Welsh elections, suffrage is not an issue that receives much media or political attention in this country. There seems little appetite for change. Pearse's chapter is therefore both thought-provoking and confronting.

Box 6.1 Reflections by Elise Kinnear

Harry Pearse's manifesto forced me to challenge my own views on the issue of child enfranchisement, to consider how and when these ideas were formed, how much was down to my own thinking and how much was a passive acceptance of societal norms. Pearse's argument served to highlight the lack of policy cohesion and seeming arbitrariness in the allocation of rights and responsibilities to British children. Why are we held criminally responsible from the age of ten (or twelve in Scotland) yet deemed unable to assume other responsibilities until much later? Why can we join the military at sixteen but not drive a car until seventeen? Why can we have sex, and become parents with responsibility for raising a child, at sixteen, while still legally a child ourselves, and yet must wait until eighteen for marriage, cigarettes or alcohol? When forced to stand back and look at the issue, it can be hard to identify a shared rationale that binds these individual pieces of legislation. However, if childhood continues to eighteen as legally recognised by international law, is there not an argument for increasing the threshold for all these activities to eighteen? As Pearse notes, such an approach would fail to acknowledge the different levels of risk posed to either the individual or wider society. So, why the need for a minimum voting age level at all? It can't be to ensuring a competent and informed electorate because, as Pearse points out, no such criterion exists for the adult electorate.

Overall, I found myself more open to a review of current voting laws – indeed a comprehensive review of the current system – and a national conversation about what a modern democracy should look like and who should have a voice. Although I question the merit in granting universal suffrage from birth, as advocated in the manifesto, I am open to the right being afforded earlier than eighteen, not least because of compelling evidence that surfaced during the aforementioned democracy research project, namely that the most pressing issues for the children in our school – including climate change, the plight of refugees, education and artificial intelligence – do not reflect the policy concerns of adults (in the UK in 2024 these are the economy, health and immigration/asylum; YouGov, 2024). If policy is driven by citizen demands, and citizens express those demands by voting – a process illustrated by the disproportionate attention given to the policy concerns of the 'grey vote' – then any group that cannot vote is placed at a disadvantage. Just as the introduction of female suffrage compelled political parties to develop policies that would resonate with women voters, suffrage for younger people would seem likely to drive policy commitments in areas that matter to younger generations. Thankfully, I am not tasked with driving policy change. I am, however, persuaded that we cannot afford to accept the status quo without question, and that children have the right to understand these important issues, form their own opinions on them, and use their voices to ensure their opinions are heard.

At the conclusion of Pearse and Runciman's democracy research project, the school conducted a review to identify its strengths and limitations and to determine how we could further refine and improve it and embed it within our school curriculum for annual delivery. To ensure maximum effectiveness, we thought carefully about the target age group. The original research project was delivered to children in Year 2 (aged six to seven), Year 4 (aged eight to nine) and Year 6 (aged ten to eleven). Based on feedback from participating children and teaching staff, it was agreed that it would be most productive to work with children aged between eight and ten, namely in Years 4 and 5. Observations from the research project revealed that younger children were less likely to participate in discussions, whilst older children, sadly, had already developed a degree of cynicism about democracy and politics. Overall, children in Year 4 participated well in the research study with a wide number of children contributing ideas and showing a willingness to reflect and alter their opinions.

Box 6.2 Reflections by Aliabbas Dhanji

The initial research project, conducted by Harry Pearse, David Runciman and Ella Bradshaw between 14 October and 2 December 2022, comprised six forty-minute workshops, each conducted with a single class from Years 2, 4 and 6.

As the teacher of the Year 2 class, I had the opportunity to observe as a bystander, having very little active participation or influence in any of the sessions other than managing class behaviour and facilitating logistics. This included arranging groups, and giving children instructions to efficiently move around the classroom when necessary. My lack of active participation, although not an explicit instruction conveyed by the research team, was to ensure the children felt they could freely express their opinions and ideas in relation to the questions being posed to them. Upon reflection, however, I do wonder whether my presence and their awareness of me as their class teacher could in some way have influenced or restricted their responses.

While my presence was required as the adult with the responsibility for those children within the classroom, it did lead me to reflect on the potentially problematic nature of trying to elicit children's authentic opinions on issues like independence and autonomy when the environment in which they are expressing their opinions is explicitly structured. Could this in fact impact the authenticity of the children's responses? I found myself wondering whether children were able to fully express their thoughts and opinions and whether – had I not been in the room – their thoughts and opinions would have been expressed differently, or whether more or less children would have felt comfortable conveying their ideas.

The initial session began with an exercise to gauge the children's existing understanding of power structures within Britain. Later, the researchers explored children's views on whether they should be allowed to vote or not. The opposition towards child enfranchisement from just over half of the children in the class (52 per cent) took me by surprise, as did the rationale (cited frequently by the children) that children lack the knowledge and terminology to appropriately convey their ideas, thoughts and beliefs. I was struck that most of the children who made this argument were students who had an existing understanding of the definition of democracy, as well as an awareness of current affairs, such as the war in Ukraine, and matters related to the environment – often speaking about and conveying their thoughts on these issues during class discussions.

Beforehand, I had wondered if the children who usually express their political opinions in class would be more proactive in the research project discussions? The facilitation and structure of the sessions allowed all children to actively take part in the discussions to some extent. However, I felt there was a disparity in the participation levels of children who had previously expressed opinions on current affairs at school or at home, and those who had not. From a teacher's perspective, this led me to ponder how a subject matter such as democracy and child enfranchisement could be made more accessible to those children who are not actively exposed to or partake in such discussion with adults at home. If we discuss such matters without ensuring all children have a base understanding of the concepts, will all children to be able to equally contribute to the discussion? To effectively discuss such matters and form an opinion, a certain amount of subject knowledge and teaching – for example about power structures and their histories – is required. Without it,

> we end up with discussions that assume all children can keep up with each other. Will this allow conversation to be truly equal? Or are the children who are exposed to democracy 'dinner table talk' at an advantage?
>
> The findings of the research project provided interesting insight into children's opinions on a subject matter they seldom have the opportunity to discuss within a primary school context. As a result, it led me to reflect on the impact that providing an open forum for young children can have, and how, regardless of their differing opinions on child enfranchisement, simply exposing children to the ideas of democracy, power structures, world affairs, and the prospect of child enfranchisement, and equipping them with the skills and knowledge they need to engage and form opinions, is hugely significant.

Working in partnership with Pearse, we created an eight-lesson work plan based on some of the findings of the democracy research project. This mini curriculum will be used in the UCPS and eventually made available to other educators and educational establishments free of charge. The curriculum combines the academic and research expertise of our colleagues at the University of Cambridge and feedback from the research study with the pedagogical knowledge of our teaching staff.

Our key objectives were to develop a curriculum that

- Is child focused and child led
- Develops and enhances children's oracy skills
- Enables children to form opinions on important issues
- Promotes British values as defined by the British Government, such as democracy, the rule of law, individual liberty and mutual respect and tolerance
- Provides an education in citizenship ahead of the UK National Curriculum KS3 requirement

The lessons are intentionally flexible rather than prescriptive and can be tailored to meet the needs of different cohorts and environments. Although aimed at children in Years 4 and 5, the curriculum design and delivery could be adapted for an older or younger audience as desirable. Similarly, schools can choose whether to deliver the eight lessons weekly over a half term, fortnightly over a full term, or intensively over a single week – combined, perhaps, with a visit to a seat of democracy, like a local council, regional mayor's office, Downing Street, the Houses of Parliament, the Scottish Parliament, the Welsh Assembly or the Northern Irish Assembly.

To maximise the benefits and impact of the curriculum, children need to be equipped with oracy skills so that they can articulate their thoughts, listen actively, purposefully engage in discussion – whether by concurring, building on an argument or disagreeing respectfully – and feel confident to change their opinion and explain their reasons for doing so. Oracy is already embedded into the UCPS' curriculum, so the democracy lessons provide another opportunity to embed and practice them. However, other schools may need to formally teach oracy skills in advance or alongside the democracy lessons to support children to fully engage.

The curriculum is easy to deliver with minimal preparation and limited teacher input. The first five lessons are framed around enquiry questions, whilst the final three sessions involve preparations for, and the delivery of, a presentation to an audience of decision-makers – for example the school governors, a local MP or local councillors. Over the course of the first five lessons, children are provided with information to help them understand societal structures (past and present) and the British democratic system and suffrage, as well as explore enquiry questions (such as, What is power? Who rules Britain? Should children have the right to vote? What really matters to children? Are children heard?). The course material is intentionally neutral in tone – its purpose is simply to provide children with the relevant information on which to form their own opinions, just as they will need to do when they become enfranchised and can exercise their right to vote. Teachers are provided with a series of follow-up questions to help deepen the discussion and challenge thinking if required. We found, however, that within a supportive classroom environment, with sufficient thinking time and drawing on their existing oracy skills, children in the target age group often pose these deeper, thought-provoking questions themselves. The final three sessions allow children to wrestle with democratic decision-making first hand. What should be included in the final presentation? Who should deliver it? Who should be invited to listen? What is the fairest way to reach a decision on these issues? Children all too often have to relinquish decision-making powers to other people. Not this time. The teacher will not resolve any disagreements or tell them what to do or how to do it. The power is theirs. And, through this series of lessons, they should come to understand what it means to exercise such power.

A similar example of child empowerment is presented below. This case study comes from colleagues in Germany, who likewise work in a school linked with a university, with strong commitments to equality and democratic process.

Box 6.3 Practitioner Wisdom from Germany: Solving Conflicts Peacefully – a Basis for Democratic Education at Laborschule Bielefeld

Nicole Freke (Laborschule Bielefeld) and Christian Timo Zenke (Bielefeld University)

The complexity of developing democracy within adult society is not dissimilar to creating educational opportunities that adhere to the principles of democracy. We know that democracy is diversely lived and experienced in countries across the world and so defining what we mean is an ongoing endeavour. In this section, Nicole and Timo explain how democracy is lived out in a school in Germany.

Laborschule Bielefeld, which is German for Laboratory School Bielefeld, had held a unique position within the German educational landscape since its founding in 1974. This is due to its focus on democratic education, but also its conceptualisation as a public experimental school of the federal state of North Rhine-Westphalia. As a progressive public school, Laborschule Bielefeld currently teaches 710 students from Year 0 (the final preschool year) to Year 10 (end of lower secondary school), ages five to sixteen.

Living together in a democratic society can only work in the long term if the members of this community are able to solve conflicts in a constructive and peaceful manner. Since this applies to both our society as a whole and the embryonic society at each school, Laborschule Bielefeld has made it its mission to include peaceful and sustainable problem solving as a central part of everyday school life. In doing so, we not only want to make our own school a more peaceful and democratic place, we also want to ensure our society becomes a space for living together peacefully.

It all started with us looking for an answer to the question, How can children learn to resolve conflicts peacefully and sustainably? While searching for an answer, we eventually came across the notion of nonviolent communication. To us, this form of communication is not just a tool; it is also (and more often) an attitude. The younger children know this form of communication as 'giraffe language', whereas the older children, adolescents and adults know it as 'mindful or respectful communication'. Giraffe language is a metaphor for communicating with heart and with a higher purpose: giraffes have the biggest hearts, as well as the longest necks.

Initially, three colleagues enrolled in training on the topic, leading to the implementation of the principles of nonviolent communication in everyday school life at Laborschule Bielefeld. Many of the ideas felt familiar, as though they were already a part of our school structure. Not all of them were, however – at least not yet. Over the following months, more and more of these ideas made their way into our classrooms. It was a like doing a puzzle in which some parts had been missing until now.

Since then, all the primary school teachers have been introduced to the principles, and every classroom has a poster setting out support measures to solve problems in a mindful way. This poster introduces the four steps of solving conflicts in nonviolent communication:

- Observation ('I have heard ...', 'I have seen ...' etc.)
- Feeling (e.g. 'I am now happy/angry/lonely')
- Need (e.g. 'I need trust/justice/openness')
- Request ('I would like to ask you to ...')

The visualisation of these four steps helps the children (and the adults) to develop an attitude that is about communicating what is going on inside oneself instead of blaming, threatening or accusing others. In addition to this, we created feelings and needs cards for each class, which illustrate the terms presented on the poster. This helps children to develop a shared vocabulary for solving conflicts.

More information on the project and the materials mentioned can be found at www.labschoolseurope.eu/solving-conflicts-peacefully/.

Over to You

In his manifesto, Pearse articulated the reasons why we should give children the vote. For us, this brought up questions about children's agency. Giving children opportunities to engage meaningfully in their education (or the decisions about what education could be) and asking questions about how we view childhood represent serious lines of enquiry. In a post-COVID-19 world, in which mental health, identity crises and economic and social uncertainties abound, it feels right that we reflect, reconsider and reimagine how we engage children as citizens; people who have a voice and should be listened to and heard! As we end this practitioners' response, we invite the reader to reflect on the following questions drawing from their own wisdom and practices in their own classrooms, schools, social, cultural and educational contexts:

- How could a school become democratic in both philosophical, theoretical and practical terms?
- Where does the power lie in a classroom or school or youth group? Are there opportunities to speak to power? To challenge authority in a way that is respectful and considerate?
- Where do children debate, disagree and argue?
- Where are the spaces of uncertainty – where teachers and school leaders allow confusion, disagreement and a little bit of organised chaos – to show children there are diverse ways of being, feeling, existing and responding to the world and to life's challenges?

References

Pearse, H. (2023) *Do children want the vote? Lessons from a primary school.* Cambridge: Centre for the Future of Democracy. Available at: www.bennettinstitute.cam.ac.uk/wp-content/uploads/2023/03/Do-children-want-the-vote.pdf.

United Nations (1989) *Convention on the rights of the child.* Available at: www.ohchr.org/en/instruments-mechanisms/instruments/convention-rights-child.

YouGov (2024) *The most important issues facing the country.* Available at: https://yougov.co.uk/topics/society/trackers/the-most-important-issues-facing-the-country.

7 | *Manifesto 4*

A (Post-Human) Transdisciplinary Manifesto for Future-Making Education

PAMELA BURNARD

What does it take to imagine, design, and inhabit spaces of experimentation, collaboration, and reflection together? How can situations of this kind be crafted? How do we – design educators, practitioners, change-makers – come in close proximity with each other to create togetherness?[1]

7.1 Introduction

Education is how a society ensures its own future. Education has the potential to bring generations together in the common task of making a future for all. But does it currently do so? In this manifesto I call for a move away from the traditional view of education as preparation for a predictable future towards a model where education equips individuals to embrace a complex, rapidly changing world. I bring a new lens to consider a future-making education. I explore how transdisciplinarity – that is, collaboration across the sciences and arts – can move education beyond siloed thinking and practices. Such 'compartmentalised' ways of being, thinking and working lead to prescription and enculturation, whereas transdisciplinarity ensures education becomes more than simply preparing for a predicted future – instead, we can make it together. Making the future is a key aspect of transdisciplinary thinking and enacting, which I discuss in what follows. Transdisciplinary research integrates knowledge across academic disciplines and with non-academic

---

[1] From "Stacking Complexities: Reframing Uncertainty through Hybrid Literacies," by Betti Marenko, *Design and Culture* 13, no. 2 (2021), reprinted by permission of Informa UK Limited, trading as Taylor & Francis Group, tandfonline.com.

stakeholders to address societal challenges. Whilst there is contested views about such bridging and merging and co-creating of new disciplines, there is broad consensus around seeking to value and integrate the knowledge from non-academic stakeholders. This implies processes of mutual learning between science and society, which embodies a mission of science *with* society rather than *for* society. So for the purpose of this manifesto, transdisciplinary is about including the diverse voices beyond the academic to consider ways of addressing the challenges of the day – including the voices of children and families.

The participation of children and young people in transdisciplinary education could be the key to achieving transformative school evolution. But what will the transformation be? Thinking, being and enacting in transdisciplinary education is about reimagining the knowledges and wisdoms that are interconnected. It is about seeing humans as part of nature, rather than separate from, or reified within, it. And it means connecting ideas and cultures and epistemologies that have been historically separated, as well as expanding our definitions of being and knowing.

It's arguable that the modern world is changing more rapidly than at any other time in history. In education, questions continue to arise about how disciplines shape how we perceive, interact with, and respond to the world, and how we should position different types of intelligence at the centre of schooling. Do we arrange knowledge and ways of knowing into silos (e.g. English, maths, geography), or is knowledge more interwoven? Research on transdisciplinary practices challenges the notion that disciplines are separate, and calls for new approaches that transcend traditionally defined disciplinary practices. Teaching has always been a complex task; however, today, working in schools is a highly complex, sophisticated and stressful endeavour. In a fast-changing world, are our education systems and school-based practices changing at similar pace? As the production of knowledge is being destabilised and deconstructed, the classic academic divides between human, social, technical, medial and natural sciences are being disrupted. In a world in which the direction of globalisation is uncertain, and climate change is requiring greater collaboration across nations and peoples, what does this mean for domain-specific skills and knowledge, and transdisciplinary education? What does it mean for teachers and learners reimagining the world and our placed within it? How will it affect our ability to foster creative teaching and learning?

Put simply, it is no longer sufficient to teach and learn in single disciplines and subject-specific domains.

7.2 From Disciplinary to Transdisciplinary

Disciplines dominate the educational landscape, and teaching and learning still exist within disciplinary boundaries. Disciplines have their own languages, relationships, materials and practical habits. And disciplinary structures and hierarchies are the focus of our curricula, whereby different skills and types of understanding are specified, sequenced and measured by standardised metrics, such as the Organisation for Economic Co-Operation and Development's Programme for International Student Assessment. Consider most exam syllabi, which remain wedded to the notion of subject disciplines with little thought for the interconnections possible with a transdisciplinary way of thinking. Teachers are also affected – trained in, and committed to, discrete disciplinary tropes, languages and practices.

Transdisciplinarity, on the other hand, is a practice that transgresses and transcends disciplinary boundaries, offering us the potential to respond to new demands and imperatives. It does this by decoupling discipline-specific language and knowledge and allowing both to be opened up to new ways of seeing and experiencing. This is more than simply cross-curricular learning and teaching, which has been criticised for not acknowledging the complexities within disciplines and across disciplines. Transdisciplinarity involves a deeper form of disciplinary interpenetration. For example it might involve using the language of dance (movement, flow, choreography) to explore scientific concepts (water, cycles, change, material).

Typically, disciplines are expressed and understood through language. Even the 'highest' form of knowledge – the university doctorate – is realised through a long piece of text. However, movement and bodily senses are essential to transdisciplinarity and the development of *new forms of relationalities* (Bennett, 2010). So, instead of thinking with only language, we can also think about the body and embodying knowledge. Think of a five-year-old child; they are constantly moving – touching, jumping, jiggling, talking, disrupting, falling and so on – and they experience the world through their bodies, not purely in or through language. The problem with our language-focused education is that words have 'become "numbed" or seem to have "lost touch" with life' (Bennett, 2010, p. 54). Educational practices usually assume that children learn best *about* a subject without being in touch (literally) with the real world. However, all things – humans and non-humans, including materials and objects – are in complex and dynamic relational entanglements. When we bring the body to the fore with children, we literally 'stick together' and the learning is 'felt' differently on the skin (Barad, 2007). When we bring a group of ten-year-olds to experience what it might be like in the trenches in the First World War, they have an embodied experience – the knowledge is felt: they smell the damp Earth, they can use their intuition to empathise with those soldiers far away from home, they can imagine the living conditions. It is a different experience to a teacher setting a task to 'write a letter about being in the trenches'. This body-focused process is amplified through transdisciplinarity. For example, when we bring the sciences and arts together, and we bring scientists and artists together, classic discipline boundaries are transgressed and transcended; new and shared language evolves, and education moves beyond siloed practices of prescription and enculturation.

At the root of transdisciplinarity is the idea that knowledge, understanding and intelligence come in many forms (see Burnard and Loughrey, 2022). Creativity, imagination, play, making, culture, thinking and so on are not fixed and clearly defined. And hegemonic and hierarchical traditions of creativity (usually Western, heroic, individual, exceptional, male and white) can and ought to be challenged. To teach *for* diverse creativities – transgressing and transcending disciplinary boundaries – the teacher has to consider which creativity is being developed.

What do these transdisciplinary creativities look like? And how might they stimulate new ways of thinking, as well as foster closer collaborations between teachers and students? In the next section, I focus on the sciences and the arts: exploring how can they connect and stimulating different forms of logic, rationality and affect – constituting a form of an inquiry that is rooted firmly in the world, not just the school or classroom (Burnard and Colucci-Gray, 2020; Burnard and Loughrey, 2022).

7.3 The Possibilities of Transdisciplinary Creativities Education

To understand the overlaps between the sciences and the arts is – by definition – to question existing subject silos. We must find new ways of understanding disciplines – not simply as vehicles for acquiring specific knowledge and skills but also as spaces to explore multiple subjects in a shared and collaborative fashion (Burnard et al., 2022). This is a creative act. We must depart from the traditional view of 'siloed' education to engage in a creative process of destruction and co-construction. We must imagine a *transdisciplinary* form of education in which students and teachers collaborate in knowledge production.

I propose a *post-human transdisciplinary manifesto*. Post-humanism recognises the value of non-human objects, and it posits that human and non-human agents and objects cannot be understood separately but rather are entangled. A post-human transdisciplinary way of thinking could act as a catalyst, expanding our educational values and practices and leading us towards truly holistic learning. I suggest that we push against the conventional divisions: sciences 'versus' arts, human 'versus' non-human and culture 'versus' nature. A commitment to a post-human view of the world challenges human exceptionalism and sees 'culture' and 'nature' as inseparable. We, too, are dirt made flesh; iron made blood; water made tears, sweat and urine.

In Figure 7.1, I present a different way of seeing the relationship between the sciences and the arts. It is what Anna Hickey-Moody (2016, pp. 173–174) calls rhizomatics – or a network of relations – which, she says, 'draw on multiple fields and ... piece together multiple practices ... and practical arrangements that initiate change'. To make a rhizome is to generate questions, pull things apart to see how they work and put them together again in a different way to see what else they can produce or how they might generate inspiration. This 'rhizomatic of transdisciplinary practice' or a 'manifesto poem' is intended to inspire, to invite curiosity; it is an example of science–arts boundary crossing. Enacting new transdisciplinary combinations and/or pairings of subject disciplines, creating new paths and new 'rhizomatics' of practice, involves professional collaboration. As Tim Ingold (2020, p. 438) asks, 'What knowledge do we need for future-making education? ... Such education, rather than teaching us *about* the world, allows us to be taught by it.' Some of these *knowledge-making practices* and *material enactments* are featured in Figure 7.1 as 'lines of flight'. These lines interfere and show the complexities between subjects, just as there is complexity between humans and environments.

Rhizomatics are an invitation for you to think, act and read *differently*. Readers are invited to reimagine, rethink and review what

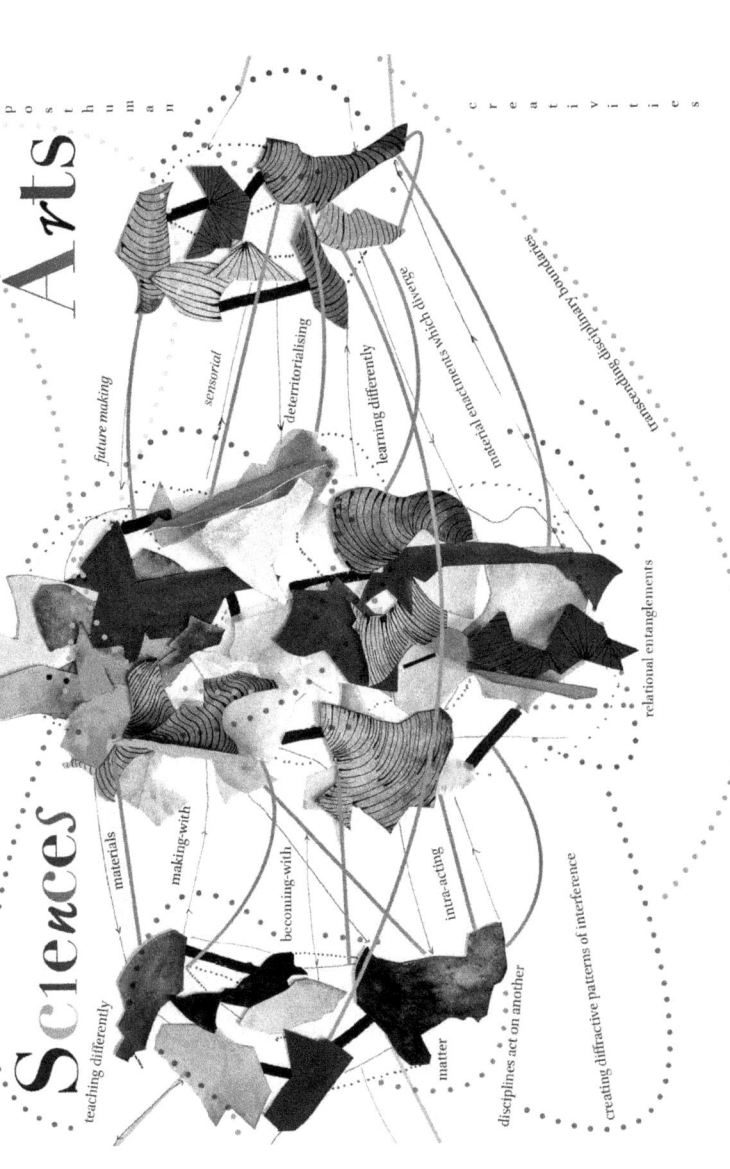

Figure 7.1 A rhizomatic of transdisciplinary practice. A non-linear, boundary-crossing constellation of routes into transdisciplinary practice is depicted as intersecting lines of flight that are co-produced in and through matter and where all things (humans and non-humans, including materials and objects) are experienced in complex and dynamic relational entanglements.

happens in the classroom, in learning and between adults and children. Rhizomatics invite the reader also to engage in (re-)viewing, (re-)framing and (re-)doing transdisciplinary practice that breaks away from traditional practices of STEM (science, technology, engineering and mathematics) or STEAM education (where the A represents the arts), to create new paths and new practices, using diverse creativities to achieve 'new normal' in learning and teaching in the twenty-first century. The reader could start by asking themselves, What knowledges are being taught? How are they being taught? What is the learning journey and what are the reasons for choosing this particular journey? Where is the knowledge siloed and where can it/they be disrupted? This is an invitation to you to think, act and read *immersively*. How? Readers can read with a certain sense of resistance but also an openness to departures from conventional practice. It is an invitation to think, act and read *reflexively* by shifting attention to new pedagogies by decoupling the language of a discipline from its original context. My proposal is that in thinking differently about knowledge and transdisciplinary knowledges, we transcend our previous assumptions, views, attitudes and ways of life to consider the new – towards future-making mindsets that ask, 'What if?'

7.4 Stimulating New Thinking and Practices of Future-Making through Transdisciplinary Education

This manifesto was written against a background of global environmental and political turmoil. Daily reports on the impact of climate change on soils, on biodiversity and on sea levels are challenging what is known and assumed to be good and true about the world. In this manifesto, I am concerned with how education across the arts and sciences can move beyond ideas of prescription (where education is viewed as preparing for a future which may be predicted or expected). Future-making in education is what fuels this manifesto – enabling people and communities to respond resourcefully and creatively to ongoing changes. In this context, transdisciplinarity is not a site of disciplinary multiplication – that is, making new disciplines – but rather a practice which transgresses disciplinary habits, learnt responses and defined boundaries; a relational space in which humans and non-humans (materials, environments) are inter-reliant *with* each other, neither being more important than the other but entangled in practices of discovery and making.

This transdisciplinary manifesto pays particular attention to three interrelated concepts: (1) making-with, (2) materiality and (3) enacting learning differently. I take each in turn. Making-with engages humans and non-humans in *intra*-action with material objects. The term *making-with* was coined by Donna Haraway (2016, p. 58). It is a pedagogical construct for enacting transdisciplinary practices, involving diverse materials, objects, bodies, instruments, tools, technologies and environments (Barad, 2007). This is different from 'learning about'. It is about connecting with others, about physically making and being aware of the complexities of learning in the same way as Figure 7.1 shows the complex relationships between two subject disciplines. The second is materiality. This refers to the materials that matter in learning. The term *materiality* can also refer to objects and things and also applies to the materiality of a person, of laughter, of an object and of an environment. Materiality includes 'the capacity of things – edibles, commodities, storms, metals ... to act as quasi agents or forces with trajectories, propensities, or tendencies of their own ... to articulate a vibrant materiality that runs alongside and inside humans' (Bennett, 2010, p. viii). These forces are a source of action that can be either human or non-human. Thinking in a material way brings out practices that are not easily codified into view (Sorensen, 2009). Thirdly, enacting learning in a material way provides the possibility for viewing learning differently and for challenging as well as complementing, established forms of learning, as for multiple creativities. It disrupts teachers and student by creating conditions for new ways of being, thinking, and enacting (Aberton, 2012). Recognising that our relationship with the physical world, and how we engage with it, impacts how we learn. All of this opens up a new way of knowing, being and doing future-making education that displaces acquired habits and perceptions and enables our students to seek new insights into the nature of a world that continually changes.

The sense of making is an important one. By *making-with*, we recognise that nothing makes itself – we are in a constant state of 'becoming' with materials, environments, bodies and constructs. This is countercultural in a world that seeks security and definitive answers. Making-with requires a process of 're-seeing' ourselves not only with(in) the world, but in the making of educational futures. Being open to the world's aliveness – literally being in touch with its material and affective configurations and reconfigurations – invites *material enactments*: our using and remaking of materials, resources, people and so on through teaching and learning. If this seems obvious, consider how much making takes place in most classrooms, relative to how much time is spent speaking, writing and thinking. More material enactments could allow for new thinking about the way we construct knowledge.

I am suggesting that we move away from the idea that meaning is exclusively made with the symbols of verbal and written language. Could a doctorate involve a performance of new science knowledge rather than the presentation of 80,000 words of text, for example? Transdisciplinary education brings the material back to the forefront of knowing and knowledge, making the case that the material world and the thinking (or symbolic) world are inextricably entangled, as are sciences and arts. For example, in a Scottish project called 'STEAM gardens' (Gray, Colucci-Gray and Robertson, 2022, p. 146), 'STEAM' refers to the synergies that can be created from 'the dialogue and interpenetration amongst previously distinct subjects'. The authors draw on the particular nature of the garden as both art and science, 'thus affording the opportunity for a plurality of educational experiences supporting an array of diverse creativities'. They go on to say that 'a garden can be known scientifically through the classification of plant and animal species and their particular properties and behaviours. However, the garden can also be known qualitatively for its artistic aspects, recognising that colour, pattern and design are integral dimensions of the garden's own creative way of responding to the environment in which it takes its own form' (p. 159). The meaning we make of the world is created through our relational material enactments, or the 'doing' of learning. This demands a shift from 'knowing' as the acquisition of specialised knowledge, to 'knowing' through the mutual relationships – relationships between the child and the material of the garden, between the living and non-living material of the garden, and between the garden as a whole and the gardener.

By extension, we need to stop regarding the arts and sciences as separate or even separable endeavours. They are connected in the complex ways I demonstrate in Figure 7.1. The material enactment (or *doing* learning) – in this case, merging or intra-connecting the arts and sciences – is made possible through transdisciplinary dialogue between human and non-human.

7.5 So, How Can We Co-Author the Bringing Together of Sciences and Arts?

Political, social, environmental, human and personal certainties have been disrupted in the wake of the COVID-19 pandemic. There is a growing sense of helplessness and cynicism across the globe. Within professional learning communities, this transdisciplinary manifesto is a call for experimentation, imagination and transformation: a call to think differently, immersively and reflexively. To do this, we need to believe in the potential of multiple creativities – and particularly transdisciplinary creativities – to shape how we conceive curricula, teacher training and development. While I appreciate the usefulness of established rules – the norms and conventions of our fields and disciplines – we have to destabilise the boundaries between the sciences and the arts and, in so doing, enrich them both.

As I end this manifesto, I will resist giving statements about what to do – to define the disciplines. Rather, I ask questions to bring further disruption. How can leaders model transdisciplinarity? How do they show uncertainties and vulnerabilities? How do they respond to challenges and changes? Where are the opportunities to ask questions about the purpose of schools, and how do schools navigate the choppy waters of government policy? At a systems level, how do teachers and school leaders imagine new languages for their work? Is there a documented and shared choreography of a school development plan? What would this involve? Where can we teach collaboratively across disciplines? Finally, at an individual level, how do we all empower ourselves to reimagine anew? Again and again?

There is a vulnerability in leaping forward into the unknown, but such leaps are full of potential, whether they end up in failure or a tentative grasping of something genuinely new. This requires some unlearning. This demands courage. Transdisciplinary education draws its very strength from not knowing in advance. Boundaries do not sit still.

In ending with a manifesto poem, I take the lead from Tim Ingold (2020, p. 124), who argues for educating creativities that move away from the consumerist focus on novelty and final products, as well as internal and intellectualist notions of creativity, to one

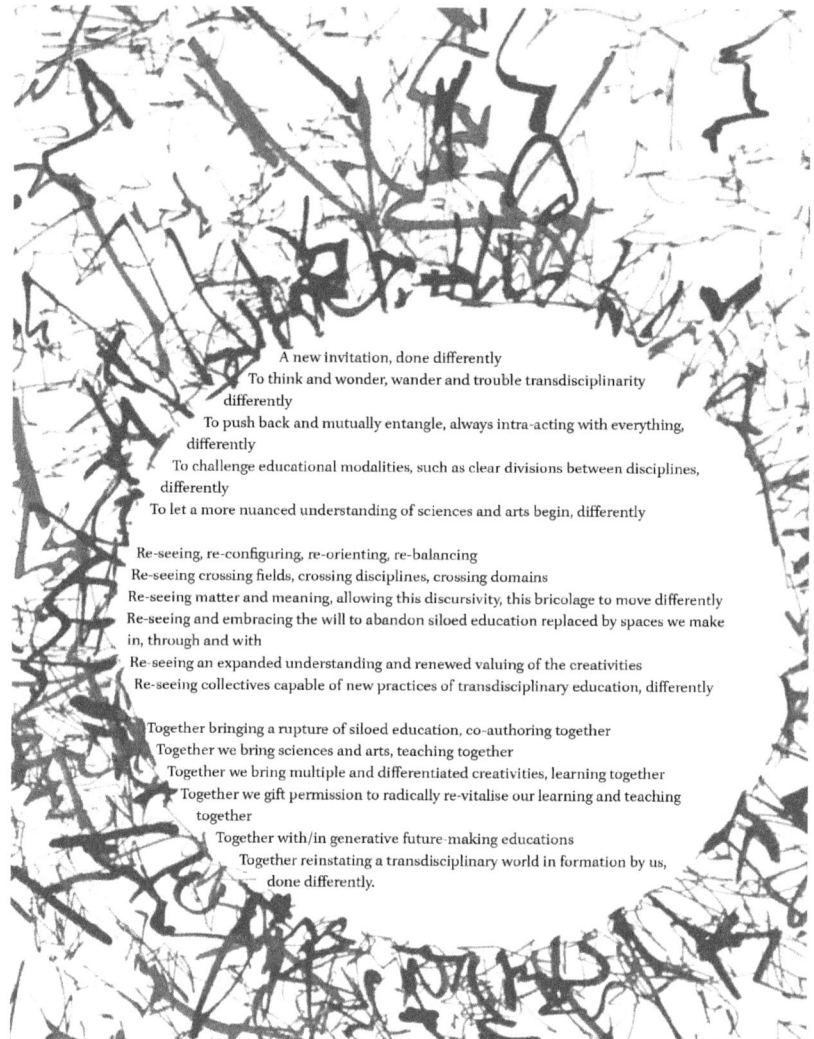

Figure 7.2 A manifesto poem for re-visioning transdisciplinary future-making education.

in which 'the wellsprings of creativity lie ... in their attending upon a world in formation'. So, what this manifesto heralds anew is given in Figure 7.2.

References

Aberton, H. (2012) 'Material enactments of identities and learning in everyday community practices: implications for pedagogy', *Pedagogy, Culture and Society*, 20(1), 113–136. https://doi.org/10.1080/14681366.2012.649418.

Barad, K. (2007) *Meeting the universe halfway: quantum physics and the entanglement of matter and meaning*. Durham: Duke University Press.

Bennett, J. (2010) *Vibrant matter: a political ecology of things*. Durham: Duke University Press.

Burnard, P. and Colucci-Gray, L. (eds.) (2020) *Why science and art creativities matter: (re)configuring STEAM for future-making education*. Leiden: Brill-i-Sense.

Burnard, P., Colucci-Gray, L. and Cooke, C. (2022) 'Transdisciplinarity: re-visioning how sciences and arts together can enact democratizing creative educational experiences', *Review of Research in Education*, 46(1), 166–197. https://doi.org/10.3102/0091732x221084323.

Burnard, P. and Loughrey, M. (eds.) (2022) *Sculpting new creativities in primary education*. Abingdon: Routledge.

Gray, D., Colucci-Gray, L. and Robertson, L. (2022) 'Cultivating primary creativities in STEAM gardens', in Burnard, P. and Loughrey, M. (eds.) *Sculpting new creativities in primary education*. London: Routledge, pp. 146–161.

Haraway, D. (2016) *Staying with the trouble*. Durham: Duke University Press.

Hickey-Moody, A. (2016) 'Manifesto: the rhizomatics of practice as research', in Hickey-Moody, A. and Page, T. (eds.) *Arts, pedagogy and cultural resistance*. Lanham: Rowman and Littlefield, pp. 169–192.

Ingold, T. (2020) 'What knowledge do we need for future-making education?', in Burnard, P. and Colucci-Gray, L. (eds.) *Why science and art creativities matter: (re)configuring STEAM for future-making education*. Leiden: Brill-i-Sense, pp. 422–439.

Sorensen, E. (2009) *The materiality of learning: technology and knowledge in educational practice*. Cambridge: Cambridge University Press.

8 Practitioners' Response to Manifesto 4
Adopting a Transdisciplinary Approach

LIAM CONNOLLY, AINO UKKONEN AND CONSTANTINOS XENOFONTOS

8.1 Introduction

The manifesto is a call to arms in a battle that has long been fought: defining the purpose of education. In a world that seems so complex and confusing, how do we know what knowledge is relevant for children and young people? As Marenko (2021, p. 166) said, 'What does it take to imagine, design and inhabit spaces of experimentation, collaboration and reflection together? How can situations of this kind be crafted?'

In this chapter, Liam, a primary school teacher from Cambridge, presents two responses. The first response is his own experience from the University of Cambridge Primary School (UCPS). The second is from Oslo, Norway, where Aino is a doctoral student studying computational thinking and formative assessment, and Constantinos is professor of mathematics education, specialising in social, cultural and political dimensions of mathematics education; both have worked in schools. The manifesto is a challenging one. It requires different thinking about how we organise and make sense of knowledge(s) and how we craft an education experience that is future-making and dynamic.

8.2 Practitioner Wisdom from Cambridge, UK

My initial reaction to reading Pamela Burnard's manifesto was to feel overwhelmed. I suspect I am not the only teacher who would feel this way.

The scale of the transformation described is staggering and, in some contexts, difficult to envisage. I read the manifesto again, and again. It brought me more questions than answers. When does cross-curricular, or 'STEAM' (science, technology, engineering, arts, mathematics), become transdisciplinary? Do we need to be transdisciplinary? Are silos important sometimes? I read the manifesto again. I thought a lot. I had the pleasure of meeting with Pam to discuss her ideas.

I am not suggesting that you re-read the manifesto umpteen times and seek out the author. What I am suggesting is that you try to keep an open mind when reading the case studies I share with you. Why? Because since reading this manifesto and hearing the term *transdisciplinarity*, I now – in an eerie Baader-Meinhof way – keep hearing it. I attended a talk by an assistant headteacher turned educational consultant and Ofsted (UK Office for Standards in Education, Children's Services and Skills) inspector – she referenced it. Then I heard about a local Cambridge primary school becoming part of the International Baccalaureate's Primary Years Programme – I did some research and found out that the programme is 'an inquiry-based, transdisciplinary curriculum framework', 'guided by six transdisciplinary themes of global significance' (International Baccalaureate, 2023).

Transdisciplinarity is not a far-flung idea impossible to create in our current education system, because it is already happening. When I can, I am trying to be transdisciplinary in my own classroom, and just down the road from where my own school is, more schools, and more teachers, are trying it too; more children are undergoing a transdisciplinary education than we might think.

To speak in the clearest terms possible, I see transdisciplinarity as a style of education in which the boundaries between subject-specific languages and themes are eroded (Burnard, Colucci-Gray and Cooke, 2022) and so 'disciplines' are explored in tandem, through inquiry-based learning, guided by teachers, but not in a purely instructional manner. Teachers may have a plan, but when the pupil leads them in another direction, they may choose to let this happen. It calls to mind the famous Reggio Emilia approach (Brunton and Thornton, 2015), which also challenges the false dichotomy between the arts and sciences (Gardner, 1998). However, Pam is also developing new ideas, such as learning through forms of expression other than language. In my view, to begin with, we should not overthink transdisciplinarity, or worry about whether our practice is transdisciplinary *enough* – the important thing is to move from seeing education as comprising different, largely discrete subjects, to understanding those subjects as blended and interrelated, as they often are in everyday, adult life. If you are a primary teacher, you may well already be doing this in various different ways.

As Pam says, the future our children will inhabit as adults will be different from the world we currently inhabit, and this requires an evolving approach to education. A transdisciplinary education may better prepare our children for a world markedly changed by AI, climate change and shifting lifestyles, because these features of our lives are intersecting more and more. Many of the professions we now consider ordinary may soon be automated, but AI will also create new jobs that require 'twenty-first-century skills' (Holzer, 2022). School is absolutely about more than preparing children for the world of work, but stop to consider what you currently teach; while much of it may be crucial to children's lives, much of it may no longer be relevant in its current form.

How can we enact large-scale change? Maybe we start small. If you teach maths and English by direct instruction in the morning, why not let children explore a project of their choosing in the afternoon? With the right stimulus and resources, children can engage in transdisciplinary exploration themselves – a child interested in science may attempt to give artistic representation to their (scientific) learning, for example. Can you integrate a transdisciplinary approach one morning a week? At my school, we replaced one afternoon science lesson – which we felt undervalued the science learning by squeezing it into the short postlunch slot at the end of the day – for a weekly 'STEM morning', where science, maths, literacy and other subjects can convene. 'STEM' easily became 'STEAM' (to include art).

A transdisciplinary education ought to furnish learners the communicative, creative and analytical skills necessary to work alongside powerful AI systems or solve issues posed by climate change. At the same time, different things work in different settings and teachers must lead using their professional judgement.

Let me share with you some of the transdisciplinary learning I undertook with my children at the UCPS, based around enhancing some of these crucial 'twenty-first-century skills', namely creativity and innovation.

Title

Constellations: Transdisciplinary Learning across Scientific, Historical, Creative and Literary Boundaries
Liam Connolly

Context

The UCPS is a large, state-funded school established by the University. The open-plan design – the doorless classrooms are arranged around the 'learning street', a space that children and adults can use to learn independently or collaboratively – lends itself well to transdisciplinary learning, as does some of its resources; the school has vast outdoor spaces, including a forest area and outdoor classrooms. There is also the advantage of the link to the University and some of its academic departments, as you will see detailed in what follows.

What You Did

We had been learning about Earth and space for some time. We had already been talking about the night sky, the solar system and stars in a literary context through our work on the poetry collection *Dark Sky Park* by Philip Gross (2018), and this blended naturally with our science learning.

One week in April, we were privileged to visit the University of Cambridge's Institute of Astronomy, where Dr Matthew Bothwell and his colleagues gave us a tour of the universe and its history. The children were enthralled by the images and information, and their interest was piqued by the Northumberland Telescope, housed in a steel dome, which was once one of the largest refracting telescopes in the world, with a clock-driven equatorial mounting. 'I never imagined a telescope would need to be so big!' one of the children said, and they were even more surprised when Dr Bothwell told them there are many larger telescopes.

Back at school, we carried on a discussion about constellations that had begun at the institute. Using cardboard tubes and black paper precut into squares, as well as pins, glue, cardboard boxes and paper, we made constellation tubes. To do this, I had printed some constellation patterns for children to cut out and stick to the black paper. Students then poked holes in the paper to make constellation patterns. Later, they used plain paper to create their own constellations. The children researched the names of the constellations and wrote them on the tubes, then swapped with each other to see the different constellations as they would be in the night sky. At the institute, they had been shown a very old book that featured drawings of the constellations and what they represented. The children were interested by the constellations that took the shape of animals. They were quickly able to spot parallels between the Latin names of the constellations and the modern English animal names, like Cygnus and cygnet, Delphinus and dolphin.

Later on, some children chose to create similar drawings, designing their own constellations and creatures to go with them, or redrawing historical ones, such as Ursa Major. They researched the stories behind the constellations and journalled their findings. A particular point of interest for many of the children, and one that was straightforward to capitalise on, was the fact that many of the constellations were based on animals. A very interesting point a child brought up at the institute was how some of the drawings of the animals differed to what they looked like in real life, and a staff member explained this was because the nineteenth-century illustrators had likely never seen the animal themselves and were drawing from someone else's description. The children factored this into their work.

One child said that learning about constellations had made her think about the poem 'Night Walker' from *Dark Sky Park* and wrote her own poem about constellations that would sit alongside Gross' collection. Later, we followed this up as a class, and more children wrote poems about what they had seen and learnt, mimicking Gross' style, invoking techniques like enjambment to mirror the shape of the real constellations.

At the institute, the children had encountered real historical artefacts of a scientific nature, and they truly felt like astronomers. Coming back to school, I was able to engage them in a project that covered substantive knowledge from the science curriculum but invoked creative skills. The learning was not without challenges; the children's interest in astronomy was not always equal. I encouraged those who were less interested in the constellation tube to find a different way of exploring the content, whether that was writing, carrying out their own research or something else. To ensure adequate rigour, it helps to have contingency ideas ready to prompt children who are unsure.

I wished to take the children somewhere to look through telescopes at the night sky and look for constellations themselves, though resources at the time did not allow for it. Fortunately, the community centre near the school sometimes holds such an event, and I encouraged the children to look out for it.

The trip to the institute was key to helping the children feel inspired and excited about constellations, which would not have happened had I introduced the subject by showing them pictures in the classroom; real-world experience is key for transdisciplinary learning and also a stepping stone for teachers to introduce a blend of disciplines. I would recommend beginning in this way – a trip, a visitor, an interesting object, a story, a problem (Russell, Wickson and Carew, 2008) – whatever resources you have, they can be contextualised in the real world. And, outside of school, it is quite rare that disciplines and skills remain siloed in the same way. Transdisciplinary learning has a power to break down boundaries and encourage new forms of creativity – many of the children were very proud of their achievements that day and were able to reflect on their successes in developing skills they did not previously consider themselves proficient in.

I am still learning about transdisciplinary practice, as we all are. I do not believe the example I just shared is a paragon of transdisciplinary practice, but it was one of the starting points for me, and a similar approach could be useful for you.

8.3 Practitioner Wisdom from Oslo, Norway

In an increasingly difficult time for state schools, resource scarcity may be one of your biggest challenges. Perhaps your resources align more fully with this second case study, from Aino Ukkonen and Constantinos Xenofontos; you will notice it could not be more different from my own example, and yet it moves easily through subject disciplines, guided by real-world application, in a somewhat similar style.

Title

The Selburose: A Meeting of Computational Thinking, Programming, Mathematics and Arts and Crafts
Aino Ukkonen and Constantinos Xenofontos

Context

In Nordic countries, like Finland and Norway, computational thinking (CT) and programming have been integrated into different school subjects (e.g. mathematics and science) for all school levels (from early years to upper secondary; ages six to eighteen). The lesson presented here provides a transdisciplinary platform for connecting computational sciences, mathematics and arts/crafts by making the computational practices visual and culturally embedded. This proposed lesson brings together ideas developed and applied in two different contexts, though with necessary adaptations to the Norwegian setting. Specifically, we draw on the work of Papageorgiou and Xenofontos (2018) in Cyprus, who used ancient mosaics to elicit connections between geometric transformations, cultural awareness and the arts, and the work of Markkanen, Perttuli-Borobio and Juuti (2022) in Finland, in which pupils designed tote bags inspired by curricular goals for sustainable development. The lesson featured a *selburose*, a symbol of the Norwegian knitting culture (see Figure 8.1).

What You Did

This proposed lesson is adaptable, depending on each classroom and the experiences of the children. It can be used for Grades 6–9 (approximately ages eleven to fifteen).

Key Concepts
Mathematical Key Concepts

- Geometric patterns
- Translation: sliding a figure in any direction
- Reflection: flipping a figure over a line
- Rotation: rotating a figure, a certain degree around a point

Figure 8.1 The selburose

CT Key Concepts

- Abstraction and patterns: recognising patterns in the structure of a selburose
- Algorithms: designing the steps of instruction for drawing a selburose
- Abstraction and efficiency: exploring how repetitions can be automated
- Debugging: detecting and identifying errors in code

Tools

- Pen and paper
- Scratch on pad or computer (this project requires basic knowledge of Scratch)
- Crafts: tote bag or knitting tools

Stage 1

Pupils first explore geometric patterns in their environment, and specifically, the selburose. This can be done by drawing with pen and paper and discussing the repetitions that occur in the pattern (Figure 8.2). Alternatively, or as an extension activity, pupils can create their own variations of the selburose by designing other patterns.

Stage 2

Mathematical and CT share similarities, such as problem solving and abstractions (Rich *et al.*, 2020; Shute, Sun and Asbell-Clarke, 2017). The exploration of geometric patterns (either repeating or growing) can provide transdisciplinary learning opportunities for developing mathematical and programming skills simultaneously. As a subsequent activity, children can draw the selburose in Scratch, a free programming language and website widely used as an educational tool for children of ages eight

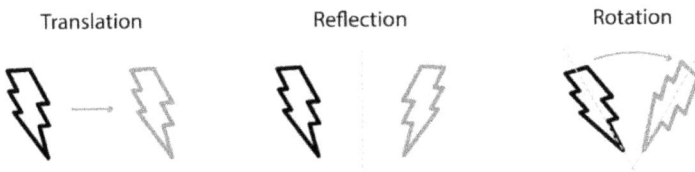

Figure 8.2 Geometric transformations

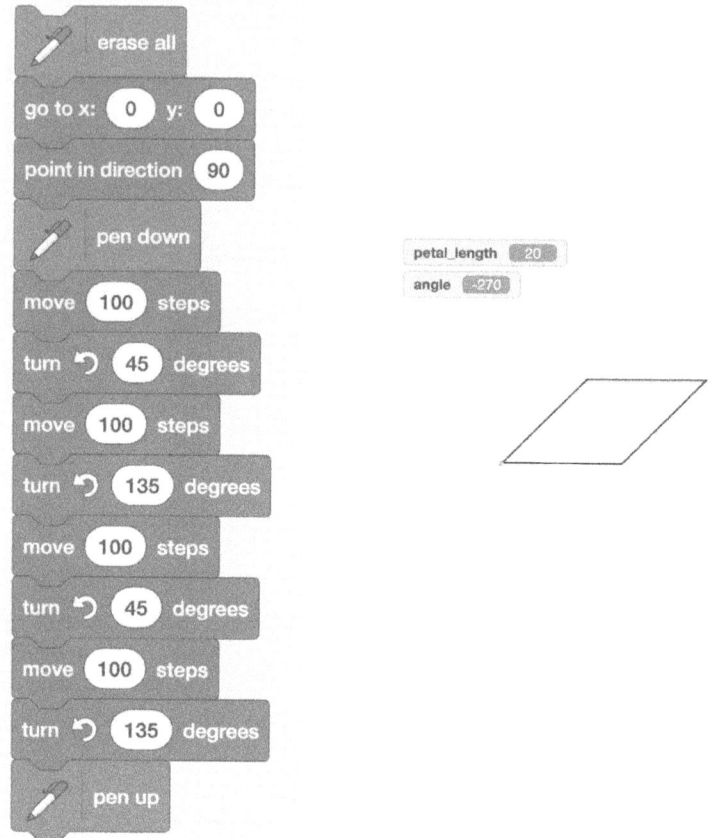

Figure 8.3 One petal leaf and a Scratch code that produces the one leaf.

to sixteen (see https://scratch.mit.edu).[1] They can start by drawing one petal leaf, and then use functions in Scratch to create the next leaf by rotating the initial one (see Figure 8.3). Later, they can use other functions to draw multiple roses (see Figure 8.4 and 8.5 variations).

[1] For an example project in Scratch, see: https://scratch.mit.edu/projects/872136983. Scratch is developed by the Lifelong Kindergarten Group at the MIT Media Lab. See http://scratch.mit.edu. The project outlined in this chapter is an example of a completed project. However, a good start for students would be to explore how to draw one petal leaf, replicate it and make functions for the parts which are repetitions (translations, rotations or reflections), and only gradually build towards their own project. There is not one single way of writing the Scratch code, and the variations in code can be discussed in the classroom.

Practitioners' Response to Manifesto 4

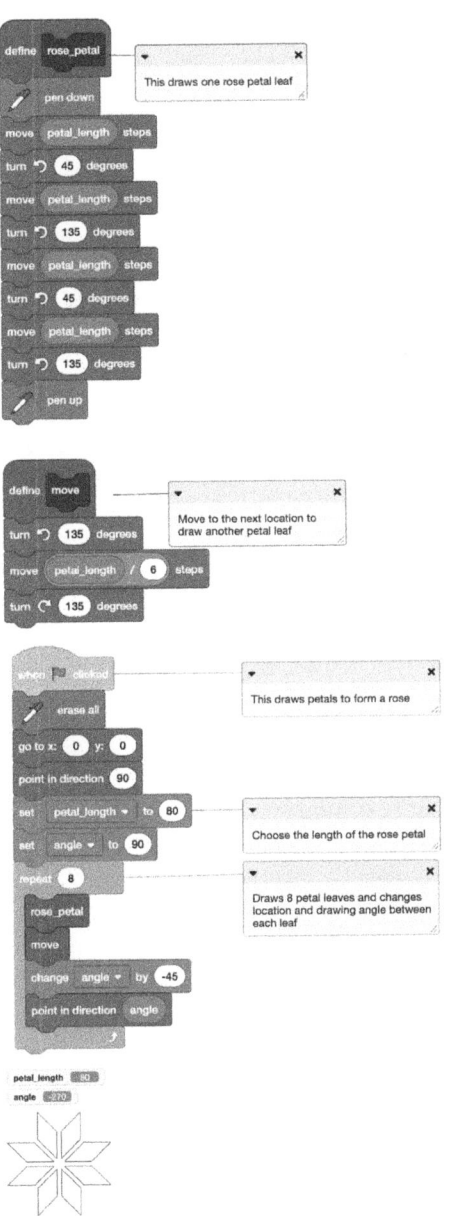

Figure 8.4 The selburose drawn by having a function drawing each leaf.

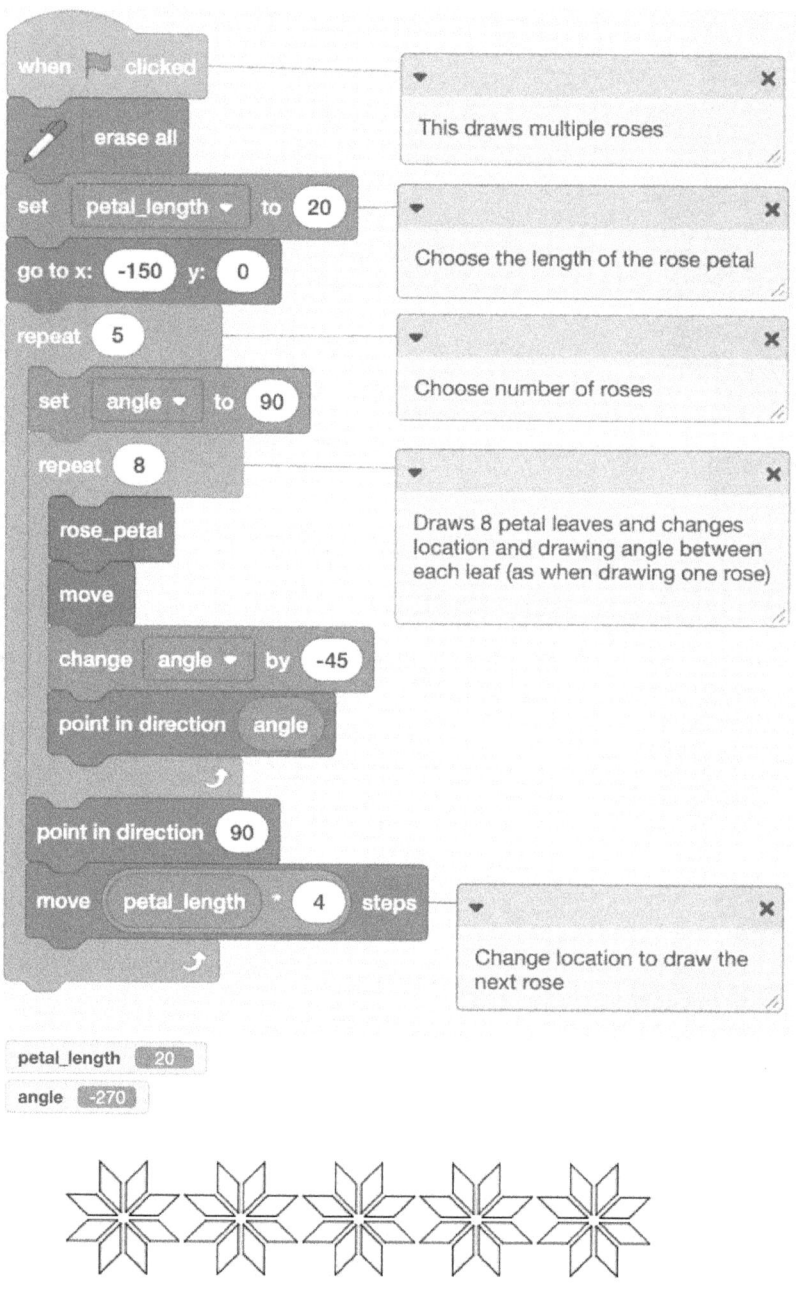

Figure 8.5 Repeating the selburose five times.

In Scratch, visualisation is integral. Therefore, pupils get immediate feedback when running a piece of the program code. The instructions given to the computer (the algorithm) for drawing geometrical patterns can be explored; there are possibilities for refining it with abstraction, and debugging (finding errors in code) can be learned in the process. When drawing geometric figures in Scratch, the computer can be used to automate some of the repetitions. There are numerous ways to automate the process, and drawing the selburose in this program allows students to explore different forms of automation and abstraction. Hence pupils can explore CT and mathematics in conjunction.

Stage 3
Tote bags (Figure 8.6), usually made from a range of fabrics, such as canvas or cotton, are widely available and often considered a good alternative to plastic bags. In the next activity – one that can be linked to curricular goals about sustainable development, as well as arts/crafts – the designed pattern can be printed on tote bags with the use of a laser printer.

Reflecting Thoughts
This lesson can be extended to include ideas and concepts from different school subjects. For example pupils can find out about the history of the selburose, investigate how other cultures use similar or different patterns for crafts and be involved in writing activities. We believe such transdisciplinary approaches provide great opportunities for exploring issues of social justice by bringing discussions about cultural awareness and sustainability to the fore.

Figure 8.6 Tote bag

8.4 Conclusion

From these two case studies, you can see the reach and some of the potential of transdisciplinary practice.

That is not to say that becoming 'a transdisciplinary teacher' is easy, or even obligatory. Indeed, many practical barriers stand in the way; the datafication of our education system and the complex infrastructure of assessment and accountability that surrounds our classrooms make many people nervous of creative pedagogy. Transdisciplinarity does not always lend itself to recording and assessing in an Ofsted-friendly way (Allsup, 2016; Fautley, 2015; Regelski, 2016).

In the UK, schools are more challenged for resources than they have been for some time, and the lack of adult support (teaching assistants, learning coaches etc.) for teachers can undercut the potential for project-led learning. Balancing the needs of all learners is complicated, and if some children want to try something completely separate from the rest of the class, there is often the simple safeguarding issue that you do not have an adult to go off with them wherever they want to go.

To change quickly and on a grand scale would require a seismic effort (and a seismic cost). But we can be reflective and developmental in our own settings, to benefit our children, our schools and ourselves. For this, collaboration is key. Teachers have an enormous number of tasks in their existing remits, but if we work together, we can pool expertise and ideas. Professional learning communities are always a good place to start and are a key method of discussing and developing practice (Dimmock, 2016; Hord, 2009). Working together, we can learn to be agile and creative.

Creativity has vast benefits for children's cognition, motivation, confidence and engagement (Kaufman, 2016; Kaufman and Sternberg, 2010). And to foster creativity, it is imperative that we (educators and other adults) step back and allow learners to make choices (Cremin, Burnard and Craft, 2006). Creativity is indisputably one of the 'twenty-first-century skills' (Holzer, 2022). Flexibility, adaptability and innovativeness will also be essential to the future lives of our learners (Zhao, 2012).

Transdisciplinarity is a way of engendering such skills and supporting our children to become well-rounded individuals who, as well as solving abstract problems in isolation, can merge what were once seen as subject-specific skills and languages and apply solutions to real-world issues. These are the skills that future generations will need: to find new ways of working, to circumvent climate change issues and to complement AI automation rather than being supplanted by it.

Over to You

These challenges are not challenges for the distant future; they are of the here and now. And education needs to adapt to face them. We must not be daunted, but excited. Upheaval – or disruption of the status quo – can be challenging. But it can also bring real positive change, of which educators can be a part. Read the case studies presented here again, and think about how you can start to make these 'small' changes in your classroom, because 'big' change is coming. As we end this practitioners' response, we invite the reader to reflect on the following questions, drawing from their own wisdom and practices in their own classroom, school, social, cultural and educational contexts:

- How can transdisciplinary thinking be developed in your school or educational context?
- How does your curriculum design allow for opportunities to connect, reimagine and evolve the ways we present knowledges?
- Where are the tensions and releases in curricula and pedagogy? Where do you find it confusing, difficult and frustrating? Are these the spaces for intercultural and transdisciplinary thinking?
- In your context's professional learning and development strategy, are there opportunities that challenge our assumptions about what learning, teaching, curricula, pedagogy, culture and spaces are? What do they mean for individuals and children, and what are the areas for discussion?
- Are you and your team open-hearted and open-minded enough to reimagine what could be?
- When and where do you ask, 'What if?'

References

Allsup, R.A. (2016) *Remixing the classroom: towards an open philosophy of music education*. Bloomington: Indiana University Press.

Brunton, L. and Thornton, P. (2015) *Understanding the Reggio approach: early years education in practice*. London: Routledge.

Burnard, P., Colucci-Gray, L. and Cooke, C. (2022) 'Transdisciplinarity: re-visioning how science and arts together can enact democratising creative educational experiences', *Review of Research in Education*, 46(1), 166–197. https://doi.org/10.3102/0091732X221084323.

Cremin, T., Burnard, P. and Craft, A. (2006) *Pedagogy and possibility thinking in the early years. Thinking Skills and Creativity*, 1(2), 108–119. https://doi.org/10.1016/j.tsc.2006.07.001.

Dimmock, C. (2016) 'Conceptualising the research–practice–professional development nexus: mobilising schools as "research-engaged" professional learning communities', *Professional Development in Education*, 42(1), 36–53. https://doi.org/10.1080/19415257.2014.963884.

Fautley, M. (2015) *Music education assessment and social justice: resisting hegemony through formative assessment*. Available at: www.open-access.bcu.ac.uk/3903/.

Gardner, H. (1998) 'Complementary perspectives on Reggio Emilia', in Edwards, C., Gandini, L. and Forman, G. (eds.) *The hundred languages of children: the Reggio Emilia approach – advanced reflections*. 2nd ed. Stamford: Albex, pp. xv–xviii.

Gross, P. (2018) *Dark sky park: poems from the edge of nature*. Hereford: Otter-Barry Books.

Holzer, H.J. (2022) *Understanding the impact of automation on workers, jobs, and wages*. Washington, DC: Brookings. Available at: www.brookings.edu/articles/understanding-the-impact-of-automation-on-workers-jobs-and-wages/.

Hord, S.M. (2009) 'Professional learning communities: educators work together toward a shared purpose', *Journal of Staff Development*, 30(1), 40–43. Available at: https://eric.ed.gov/?id=EJ827545.

International Baccalaureate (2023) *Primary years programme*. Available at: www.ibo.org/programmes/primary-years-programme/.

Kaufman, J.C. (2016) *Creativity 101*. New York: Springer.

Kaufman, J.C. and Sternberg, R.J. (eds.) (2010) *The Cambridge handbook of creativity*. Cambridge: Cambridge University Press.

Marenko, B. (2021) 'Stacking complexities: reframing uncertainty through hybrid literacies', *Design and Culture*, 13(2), 165–184. https://doi.org/10.1080/17547075.2021.1916856.

Markkanen, A., Perttuli-Borobio, E. and Juuti, K. (2022) 'Learning computational thinking within middle school STEAM project'. Available at: www.ucviden.dk/files/190654232/Symposium_Designing_opportunities_to_learn_computational_thinking.docx.

Papageorgiou, E. and Xenofontos, C. (2018) 'Discovering geometrical transformations in the ancient mosaics of Cyprus: an instructional approach to Grade 6', *Australian Mathematics Teacher*, 74(2), 34–40.

Regelski, T. (2016) 'Music, music education and institutional ideology: a praxial philosophy of music sociality', *Action, Criticism and Theory for Music Education*, 15(2), 9–45.

Rich, K.M. *et al.* (2020) 'Synergies and differences in mathematical and computational thinking: implications for integrated instruction', *Interactive Learning Environments*, 28(3), 272–283. https://doi.org/10.1080/10494820.2019.1612445.

Russell, A.W., Wickson, F. and Carew, A. (2008) 'Transdisciplinarity: context, contradictions and capacity', *Science Direct Futures*, 40, 460–472. https://doi.org/10.1016/j.futures.2007.10.005.

Shute, V.J., Sun, C. and Asbell-Clarke, J. (2017) 'Demystifying computational thinking', *Educational Research Review*, 22, 142–158. https://doi.org/10.1016/j.edurev.2017.09.003.

Zhao, Y. (2012) *World class learners: educating creative and entrepreneurial students*. Thousand Oaks: Corwin Press.

9 Manifesto 5

The Biology of Stress – Implications for Education and Lifelong Health

SARAH TEMPLE AND ISABELLE BUTCHER

9.1 Introduction

We all experience stress. It is a fact that at some point in our lives, we will face an event or moment that triggers a stress response. How we deal with stress is very different. How children deal with stress is also related to their own childhood experiences as well as the biological responses. Sometimes children find their experiences so stressful that the response is 'I just can't do it anymore'. And this is why our manifesto calls for new thinking about how we respond, as caregiver and educator, to the children in our schools.

I'll start with a confession: I (Sarah Temple) am not a qualified teacher. In fact, for the last thirty-five years, I have worked across the UK in a number of different health, care and education settings. Although my main role is as a general practitioner (GP), I have also worked within community paediatrics and child and adolescent mental health services. In 2014 I founded EHCAP Ltd – a social enterprise committed to finding innovative solutions for education, health, care and prison services. My work with EHCAP was initially school based – ranging from working with early years teams through to secondary schools. More recently I have provided webinar-based training on adverse childhood experiences and the biology of stress for the Royal College of General Practitioners, the Association of Child and Adolescent Mental Health, the European Mentoring and Coaching Council and the Personalised Care Institute. In writing this manifesto, I collaborated with Isabelle Butcher. Isabelle is a postdoctoral researcher working on the ATTUNE project (understanding mechanisms and mental health impacts of adverse childhood experiences to

Manifesto 5

co-design preventative arts and digital interventions), Oxford University (Bhui *et al.*, 2022), and I am a senior advisor on the board of the project.

Over the years, I have heard countless stories of parents, caregivers, young people and children struggling to make sense of themselves, their relationships and the systems of schools and other services they draw upon to thrive (or survive). This manifesto aims to show the vital importance of three aspects for the healthy development of children and for improving outcomes for children, young people and families:

- The biology of stress
- Responsive relationships and stress management
- Strengthening skills and capabilities in the core life skills of adult caregivers

9.2 The Biology of Stress and the Importance of Responsive Relationships to Stress Management: Raising Awareness of the Science for Teachers

For educators working closely with children, knowledge about stress and stress responses will support them in knowing how to support the children in their care. To reduce sources of stress, we need first to understand the biology of stress responses. Shonkoff (2018) talks about the 'biology of stress' in terms of the body's physiological response to differing levels of stress. Let us consider three different responses: positive, tolerable and toxic (Figure 9.1).

When there is a *positive stress response*, it is a normal and essential part of healthy development, characterised by brief increases in heart rate and mild elevations in hormone levels. Examples include things like getting to an appointment on time, getting children ready for school or preparing for a deadline.

At some point in our lives, we may face an event or moment that triggers a *tolerable stress response*. In this situation, the body's stress response systems are activated at a higher level with more severe, longer-lasting difficulties. An example of this could be the death of a much-loved grandparent. Many families experienced this level of stress during the COVID-19 pandemic. In order to understand the difference between this tolerable stress response and a toxic stress response, we need first to understand what is meant by *responsive relationships*.

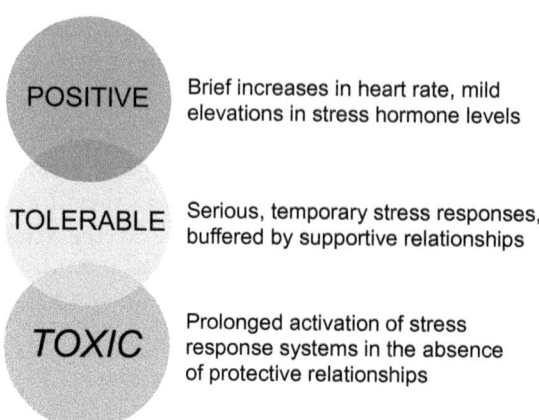

Figure 9.1 Center on the Developing Child (2021) model of positive, tolerable and toxic stress.

The concept of responsive relationships can be difficult to explain (see Table 9.1 for examples of emotion-responsible phrases and their opposite dimissing or disapproving phrases). In essence, responsive relationships are about an emotional connection between the responsible or close adult and the child or between two adults. The terms *emotion coaching* (Gottman and Katz, 1996) and *emotion validating* (Lambie, Lambie and Sadek, 2020) are often used to describe responsive relationships.

Sometimes it can be easier to understand what a responsive relationship is by looking at relationships that are not emotionally responsive – for example emotion-dismissing or emotion-disapproving relationships. The following examples may help explain the difference between these relationship styles. In the first, Mum dismisses Max's feelings, and in the second, Mum disapproves of Max's feelings.

Example of a Non-Responsive, Emotion-Dismissing Relationship Style

MUM: Max, it's time to go.
MAX: I don't want to. I hate school.
MUM: Come on Max, you know you enjoy school. Of course you're going.
MAX: No, I hate it. Why do you always tell me what I like? You never listen.

Table 9.1 *Emotion-responsive phrases compared with emotion-dismissive or -disapproving phrases*

Emotion-responsive phrases	Emotion-dismissing or -disapproving phrases
It's understandable you would feel ...	Don't worry about it.
It's hard when you lose something.	Stop crying!
I know what you mean.	Cheer up!
Everyone feels like that sometimes.	There's no need to be angry/anxious.
It's annoying when someone takes your ...	What you should do is ...
It's OK to feel like that.	Come and look at this.
Are you having any tummy pain?	You are worrying over nothing.
Do you think you might be feeling sad?	Stop whining/complaining.

MUM: What do you mean I never listen? Now come on we need to go- I've got a meeting I need to get to this morning.
Max comes out of the kitchen banging his bag on the door and kicking the chair. They drive to school in silence.

Example of a Non-Responsive, Emotion-Disapproving Style

MUM: Max, it's time to go.
MAX: I'm not going.
MUM: What do you mean, I'm not going?
MAX: I hate school.
MUM: That's ridiculous, you love school.
MAX: Jake's being mean.
MUM: That's quite enough now get into the car. You need to calm down and get your things together. Stop making such a fuss.
They drive to school in silence.

For young and pre-adolescent children, a responsive relationship with an adult caregiver means pausing, noticing and describing physical sensations associated with emotions as well as expanding the child's awareness and understanding of different feelings associated with their emotions. Gottman and Katz (1996) coined the term *emotion coaching* in their research, whilst Lambie, Lambie and Sadek (2020) use the term *emotion validating*. Both are emotionally responsive relationships. Let's take a look at Mum and Max's interactions where Mum is curious, is emotionally present for her son and validates how he is feeling. This in turn allows Max to speak more and for his mum to model how an emotional response to a situation can be 'worked through'.

Responsive Emotion Coaching Relationship Style

MUM: Max, it's time to go.
MAX: I'm not going.
MUM: What do you mean, you're not going?
MAX: I hate school.
MUM: Oh dear, what's happened?
MAX: It's Jake, he doesn't choose me for five-a-side now and I'm on my own at break time.
MUM: Oh dear Max (pause) – mmmm. I wonder how you are feeling about that? Are you feeling sad? Are you feeling any pain in your body?
MAX: I'm feeling sick and my tummy hurts.
MUM: (pause) Yes, I understand that. When you're feeling sad sometimes you might notice your tummy hurting or feeling sick. Are you a little bit disappointed as well?
MAX: Yes. Jake used to be my best friend.
MUM: It's OK, it's normal to have these feelings – let's get your stuff in the car and we can talk more on the way to school.

Max picks up his bag and walks to the car.

Adolescents respond best when adult caregivers facilitate their progression towards becoming autonomous (Havighurst *et al.*, 2010) by pausing and allowing the adolescent to express themselves – acting in a consultant role (as opposed to managerial) as the adolescent talks through their physical sensations, emotions and feelings and considers possible solutions. In countries like the UK – where children are in full-time education for as long as they are – this adolescent phase lasts into the mid twenties.

For pregnant women, responsive relationships with their partner and other adults' buffer against the physiological impact of stress on both themselves and their developing baby or babies. Responsive relationships (e.g. emotion coaching or emotion validating) buffer against otherwise potentially damaging physiological changes of the tolerable stress response (Center on the Developing Child, 2021). This buffering effect is particularly significant in the critical phase of development between conception and the third birthday but is relevant to all ages.

A *toxic stress response* occurs when the body's stress response systems are activated at a higher level with strong, frequent and/or prolonged adversity in the absence of an adult caregiver able to provide responsive relationships. Adverse childhood experiences (ACEs) are some of the most intensive sources of stress that children can suffer whilst growing up (Bellis *et al.*, 2023). In their research on ACEs, Felitti and Anda (1998) devised a series of questions that intentionally included family dysfunction (mental health difficulties, addiction, domestic abuse, incarceration) as well as more traditional neglect and abuse. These difficulties make it almost impossible for adult caregivers to provide their children with responsive relationships unless they access support of some sort – for example coaching, counselling, medical input including medication or therapy.

Crucially, without responsive relationships, the stress response systems are activated at a level that can cause long-term physiological changes. As humans, we are particularly vulnerable to these changes while in the womb and during the first three years of life while our biological systems are developing. This is termed the *critical developmental phase*. A toxic stress response involves prolonged elevation of stress hormone levels as well as chronic inflammation. The impact during the critical developmental phase is on the laying down of hormonal systems, immune systems, metabolic systems, brain architecture and genetic systems (epigenetics).

The experience of a toxic stress response in the critical phase of development may mean a child

- Is emotionally reactive
- Has difficulty managing their emotions, behaviours and executive function
- Has difficulty understanding what nurturing relationships and nurturing self-care are

- Has difficulty with relationships (brain architectural difference)
- Is cast into out-groups and has few friends
- Is less able to make healthy lifestyle choices and be more likely to have difficulty with addiction, over or under eat, smoke or take drugs
- Has long-term emotional, mental and physical health difficulties, including a higher risk of ischaemic heart disease, cancer, metabolic conditions such as diabetes and pulmonary conditions such as emphysema

As the child develops, there may be a period of latent vulnerability where the difficulties the child is experiencing are not recognised. When this happens, the child is likely to present to health or care services at about the age of eight or nine with behavioural issues that are causing difficulties in school and at home.

9.3 Strengthening Skills and Capabilities in Core Life Skills of Adult Caregivers

As a society, we need to notice the children who are experiencing a toxic stress response and support both them and their adult caregivers by providing education about the biology of stress as well as psycho-educational tools that strengthen core life skills in emotion literacy and emotion intelligence. It is important to maintain compassion and a clear sense of hope.

When children who experience a toxic stress response in the critical phase of their development become parents and caregivers themselves, they are likely to struggle with parenting effectively. This is sometimes referred to as intergenerational adversity. By educating whole communities we can together get better at compassionately noticing parents and caregivers who are struggling with emotional aspects of parenting – whether related to unresolved mental health difficulties, being genetically neurodivergent, having experienced a toxic stress response, or (more likely) a mix of these. The beauty of an approach that takes psycho-education tools into the whole population (universal approach) is that it avoids the pitfalls of assessment, thresholds, 'fixes' and referrals. This moves us away from the traditional trauma model of 'identifying that family over there' and then 'doing something to them', and moves us toward a coaching approach that encourages people to tap into and grow their internal resources; it is an affirmative model rather than a deficit one, using partnerships, collaboration and relationship development; a working-with approach to understanding that finds and explores ways to strengthen core life skills and executive function. Individuals are more likely to feel included and cared for and less likely to find themselves cast into out-groups. Understanding the biology of stress and what it means to hold responsive relationships gives whole communities the opportunity to notice those individuals who are struggling and offer compassionate support earlier.

The current system of safeguarding and child protection identifies and supports children who are experiencing high levels of stress, but unfortunately, some children 'slip through the net' or are identified late. We are advocating that this universal coaching approach run alongside existing services to complement and enhance their effectiveness.

The detail of the psycho-education tools that we use within EHCAP's family wellness (sometimes known as school readiness) programme (Temple, 2022) is beyond the remit of this manifesto, but in principle we use

- Biology of stress (positive, tolerable, toxic)
- An adapted version of Dan Siegel's hand model (Siegel, 2015)
- An adapted version of Dan Siegel's river of well-being (Siegel, 2015; see Figure 9.2)
- Emotion coaching and emotion validating
- Mindful activities

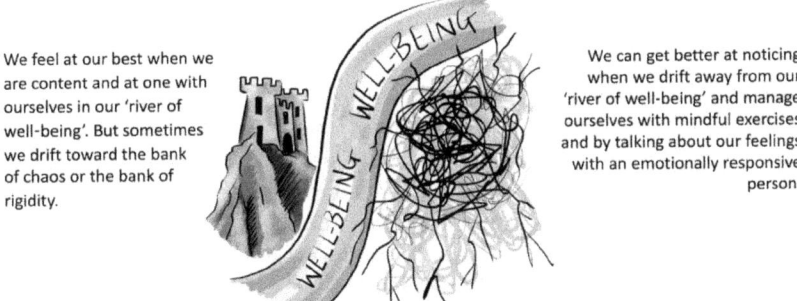

We feel at our best when we are content and at one with ourselves in our 'river of well-being'. But sometimes we drift toward the bank of chaos or the bank of rigidity.

We can get better at noticing when we drift away from our 'river of well-being' and manage ourselves with mindful exercises and by talking about our feelings with an emotionally responsive person.

Figure 9.2 EHCAP's adaptation of Dan Siegel's metaphor 'the river of well-being'. Illustration: Sarah-Leigh Wills.

Whilst, as a society, we are becoming increasingly aware of the relevance of emotionally responsive relationships to well-being and to the healthy development of the brain (Center on the Developing Child, 2011; Dalton *et al.*, 2021), there are significant gaps in understanding the broader issues to do with how emotionally responsive relationships buffer against the wider physiological changes associated with a toxic stress response.

Between conception and the third birthday a complex interplay of factors such as genetics, environment (including diet, medicines, drugs or alcohol) and relationships (Shonkoff, 2018) affect the development of an individual child. A toxic stress response may impact

- Learning and readiness to succeed in school
- Lifelong emotional, mental and physical health through physiological changes to the
  - brain architecture
  - developing immune and metabolic systems
  - developing genetic systems (epigenetics)
- An individual's ability to adapt, self-manage and thrive (manage life's ups and downs)
- An individual's ability to engage with learning and education
- An individual's ability to manage relationships
- An individual's ability to parent effectively
- Likelihood of being cast into an out-group

I recall a reflection from Jasmin (*pseudonym), a teacher and mum of two young children. Jasmin's words point to the key principle of this manifesto: to listen with compassion, to draw from the biology of stress and to develop emotionally responsive school communities. Jasmin kindly provided this quote:

Jasmin, Primary School Teacher and Mum of Two Young Children (2022)

As a child who experienced adversity, I often struggled to identify and manage the emotions that I felt. During adolescence I remember feeling confused, unliked and worthless. My relationship with both parents was fractious, they were quite authoritative, and I often experienced what I now know as a lot of shame, blame and fear. I didn't know how to cope with the feelings I had, for I didn't even really know what a feeling was. Our emotional world was rarely discussed and was never deemed as an acceptable reason for any behaviour.

Looking back, I now understand that the child in me never developed the coping skills, language or ability to recognise and express how I was feeling. Because feelings were laughed at, it felt weak to show any struggle and I felt too vulnerable to express my true worries. At the same time, I didn't want to burden my mum, who already had enough stress to contend with. I often hid my emotions or if I expressed them, it would end in upset. I quickly learnt to repress or hide them as it was safer that way.

This way of coping followed me into my teens where I found a way to seek control and cope with my feelings through food. At fourteen, I developed an eating disorder that lasted over twelve years. It was something I was deeply ashamed of and hid for as long as I could.

In my early twenties I was fortunate to connect with someone who supported me. Feeling emotionally understood and supported meant more to me than anything material. This person validated how I felt, made me feel strong, safe and ok with who I was. It gave me permission to express and explore my feelings which is when I started to journal and explore my emotional world.

Fortunately, I recovered from my eating disorder in adulthood. However, I firmly believe that this journey would not have taken almost fourteen years if I had had an emotionally validating relationship with someone from a young age; someone who accepted my emotions, helped me understand my physical signs of stress and feelings of being overwhelmed.

Jasmin's story is not uncommon. We cannot separate people's emotional stories and journeys from their academic or social lives. They are inextricably intertwined.

Let's take a look at some possible ways forward that reduce sources of stress and enable responsive relationships. Some of the questions educators could consider follow:

- How can teachers, schools, or communities support people like Jasmin (and her children)?
- How can we move beyond the 'firefighting' of antisocial behaviour in classrooms towards a compassionate understanding of people rooted in a scientifically informed understanding of emotions and the biology of stress?
- How do we limit judgements and instead use language that connects with feelings and needs?
- How do we broaden this understanding from focusing on the brain to understanding the whole-body physiological impact of a toxic stress response and the potential impact on lifelong health and well-being?

Personalised approaches to educating and child-rearing were formally discussed in the UK by government-funded think tanks more than a decade ago (Diggins, 2011). However, for several reasons, they have been difficult to put into action. Simple concepts, such as empowerment and choice, are difficult to define and elaborate in groups, organisations and systems. Cultural differences within and between services and communities pose a barrier, as do practical-ethical implementation challenges and social inequalities and prejudices. Different experiences lead to different descriptors –words and acronyms – being used in schools by comparison with health or care settings. This gap in language – disrupting communication across professional contexts – can lead to children, young people and families not receiving the support they need. Communities and professional services can easily slip into blaming and shaming.

The Social Care Institute of Excellence published *Think Child, Think Parent, Think Family* (Diggins, 2011) as a blueprint for moving towards compassionate, person-centred care. This report advocates for an approach with children and families at the heart of discussions and decision-making about their care, having values of working together across systems (e.g. education, healthcare and justice) and creating a common language, while keeping safeguarding as the golden thread.

Munro (2011) gave us a framework for a relational approach to person-centred care. Munro states that relationships are key for healthy child development – that relationship development is *the* answer to the challenges faced by parents and children. Of course, why *wouldn't* relationships be central to the way we work with children and their families? So, the question is, How do our systems and structures of working prevent children and their families from forming appropriate and meaningful relationships? If we know the consequences of children not receiving emotional validation, what are the barriers to changing what we do and how we do it?

Healthcare research from multiple sources, including the Center on the Developing Child, shows that a personalised approach lays the foundation for responsive, caregiving and economically stable adults. When educational settings apply the principles of person-centredness and work together with families and communities (as well as other services), they can play a crucial role in enabling a child to succeed in school but also in their lifelong health and well-being.

Figure 9.3 Interplay between the Center on the Developing Child's three principles and healthy development and educational achievement when a child is engaged with adult caregivers who are responsive and economically stable. Illustration: Sarah-Leigh Wills.

From an international perspective (National Scientific Council on the Developing Child, 2020), there is evidence that the interplay between a child's genetic make-up, their environment (including diet) and their interpersonal relationships are central to their formation as individuals. Collating decades of research, the Center on the Developing Child (2021) developed three principles to improve outcomes for children and families (Figure 9.3):

- Reduce sources of stress
- Support responsive relationships
- Strengthen core life skills such as emotional intelligence and executive function

Mindful emotion coaching, the family wellness (sometimes referred to as school readiness) programme that I have created (Temple, 2022), holds these three principles as the foundation pillars in an outcome framework. In terms of reducing stress, we have developed a way of talking about the biology of stress with the intention that as community leads understand better this science they will work with their local communities and create their own innovations that reduce sources of stress. We have concluded that both emotion coaching (Gottman and Katz, 1996) and emotion validating (Lambie, Lambie and Sadek, 2020) are effective for enabling 'serve and return' responsive relationships. We have adapted these concepts into psycho-educational tools that are easy to access and use in everyday life. These tools strengthen core skills of emotion intelligence, emotion literacy and executive function.

9.4 Next Steps: How Do We Embed This Science in Educational and Healthcare Systems?

One way to strengthen understanding of responsive relationships is to engage with parents and adult caregivers in developing their own awareness of emotions, of the language and feeling of emotions, and of the physical sensations associated with them. The scientific advisor on the Disney film *Inside Out* describes seven core emotions common to all humans: joy, sadness, contempt, disgust, surprise, anger and fear (Ekman, 1992). Being able to connect with children experiencing difficult emotions, such as fear, worry, anxiety and anger, is an important aspect of emotion validation/coaching because it builds emotional literacy and emotional intelligence, which in turn enables more effective executive function.

Lambie, Lambie and Sadek (2020) show that teaching emotion validation skills to parents in a social care setting leads to children becoming calmer and more accepting of negative emotions. Lambie and colleagues have collaborated with the publishing company Skylark Online to create commercially available resources for parents and adult caregivers of babies and young children. Rose and Temple (2017) researched emotion coaching with children in schools and created lesson plans and resources for schools spanning from age three to nineteen. Havighurst *et al.* (2010) have created a suite of parenting programmes, called Tuning in to Kids, that seek to forge emotional connections between parents and children. These programmes have also been shown to improve emotion socialisation practices in parents of preschool children. The Happy Child Parenting App (Larson and Banks, 2020) provides user-friendly video footage demonstrating responsive relationships.

According to Gottman and Katz (1996), holding an emotion coaching relationship style at least 30 per cent of the time improves children's ability to nurture relationships and cope with life's ups and downs, and is likely to result in superior academic achievement. The change in emphasis from the predominant (in Western society) emotion-dismissing style to an emotion-coaching style can have surprising knock-on effects for the child as well as the parent. The following excerpt is about the experience of a mum with a baby and a toddler.

Manifesto 5

Mum of a Baby and Toddler (2022)

Initially, I didn't really understand what emotion coaching was all about but as I listened to the information about the biology of stress, and in particular the toxic stress response, I started to understand how the trauma I experienced in my childhood was impacting on my baby and toddler – as well as my marriage. Gradually, I felt able to begin working with a counsellor and healer. I started to understand how reactive I am to stress and to learn how to calm myself and manage my emotions before interacting with my children.

While schools focus on children's education, a teacher or teaching assistant could – with knowledge about the biology of stress – listen differently, respond with more compassion and resist the temptation to make judgements. They could also connect with the parents and adult caregivers with coaching style trauma–informed conversations. Consider Ellie:

Ellie, Mum of Two Daughters (2022)

I first went on anti-depressants/anti-anxiety medication after a period of undiagnosed post-natal depression and parenting a neurodivergent child. I tried to reach out for help to the GP, to school and even in earlier years to health visitors. I was a well-presented, middle-class parent who in public had well-behaved children. No one paid attention to me. I doubted my parenting and myself. I wanted and needed help but didn't know where to go and no one took me seriously. I tried to get help via various online resources but still felt misunderstood until I came upon a Family Wellness Coach. The coach not only made me feel normal, she made me feel supported and helped my husband understand how being neurodivergent can affect a child's ability to manage their emotions.

The journey is still hard, but I no longer feel alone. Family Wellness Coaching gave me the confidence to understand I had to do what was best for my child and that in turn has given me more confidence to access support.

Being involved in workshops about emotions or emotional literacy and the biology of stress raises awareness and makes a difference for those involved and their families. Listen to Amanda's experiences:

Amanda, Mum of Four (2022)

I honestly can't explain just how life changing the introduction of mindful emotion coaching has been to my family and I. . . . Although it wasn't always easy, over time it became easier to remain calm and choose an emotion coaching response in those challenging moments. I found that teaching the children to tune into the physical sensation in their bodies helped massively. They learned to notice their stress sooner and while it was at a more manageable level. The children's emotional literacy also developed significantly. One of my children went from only being able to identify good and bad feelings, to being able to identify and label complex emotions like shame, resentment and compassion.

Different sectors working in partnership is key; the siloed thinking of subject domains (e.g. health and education as separate entities) is not helping our young people to flourish. Box 9.1 illustrates the actions taken in one school in the UK where a passionate headteacher (Kate Nester) worked with a family support advisor (Andy Leafe).

Box 9.1 A Discussion with Kate Nester (Headteacher) and Andy Leafe (Parent Family Support Advisor) about Embedding This Trauma-Informed Approach in a School

Hindhayes Infant School is in Street, Somerset, UK. Both Kate and Andy trained as mindful emotion coaches in 2015 and have adapted this training to meet the needs of their community and setting, embedding sustainable, relationship-based, child-centred care by

- Creating a clear vision which they shared across staff, pupils and families and into the local community
- Developing a culture of both compassion and learning
- Focusing on relationships – staff to staff, staff to parents and carers, staff to children and child to child

To implement these steps, they developed the following:

- *Curriculum design.* Underpinned by a trauma-informed approach, following Kidd (2020) and her 'Curriculum of Hope'. The five areas of coherence, credibility, creativity, community and compassion now provide clear headings for school staff and the wider community. Stickers have been added to the children's books and a strapline created – 'Hindhayes, Kind Ways – Kind to self, others, school, community'. This approach made asking 'are you OK?' normal.
- *Recruitment processes.* Embed a need for staff to have meaningful relationships with children in their care. This led to a reduction in the use of bank staff and an expanded role for teaching assistants (TAs) as play workers.
- *A learning culture.* All staff, from TAs to senior leaders, are given space and time in the curriculum for their own learning.

- *Outdoor activities with Forest School.* Every child has one half day a fortnight, with more vulnerable children having access once a week, depending on needs.
- *Community engagement.* Volunteer roles are offered to isolated, vulnerable parents in the Forest School, which runs in both term time and holidays, providing an opportunity for connecting with parents and carers and skill building, for example by joining in with food preparation and fun activities, supporting effective parenting through play in adult caregivers.
- *Professional development (CPD).* To support positive play.
- *Solution Circles.* Once a week in a staff meeting, we talk about a challenging situation.
- *Behaviour policy transformed into relationship policy.* Both consequences of behaviour and repair happen in school through a recovery curriculum, 'correction through connection'.

Andy trained to run both Tuning in to Kids and Tuning in to Teens groups for parents (both programmes promote emotion-validating relationships). He has merged learning from Family Links and, using the mindful emotion-coaching approach, empowers parents to enhance their executive function through the use of psycho-educational tools. Andy creates his own easy-to-access resources for parents and carers, including information based on the biology of stress, emotion coaching and mindfulness. Mindful activities have been particularly helpful for staff as well as parents and carers, for example in the transition from home to school after drop-off. Kate has continued to develop her leadership skills and has drawn on multiple approaches to building emotion intelligence, recognising that no one size fits all and adapting her learning to meet the needs of children and families in her setting. This includes the innovative use of 'Oops' cards, which normalise moments when things just don't go to plan.

The key issue in this example is the combination of leadership from Kate and the skill of Andy in networking with the community to connect with both children and families with a mindful emotion coaching approach. Building emotionally supportive futures is essential if we want our children and their caregivers to flourish, to move out of toxic stress and to live wholesome, healthier and more emotionally connected lives.

9.5 Conclusion: Building Emotionally Supported Futures

An emotionally supported, trauma-informed and personalised future is very much needed, especially in a post-pandemic world that has exacerbated inequalities and left many with high or toxic stress in their lives. Feelings matter, and the emotional well-being of families and children matter, not only for them but also for communities and society at large. If school professionals can help communities improve their understanding of the biology of stress and the protective buffering effect of responsive relationships, then there is the possibility that together we can reduce the number of children in our society who experience a toxic stress response (with all the potential lifelong emotional, mental and physical health difficulties associated).

The key questions that now must be asked follow:

- How do we start conversations about the biology of stress, and how do we incorporate what we know into lesson plans, curriculum and behaviour policy as well as into our communities?
- How do we support teaching staff to talk about difficult topics?
- How do we notice and support those children who have experienced or are currently experiencing a toxic stress response?

Looking forward, further research and curriculum development needs to be orchestrated through community leaders as well as a multi-agency approach. This must include health and care professionals, educationalists, government support agencies, third sector organisations, community groups and people with lived experience of a toxic stress response.

References

Bellis, M. *et al.* (2023) *Tackling adverse childhood experience (ACEs) – state of the art and options for action.* Public Health Wales NHS Trust. Available at: www.ljmu.ac.uk/-/media/phi-reports/pdf/2023–01-state-of-the-art-report-eng.pdf.

Bhui, K. et al. (2022) 'Creative arts and digital interventions as potential tools in prevention and recovery from the mental health consequences of adverse childhood experiences', *Nature Communications*, 13(1), pp.1–5.

Center on the Developing Child (2011) *Building the brain's 'air traffic control' system: how early experiences shape the development of executive function*. Working Paper 11. Available at: https://developingchild.harvard.edu/wp-content/uploads/2011/05/How-Early-Experiences-Shape-the-Development-of-Executive-Function.pdf.

Center on the Developing Child (2021) *Three principles to improve outcomes for children and families*. Available at: https://developingchild.harvard.edu/resources/three-early-childhood-development-principles-improve-child-family-outcomes/.

Dalton, L. et al. (2021) *SEEN: secondary education around early neurodevelopment*. Oxford: Department of Psychiatry, University of Oxford. Available at: www.psych.ox.ac.uk/research/seen.

Diggins, M. (2011) *Think child, think parent, think family document – a guide to parental mental health and child welfare*. Egham: Social Care Institute for Excellence. Available at: https://jerseyscb.proceduresonline.com/files/think_child.pdf.

Ekman, P. (1992) 'Are there basic emotions?' *Psychological Review*, 99(3), 550–553. https://doi.org/10.1037/0033-295x.99.3.550.

Felitti, V.J. and Anda, R.F. (1998) 'Relationship of childhood abuse and household dysfunction to many of the leading causes of death in adults. The Adverse Childhood Experiences (ACE) Study', *American Journal of Preventive Medicine*, 14(4), 245–258. https://doi.org/10.1016/s0749-3797(98)00017-8.

Gottman, J. and Katz, L.F. (1996) 'Parental meta-emotion philosophy and the emotional life of families: theoretical models and preliminary data', *Journal of Family Psychology*, 10(3), 243–268. https://doi.org/10.1037/0893-3200.10.3.243.

Havighurst, S.S. et al. (2010) 'Tuning in to kids: improving emotion socialization practices in parents of preschool children – findings from a community trial', *Journal of Child Psychology and Psychiatry, and Allied Disciplines*, 51(12), 1342–1350. https://doi.org/10.1111/j.1469-7610.2010.02303.x.

Kidd, D. (2020) *A curriculum of hope: as rich in humanity as in knowledge*. Estonia: Crown.

Lambie, J.A., Lambie, H.J. and Sadek, S. (2020) 'My child will actually say 'I am upset' ... before all they would do was scream: Teaching parents emotion validation in a social care setting', *Child: Care, Health and Development*, 46(5), 627–636. https://doi.org/10.1111/cch.12770.

Larson, M. and Banks, R. (2020) *The happy child parenting app*. Available at: www.humanimprovement.org/the-happy-child-app.

Munro, E. (2011) *Munro review of child protection: a child-centred system*. Available at: www.gov.uk/government/publications/munro-review-of-child-protection-final-report-a-child-centred-system.

National Scientific Council on the Developing Child (2020) *Early childhood development and lifelong health are deeply intertwined*. Working Paper 15. Available at: https://eric.ed.gov/?id=ED607013.

Rose, J. and Temple, S. (2017) *Somerset emotion coaching project evaluation report phase two*. Bath: Institute for Education, Bath Spa University. Available at: https://researchspace.bathspa.ac.uk/10730/.

Shonkoff, J.P. (2018) *Protecting brains, stimulating minds: the early life roots of success in school lecture*. Cambridge: Harvard Graduate School of Education. Available at: https://developingchild.harvard.edu/resources/protecting-brains-stimulating-minds-the-early-life-roots-of-success-in-school/.

Siegel, D.J. (2015) *The whole brain child*. New York: Mind Your Brain.

Temple, S. (2022) *Mindful emotion coaching: a universal, trauma-informed, neurodiversity-inclusive family wellness coaching programme*. Oxford: ECHAP.

Resources

'All Emotions Are OK' free download, from www.allemotionsareok.co.uk.
EHCAP resources from www.mindfulemotioncoaching.co.uk.

10 Practitioners' Response to Manifesto 5

Implementing an Understanding of the Biology of Stress

AIMEE DURNING AND ELENA NATALE

10.1 Introduction

This chapter offers two sets of reflections in response to the vision for a more integrated approach to supporting children who experience toxic stress. In the first, Aimee describes the reflective 'standing back' needed when thinking about a child's needs and how they might be catered for in a mainstream school. The second is from Elena, who runs projects with children from traumatic backgrounds in Sicily, using arts, stories and yoga to help children explore the stresses they experience. Both examples illustrate the importance of starting conversations about the biology of stress, facing up to emotionally challenging circumstances, and making adjustments to a child's school day when we notice signs of toxic stress. The manifesto argues that knowledge of stress can transform our classrooms because the starting point for all education is the emotional health of the child – before we get to reading, writing and maths!

10.2 Practitioner Wisdom from Cambridge, UK (by Aimee Durning)

The University of Cambridge Primary School (UCPS) has the development of compassionate citizens at the heart of its curriculum design. Our aim is to nurture the whole child by considering their mental wellness, physical being and their academic knowledge (and where necessary we aim to nurture the child's family also). As educators, we look to research to support our pedagogical thinking. However, we can only learn so much from a textbook, webinar or an in-person training session. Sometimes knowledge and understanding comes through observation and empathetical attunement; that is, practitioner wisdom. As Sarah Temple and Isabelle Butcher state in their manifesto, there can be no separation of people's emotional stories from their academic or social lives.

In most classrooms, there is usually a student who poses a conundrum: Why do they react in this or that way? Why is writing so difficult for them? How can I help their speech and language development? As we near the holidays why is their behaviour escalating? All of these questions require moments of reflection, as well as conversations with previous teachers or special educational needs coordinators. Together we must think about the child's lived experience; whether they have secure or insecure attachments, any potential adverse childhood experiences (ACEs), and their physical and mental wellness. The list goes on. So, why do Temple and Butcher advocate a focused understanding on stress and the biological impacts of stress? And why is it a teacher's responsibility? Maybe these are obvious questions to the reader. But in a 6-hour school day, teachers face numerous, sometimes competing, claims on their time! Educators need to become behaviour detectives. Detectives trained in the scientific knowledge of toxic stress and stress responses. These behaviour detectives require a kind and loving heart and deep understanding that 'Kids do well when they can' (Greene, 1999).

How do we go about developing these detective qualities at the University of Cambridge Primary School? Firstly, we work to promote the power of relationships and non-violent communication (Rosenberg, 2002). To achieve this, we work with an educational coach to understand how teachers can coach children through difficult times whilst simultaneously nurturing the child's self-regulation (skills which promote autonomy and an understanding of the child's unique behavioural responses). Second, we choose the language we use very carefully. For example we prefer to think about self-regulation as co-regulation. We try and resist naming children's behaviour in negative terms (e.g. a meltdown, or being naughty or rude), but rather as an expression of particular needs. Third, we work as collaborators: we support one another (child and adult/adult and child) to find ways through when our stress responses become too much. We take the time to sit alongside the child and wait until the time is right to unpick their feelings and needs. Fourth, we embed knowledge about emotional health in the curriculum. The biology of stress is a teachable body of knowledge, and we teach students about emotions and the mind, as well as the body's reaction to stress. For example we use Daniel Siegel's (2012) hand model to demonstrate to children that when their emotions get very big, they sometimes 'flip their lid', and we help them to recognise these feelings in their own bodies before an episode of 'lid flipping'. For our younger children we use Lambie's (2022) resources from Skylark, as mentioned in the manifesto. In our nursery and reception classes, we use accessible and developmentally appropriate books to explain emotions and the feelings children experience. This openness, curiosity and teaching of emotions has created a culture of care and understanding between staff, pupils and parents/caregivers, which over time has fostered a community of reciprocal care and compassion. For educators, it is important we link this understanding to academic and/or specialist knowledge, providing a research-informed platform to share our work with others and exploit the benefit of those who have developed supportive strategies in other schools.

Finally, for the team at the UCPS, practitioner knowledge has been built over several years of professional development (PD). For example our team was given an in-person PD session from Cambridgeshire Virtual Schools. The role of the virtual school is to support educational settings for children who have experienced or are experiencing the care system. The work of virtual schools – in keeping with Temple and Butcher's manifesto – focuses on listening and being attuned to children's behaviour, on pausing, noticing and describing children's manifestations of stress during moments of crisis. As a school, this session strengthened our work as 'emotions detectives' – tapping into children's emotional rhythms each day and noticing patterns and triggers for explosive behaviours. We were encouraged to consider the child's so-called window of tolerance. To understanding emotional rhythms (e.g. a child's heightened emotions when they are hungry or if someone touches their belongings), children and educators must work together to notice these challenging moments and find strategies to manage them – say, through strongly formed, emotionally validating relationships.

Through the Local Authority in Cambridgeshire, members of the school team, including senior leaders, teachers and teaching assistants, have attended the STEPS (Cambridgeshire Therapeutic Thinking Framework) training. This added another layer of understanding about the behaviours teachers are confronted with in school. The STEPS philosophy reminds us that all children should be given an equal opportunity to develop socially. This training provided the school with a script to use when supporting a child during a moment of crisis. The script removes all judgemental language, questions the child about their needs and requires the adult remain calm and offer the child time to respond. The script is part of the emotions detective toolkit. It helped me engage with an autistic Year 6 child who was suffering a crisis – the child felt ignored and wanted his teacher to accompany him during the daily mile (a global initiative to run/walk a mile each day). The STEPS philosophy enabled me to carefully and reassuringly assist but not judge. How often have we as educators spared the time to sit alongside a child whilst they are volubly expressing their dissatisfaction? When do we ever stop and think about whether a child is developing socially and enjoying life? Have we come to the point where the curriculum dictates everything? Where there is only enough time in the school day to rattle through the timetable as we reduce the amount of play our young people experience?

Along with other local schools, the UCPS takes the time to attend to children's mental wellness. Some children are provided with school-based emotional support sessions. These sessions are run by our learning coaches, who are trained as emotional literacy support assistants. Coaches provide afternoon sessions in a nurturing environment where children are listened to and their emotions are validated. By helping children understand their emotions, the sessions support them to manage their anger. Several children attend weekly sessions, and some attendees are neurodivergent. Some children display overwhelming behaviours, and for some, toxic stress causes them to shut down, preventing them from coping with the demands of the school day (and as some parents report, unable to cope with the demands of home).

When attempting to understand the science of stress, but also practitioner experiences, educators can engage with external knowledge exerts. Studio 3 is an organisation that proposes an approach to managing challenging behaviour known as the low-arousal approach – appropriate for dealing with children and young people suffering from toxic stress. Its director Professor Andrew McDonnell's (2020) 'The Reflective Journey: A Practitioner's Guide to the Low Arousal' offers insight into the science behind challenging behaviour due to traumatic experiences (understanding about cortisol and adrenaline). McDonnell acknowledges that the playfulness, acceptance, curiosity and empathy

(PACE) approach is a close fit to the low-arousal approach. He discusses the low-arousal approach as non-confrontational and person centred, as opposed to a strict zero-tolerance behaviour strategy that does not take individual experiences into consideration. I would also recommend, for anyone who wishes to develop their behaviour management strategies, the work of Louise Bomber, Gerry Diamond, Jarlath O'Brien and Gareth Morewood (Studio 3).

To implement the low-arousal approach, practitioners must show bravery, courage, calmness and empathy. These attributes point towards the values and culture embodied at the UCPS:

- Nurturing the vulnerable
- Taking the time to discover the triggers that cause emotional outbursts
- Finding ways to ensure children can flourish and learn alongside others, free from labels such as 'nightmare child', 'naughty' or 'bad'
- Sensitively unravelling particular stories so that new ones of success and hope can be spun

In Boxes 10.1 and 10.2 are two stories associated with understanding toxic stress and meeting individual needs (and family needs). Billy and Jonny (both pseudonyms) represent typical experiences working with children living with toxic stress. Both stories contain insights into the ways of overcoming it.

Box 10.1 Hello Billy

Billy joined our school at the beginning of Year 2 (ages six to seven). We had been briefed by virtual schools and his social worker about his difficulties in his previous school. Billy was trapped in a cycle of toxic stress. His previous school had attempted to educate him in isolation. Mostly he was supervised by a teaching assistant and a member of the local authority specialist teaching team. He was on a part-time timetable which meant he attended school for only two and a half hours a day. We were also told that Billy was a child with experience of the care system.

As a team we set in motion a plan to support Billy as he transitioned from part-time to full-time education. The plan included our most experienced team members who were required to support him. While the external professionals pushed for a support plan of rapid academic catch up, we pushed back and promoted a timetable of play and friendships. We knew that Billy had to learn to like himself and understand that he had many qualities hidden underneath the years of abuse and multiple layers of stress-inducing cortisol and adrenaline.

Slowly and lovingly, we nurtured his spirit. We arranged numerous playtimes for Billy – playtime with a peer in which the adults stepped back. We observed that Billy lacked basic play skills, but also that he was struggling with expressive language and that he had trust issues. On reflection, and after an informal chat with Gerry Diamond (trauma practitioner), we realised that Billy was not ready to access any sort of formal learning in the classroom. The classroom environment is a step too far for a child who is suffering from toxic stress. Instead, Billy would pop into class for a few minutes each day, to build and foster a sense of belonging.

To begin with, Billy was mostly unhappy and would spend his time in school either swearing at the adults or hitting them. With each occurrence, we offered love, patience and reassurance, explaining that it was Billy's behaviour we did not like, not Billy himself, who we liked very much, and who would always be welcome at our school. We reinforced this with messages of trust, compassion and belonging. At the end of every day, we would tell him that we looked forward to seeing him in the morning or that we hoped he had a nice weekend and we would see him on Monday.

Gradually (over one academic year), his friendships and confidence grew. The team had helped to tackle and dismantle his toxic stress and Billy had learnt to recognise the signs of his stress and had developed strategies to help himself manage. At this point we knew that academic learning could begin.

Box 10.2 Listening to Jonny

Jonny joined us halfway through Year 1 (ages five to six). He came to us with very little spoken language and little knowledge of appropriate classroom behaviours. Once again, the team had to spend time observing him to understand Jonny and his quirky behaviours.

> Jonny lives with his father and younger sister. His father had fought hard for his Educational, Health, Care Plan (EHCP) – a legal document outlining a plan for a child who has educational special needs and/or health needs – and is fully invested in his education. On occasion, Jonny's father could become extremely cross and aggressive with the school team, shouting and swearing and ringing the school office several times during the day. His behaviour became impossible to manage and weighed heavily on the team. We noticed that Jonny's behaviour often mirrored his father's. At this point, our headteacher reminded us of toxic stress and fight, flight or freeze responses. Jonny's father was in constant fight mode. The headteacher told us that there was only one way we could manage this volatile situation – by responding with kindness and understanding. We needed to be emotionally validating rather than judging, well aware that his father was not only in 'flight/fight mode' in individual moments but also fighting the wider system. Because by meeting Jonny's father's needs, we would inadvertently meet his. Following this conversation, there was a shift in mindset and the team set about cloaking Jonny's father with compassion and empathy. For example, if there was a scheduled school event, we would make sure that we personally invited him. We would go out of our way to invite him into the school and make him feel welcome by fostering a sense of belonging. It was not always easy – sometimes it was very hard and our headteacher had to be tough and set new boundaries – always with kindness and not with the ego of his status of headteacher. Sometimes tough love was needed but always the father returned, this time less angry and ready to listen and also to express himself without the emotion.

The more we learn about toxic stress and trauma – from personal study or experience, or through external professionals, like virtual schools – the greater our empathic understanding and our ability to form strong, supportive relationships with children and their families. The previous examples have sketched out fairly conventional approaches. However, in the following case study, Elena Natale explains how the use of yoga, the provision of spaces for creative expression and an awareness of emotional stress in the lives of refugees were able to improve the emotional experiences children.

10.3 Practitioner Wisdom from Sicily, Italy (by Elena Natale)

Context

The Yoga Story Time project took place over one month during the summer holidays with Grade 1 children (ages six to seven) at the Goretti school – part of the Istituto Comprensivo Rita Atria in Catania. The Istituto Comprensivo is made up of seven school complexes ranging from nursery to middle school, totalling about 850 pupils. The Istituto is located in an 'at risk' area – with volumes of social housing, not enough green spaces and limited social infrastructure. Families differ in social background, culture and work activity, but the area is characterised by illiteracy, high migration, unemployment, disintegration and criminality. The Goretti school is in the village of Santa Maria Goretti.

Children in this area often suffer from economic, social and cultural deprivation and have fewer opportunities to participate in educational experiences outside school. The school therefore organises summer projects to keep the children engaged, to develop basic competencies and support the well-being of children and the wider community. The project was part of a three-year plan undertaken by the school to prevent early school dropouts and educational poverty.

Aims and Objectives

The Yoga Story Time project combined the power of picture book stories, the arts and the benefits derived from yoga to support the well-being of children and to develop collaboration and communication skills and competency in English. It encouraged children to express their emotions and, through knowledge of their own body, to communicate their personal needs and improve their physical, emotional and social well-being. Most of the children had had traumatic experiences or lived in unsafe situations that had led to toxic levels of stress, and therefore they found it very hard to interact with each other, to trust adults and to share anything about themselves. They also displayed challenging and violent behaviours, towards themselves and others.

The specific aims of the project were linked to the objectives and development of key competencies in the curriculum that can be found in the Italian Indicazioni Nazionali (Consiglio dell'Unione Europea, 2018; Ministero dell'Istruzione, dell'Università e della Ricerca, 2012). The focus was on developing the following skills:

- Multilingual skills: to develop children's ability to understand and communicate orally in the English language
- Personal and social skills: to foster children's emotional and mental well-being and improve their ability to relate to others and to take care of their emotions
- Motor and physical skills: to learn to understand one's body, to stay active and develop fundamental movement skills, to recognise and live according to principles that promote psycho-physical well-being

Structure

Through this project, children participated in creative activities, inspired by the following picture books:

- *Be Who You Are* by Todd Parr
- *The Colour Monster* by Anna Llenas
- *Here We Are* by Oliver Jeffers
- *Same, Same but Different* by Jenny Sue Kostecki-Shaw

The books were chosen because they all had similar themes, such as belonging, identity, care towards others and the environment, and the understanding and expression of feelings. To facilitate children's engagement with the themes of the books I integrated interactive and creative activities, movement-based exploration and reflective discussion. The lessons usually began with dynamic reading sessions – interactive storytelling where children enacted scenes, mimed key events and embodied characters from the narrative. Following this, thematic exploration was facilitated through the use of educational aids such as flashcards, vocabulary games and creative crafts, aimed at deepening comprehension and fostering a closer connection with the text. At this point, children were ready to delve deeper into the meaning of the stories – not through words but rather through their bodies. I introduced students to yoga poses and breathwork that aligned with key story elements and emotions. This embodied exploration provided children with a sensory experience of the story's themes in a safe and natural manner, creating opportunities for deeper understanding. Only after engaging with the narrative on a physical level did we move onto discussions. Here, children were encouraged to share their thoughts, draw connections to their personal experiences and derive meaningful insights from the story. To make them feel more at ease, I encouraged the children to communicate in their native language, fostering a sense of comfort and enabling more authentic expression. However, to encourage language development, I led all the activities in English, I repeated what they said in English and I encouraged them to use key vocabulary we had learnt.

Some of the questions we discussed were, What makes us happy? How should we react when we experience negative emotions? What are the different ways to express ourselves and our feelings? How are we similar and different to others? What makes us who we are? How can we respect ourselves and others?

After reading *The Colour Monster*, children created small 'feeling monster' puppets out of paper cups and pipe cleaners. By encouraging children to represent their emotions by drawing on the puppets, they were able to reflect on their feelings and talk about them with more distance. I then asked them to act out, using their puppets, situations where they feel those emotions, an activity that revealed how children need the space to process their stress and negative experiences. The puppet provided this space insofar as the children did not feel they were talking directly or entirely about themselves.

To explore the messages of the book *Same, Same but Different*, children were invited to explore the question, In what ways are we the same as one another, and in what ways are we different? The children were encouraged to think about their identity by representing their likes, dislikes and dreams on a puzzle piece. They then worked collaboratively to put the pieces together and reflected on how even though each piece was different and unique, they all fitted in to create the puzzle. Through this activity they realised they had much more in common than they thought, and this helped to establish a mutual acceptance. The children also painted their handprints. Getting them to compare their hands with one another illustrated that no matter where people are from – their family or social background – as humans, we are much more similar than we think.

In addition to creating physical pieces of art, the children engaged in physical activities to reflect the texts they read. For example the children enacted with their bodies through yoga the people and animals from the book *Here We Are*. This was followed by a discussion about how we can live in symbiosis with nature, other people and animals and how we can develop healthy habits that benefit us and our surroundings.

Link between Yoga and Well-Being

If we accept the manifesto pledge to reconnect the emotional health of children to the purpose of education, a case can be made for using and practising yoga in schools. All around the world, research illustrates the positive effects of yoga on children's learning and cognition, physical and mental health, emotional development and behaviour (Khalsa and Butzer, 2016; Khunti *et al.*, 2022). Many studies start by identifying the differences between yoga and physical education and explore the benefits yoga can have when integrated in the curriculum. This research is still developing in terms of its methodologies, sample sizes, assessments of long-term impact and systematic analysis. However, the results are promising and call for further explorations.

In *Yoga Education for Children*, Swami Satyananda Saraswati (1999) and others explore the value of yoga in education, explaining how it can be used as therapy, and give examples of practices suitable for use with children. They state, 'Yoga is a form of complete education that can be used with all children, because it develops physical stamina, emotional stability and intellectual and creative talents. It is a unified system for developing the balanced, total personality of the child' (p. 9). As an aspect of children's education, yoga can have an impact on their physical, emotional, mental and creative development.

At the physical level, yoga can help children develop good posture and work on their motor skills, enhancing balance, agility and coordination. It can also support the development of muscular and skeletal structure. Yoga and breathing techniques aid in maintaining hormonal balance and equilibrium between the sympathetic and parasympathetic nervous systems. Another advantage of yogic practices, particularly pranayama, is helping children learn to utilise their lungs to their full capacity. Yoga is fully inclusive and allows children with physical disabilities to participate as it does not require the same physical endurance, quick movements or strength as other forms of exercise.

At the emotional and behavioural level, yoga can help children develop a toolkit to balance their various energies. Yoga works on the brain and the endocrine system, thus facilitating emotional harmony and increasing concentration capacity. Yoga requires discipline and can help children regulate and channel their emotions.

At the mental level, yoga can stimulate both brain hemispheres, helping children develop various learning skills such as memory, creativity, concentration and reasoning. By helping children become more aware and conscious of what is happening in their minds, we can help them understand how to develop mental habits for learning. Through various asanas or nature-inspired positions and visualisation techniques, children are also encouraged to imagine, experiment and be creative.

Observed Impact on Children

The Yoga Story Time project is focused on addressing children's needs, starting from their physiological needs and moving to the self-actualisation needs described in Maslow's (1943) hierarchy of needs. By observing children's behaviours, I realised they needed to feel safe, to be loved and encouraged and to be listened to. The use of yoga and stories created the space for children's needs to be met.

Using picture books helped to tap into children's imagination and introduce new ideas in a creative and child-centred way – providing a stimulus to spark dialogue and to capture children's attention with follow-up creative activities.

Being experiential in nature, yoga helped the children to be involved in their learning and explore key themes related to their lives at both physical and mental level. It proved to be a useful tool to help the children work on themselves, starting with their outermost aspect, the body, through physical postures and gradually moving inwards through breathing and meditation techniques to regulate their emotions. Through guided meditations and visualisations on the themes of the books, the children were encouraged to use their senses and their imagination to understand the themes and messages of the stories and make connections with their own lives.

On a practical level, the use of stories and yoga helped the children interact with each other more positively, take part in shared activities and games, use nicer language when communicating with each other, react less abruptly and violently to situations and respect each other and their personal spaces. By the end of the project, children had opened up and were communicating with more confidence: they could talk about themselves and their future hopes, they shared personal stories and they started describing themselves and their surroundings in more positive terms.

Conclusion

This project highlights the role that stories and yoga can have on children's well-being. Integrating reading-for-pleasure opportunities, mindfulness, yoga and other creative practices into the curriculum could have multiple benefits for a child's holistic development. By giving children the chance to practice yoga, we are developing the whole human being, empowering children to become more aware and balanced and helping them regulate their emotions and understand themselves, their body and their learning.

Over to You

In their manifesto, Temple and Butcher invite us to consider how the biology of stress is an essential component of the educational journey of children. They also explain how toxic stress can irrevocably destroy children's life chances. The two preceding cases show the different ways practitioners have responded to these challenges. Both examples reveal the emotional intelligence and sensitivity of children and their families. However, neither provides complete answers. As we end this practitioners' response section, we invite the reader to reflect on the following questions, drawing from their own wisdom and practices in their own classrooms, schools and social, cultural and educational contexts:

- Which family in your education context could be experiencing stress? What type of stress? How do the behaviours suggest they are in stress? Could it be toxic stress?

- Are there children in your class or school or youth group who seem to find social interactions really difficult? What do you know about their life stories? What do you know about their family's life stories?
- Where do children fit in and stick out? How has your school adapted to provide pathways for families that find school, formal contexts and social interactions particularly difficult?
- What is your response to stress? Could you have lived through a period of toxic stress? If so, how could you get the support you need to evolve the ways you respond?
- How do we start conversations about the biology of stress, and how do we incorporate what we know into lesson plans, curriculum and behaviour policy as well as into our communities? A culture of professional learning and understanding needs to be nurtured, maintained and constantly revisited.

References

Consiglio dell'Unione Europea (2018) *Raccomandazione del consiglio del 22 maggio 2018 relativa alle competenze chiave per l'apprendimento permanente*. Available at: https://online.scuola.zanichelli.it/competenze/files/2019/01/Raccomandazione_consiglio_europeo_competenze_2018.pdf.

Greene, R.W. (1999) *The explosive child*. New York: HarperCollins World.

Khalsa, S.B. and Butzer, B. (2016) 'Yoga in school settings: a research review', *Annals of the New York Academy of Sciences*, 1373(1), 45–55. https://doi.org/10.1111/nyas.13025.

Khunti, K. *et al.* (2022) 'The effects of yoga on mental health in school-aged children: a systematic review and narrative synthesis of randomized control trials', *Clinical Child Psychology*, 28(3), 1217–1238. https://doi.org/10.1177/13591045221136016.

Lambie, J. (2022) *My first emotions: learn to understand and manage feelings together*. Cambridge: Skylark.

Maslow, A.H. (1943) 'A theory of human motivation', *Psychological Review*, 50(4), 370–396.

McDonnell, A. (2020) 'The reflective journey: a practitioner's guide to the low arousal approach', *International Journal of Positive Behavioural Support*, 10(1), 68–69.

Ministero dell'Istruzione, dell'Università e della Ricerca (2012) *Indicazioni nazionali per il curricolo della scuola dell'infanzia e del primo ciclo d'istruzione*. Available at: www.miur.gov.it/documents/20182/513 10/DM+254_2012.pdf/1f967360-0ca6-48fb-95e9-c15d49f18831.

Rosenberg, M.B. (2002) *Nonviolent communication: a language of compassion*. Encinitas: Puddledancer Press.

Saraswati, S. (1999) *Yoga education for children*. Vol. 1. Bihar: Bihar Yoga/ Yoga Publications Trust.

Siegel, D. (2012) *Dr Daniel Siegel presenting a hand model of the brain*. Available at: www.youtube.com/watch?v=gm9CIJ74Oxw.

11 Manifesto 6

Science and Spirituality – Cultivating Meaning and Purpose in Education

AKHANDADHI DAS

11.1 Introduction: What's the Problem?

What is the purpose of education? It is a question that remains unanswered and asked perpetually by governments, educators and parents. It is a question related to another – what is the purpose of life? The two are interrelated – one will answer the other. Carl Jung (1962, p. 326) said that 'as far as we can discern, the sole purpose of human existence is to kindle a light of meaning in the darkness of mere being'. And Viktor Frankl (1966) talks of grasping the meaningfulness of life in rational terms. So, my manifesto for education attempts to suggest ways in which we philosophise the experience for children and young people; to grapple with big questions and to consider the very point of life. I argue for the need to equip young people with the philosophical tools and critical thinking skills necessary to grapple with the complexities of existence and create meaningful lives for themselves within a rapidly changing world. This involves moving away from traditional, discipline-specific models of education and embracing a more holistic approach that encourages open-ended exploration of fundamental questions, fostering intellectual curiosity, self-awareness and a sense of purpose in life.

Life as a teenager has probably never been easy in any epoch or civilisation. It's a time of bodily transition, raging hormones and new emotions. It's also a time for making up one's mind on what we think of the world and how we fit into it. We question ideas we've been fed, rebel against the norm or endeavour to fit in – seeking self-expression or conformity. There's much to consider, especially as our minds contemplate the big questions of existence that humans have posed – argued and fought over – since time immemorial:

Who am I?
What is life?
Is there something more?

These may seem abstract and peripheral to the immediate matters of domestic life, family disruption, social interactions, exams, dating and so on, but I contend that a teenager's ability to navigate the challenges of adolescence is affected by the concepts and beliefs one holds about oneself and one's purpose in life.

In the UK, the Health Foundation suggests that the number of children aged between six and sixteen who have a 'probable mental health condition' rose from one in nine in 2017 to one in six in 2021 (Peytrignet *et al.*, 2022). Of particular concern is that this included one in four adolescent girls. These are worrying statistics. And it is therefore imperative that we deepen our understanding of, and approach to, the complex underlying causes at work in, what we euphemistically term 'teen angst'.

In both education and care, we are getting better at delivering appropriate forms of support, therapy and counselling, despite the huge challenges on public finances that is resulting in reduced access to such support. However, if we could identify common contributing factors to the mental illness, perhaps we could do more in the healing? Chapter 10 in this volume refers to the biology of stress, but I am referring to the ways in which we define who we are, how we want to engage in the world and the meaning of both. Could there be preventative mental healthcare? What would it look like? Could an educational experience that has philosophy at the heart of it bring about more articulate – socially, emotionally and intellectually – young people? This manifesto cannot provide answers to all these questions. However, it will endeavour to explore issues that might enable young people to find a deeper sense of purpose and meaning for their lives; to sustain – even inspire – them through the opportunities and challenges that lie ahead.

According to Hill *et al.* (2010), purpose and meaning are related but are not synonymous. They identify four main types of purpose as follows:

Prosocial: Propensity to help others and influence the societal structure
Creative: Artistic and creative goals and propensity for originality
Financial: Financial well-being, security and worldly attainment
Recognition: Desire for recognition and respect

People pursue these goals in various combinations and with varying degrees, though it is thought that if our goal is to increase happiness and well-being, we should focus on prosocial activities (Lyubomirsky and Layous, 2013). The aforementioned purposes do not in themselves establish *meaning*, though they can and often contribute to a person attributing a sense of meaning to their life.

Meaning is generally thought of as a mix of factors, such as proposed by Morgan and Farsides (2009):

Valuing life: Seeing life's inherent value
Living by principles: Having a personal philosophy that guides your life
Purpose: Having clear goals and intentions
Accomplishment: Setting and reaching personal goals
Excitement in life: A sense that life is exciting, interesting or engaging

Some young people may establish satisfactory meaning for their life within a prosaic interpretation of these factors without addressing wider existential questions. But they and others may benefit from a deeper understanding of what gives life meaning, by exploring the foundational questions: What is my rationale for valuing life? What principles does it give rise to? How are my values and purposes authentic to that meaning?

It is almost impossible to capture meaning without considering the broader context of one's life – and thus also, what happens to us at death. Existential questions about life are intrinsic to the quest for meaning. In *The Search for Meaning in Life and the Existential Fundamental Motivations*, Alfried Längle (1999) explains that individuals are fundamentally looking for a greater context and values for which they want to live for. Along with the issue of our personal existence is the question of the larger reality in which we find ourselves. Does the universe have a purpose for us? Is there anything beyond to which I am or could be connected that might also bestow direction and meaning to my life?

Furthermore, a major factor in deriving meaning from work, creativity, altruism and service to others is the hope that we leave a legacy, to perpetuate something of ourselves after our demise, something that made a difference. Prosocial purposes not only offer greater happiness in life; they also offer more opportunities for legacy, to pass on wisdom, wealth, opportunity, monuments, projects and so on to the next generation. Extending the impact of one's actions beyond death – and being appreciated and remembered for them – bestows a greater sense of meaning to them in the present. The question is, What might a prosocial focus look like in schools? How would children manifest this in their daily life as learners, friends, siblings and sons and daughters? and How do teachers make sense of this in their practice, beyond the substantive things they teach?

In this manifesto, I argue that modern education must provide a forum for all young people, at appropriate ages, to engage with such existential questions. If you have ever been in an early years classroom, you will know that children are curious to know what happens when we die. This is not morbid. Instead, could it be that the human condition is in the constant state of seeking and sense-making? Could it be that instead of sanitising and ordering life into easily accepted compartments, we keep the spaces of uncertainty open and alive for rich questioning and deep discussion?

11.2 What to Do about It?

If we accept that finding meaning for one's life contributes positively to mental well-being and other social aims, we should integrate and develop this endeavour within school life. Marcel Proust is paraphrased to explain that the movement through life and in seeking new landscapes must also include the vital practice of seeing – of having eyes.[1] I argue that there should be a distinct philosophical project, beyond what we currently offer in the UK in religious education (RE) and personal, social, health and economic education (PSHE). And the subjects and topics for discussion should be objective and neutral. It is not required nor desirable to tell young people what to believe, nor to

---

[1] This is a common paraphrase of 'The only true voyage of discovery, the only fountain of Eternal Youth, would be not to visit strange lands but to possess other eyes, to behold the universe through the eyes of another, of a hundred others, to behold the hundred universes that each of them beholds, that each of them is.'

suggest that they must have something to believe in to find meaning. When it comes to notions of the self, life and reality, the questions and answers must be open. But by helping young people to determine answers for themselves, they may find clarity, enrichment and optimism. My hope, therefore, is that addressing such existential questions will reduce the prevalence and intensity of mental health issues for our younger generation.

11.3 The Philosophical Forum

It is possible to address the question of meaning through the lens of personal and social identity, and their attendant obligations and responsibilities, without considering wider existential contexts. We can discuss prosocial purposes, principles and values in PSHE and RE. And in the UK, the Department for Education says PSHE should cover health, well-being, relationships and how to work and live in society. This is relatively safe and familiar ground for school education. But it is not sufficient for tackling underlying issues of young person isolation, disillusionment and pessimism.

Are the big questions of existence and meaning best left to RE? Certainly, young people may derive benefits and inspiration from exposure to a wide range of religious views and insights. But, RE tends to frame discussions on universal themes within the compartmentalised beliefs and practices of various faith communities. However, considering the diversity of beliefs within the school population, as well as those in the 'none' (no religion), or 'SBNR' (spiritual but not religious) cohorts, it may be better to brand philosophical exploration of the nature of existence as universal, rather than associated with religion. Hence, my preference is that there should be independent classroom time (without being onerous on the timetable) dedicated to philosophy. Sure, some people (mis)characterise philosophy as a plethora of unsubstantiated ideas that are more confusing than enlightening. But the ability to think philosophically is a powerful tool that can clarify how one regards oneself, one's life and one's value.

To think about the meaning of one's life, one must try to understand what it means to be in the world, to have life and to have an individual identity (Frankl, 1966). These questions then require us to consider if there is a larger picture that, in some way, defines purpose for me. There are two essential topics in this regard: (1) personal existence and

(2) reality beyond the here and now. What follows is my thinking about addressing these two topics.

11.4 Personal Existence

What's the starting point for this exploration? What can I know for certain? Let's take a step-by-step approach. We start with the statement, and this is followed by the question to problematise the statement.

'I exist.'
   How do I know this?
   'I experience things.' I see, hear, taste, smell or touch. I feel sensations: sometimes a happy feeling, or hunger, or fear or pain.
   'I think thoughts.' I am aware of them as they float through my mind when I'm awake, or at night, in my dreams.
   My thoughts and dreams may be correct or foolish, but the fact of my having these experiences and feelings is certainly real to me. So real, that I can be convinced that I do exist in the world I see around me; and that I have the privilege of knowing that I do.

This line of thinking in itself can be challenged. For example, strictly speaking, Descartes had to take a number of additional steps and make a number of additional arguments to get to the 'the world is as I perceive it' position, namely that God exists, that God is good and that a good God wouldn't condemn people to live with systematic misapprehensions about the world. The process of philosophical challenge is the process of making better sense of our positionality and purpose in the world. Moreover, an objection might be raised that certain eastern wisdom traditions assert the ultimate non-existence of a personal self. However, within those traditions, the starting point is the same: that, for now, a person believes themselves to be an existent self. Persons suffering Cotard's syndrome report they believe they may be dead, or not exist. This subjective expression of their detachment from any sense of self still entails the principle that they are the person experiencing a particular delusion of non-existence.

In the West, we credit Descartes for this insight – that I exist as a thinking thing: *cogito ergo sum*. But the idea is also evident in various meditative traditions going back into antiquity. This conviction that 'I exist' can be referred to as a 'pre-philosophical insight' or 'intuition'. It is axiomatic knowledge we possess without having validated it through the epistemologies of philosophy, science or religion. Although in English we use two separate words: 'I' and 'am', some languages combine them as one unified concept: 'I-am' as in Latin, 'sum'. I cannot separate the truth that I am from the fact that it is I who is doing the being. This leads us to a further realised axiom: that I am the subject of my experiences – it is I who feels, I who sees, I who loves and so on.

These intuitions regarding my personal existence and my capacity to experience life in a feeling way are key components of what we mean by the term *consciousness*. The phenomenon of consciousness is not easy to explain. However, we know what it is to us. It is what makes us sentient, aware of life around us and of our own existence. My awareness or consciousness belongs to me. It is what makes me, the 'I' who experiences my life. It is the 'me' who really, really cares about what I do during my life. It is fascinating to contemplate the wonder of our existence, the amazing phenomenon of being alive and sentient. For as long as I can remember it has only been 'me', the conscious self, living in this body, watching it grow and morph from a child to an adolescent to an adult. And despite how my thoughts, outlook and personality have evolved over all these years, it has always felt like the same 'me' – the prime self as the possessor of sentience – doing the experiencing.

Of course, selfhood can sometimes feel, or be perceived as, impermanent; that one's 'future self' is not really the same as one's 'current self'. Perhaps, then, one's 'current self' should not worry about one's 'future self?' – in fact, why do anything other than gratify one's 'current self' in this moment? However, this line of inquiry is unproductive. And a more pressing and more common question arrives from the opposite direction, namely how does the subjective aspect of consciousness remain so permanent in the ever-changing biological environment of our body and brain?

The following is a short summary of current thinking within science and philosophy that explores the question of what gives rise to this sense of being, of life and of sentience that we call consciousness. A question that arises is, Is consciousness a physical phenomenon or something extra-physical? Perhaps, twenty years ago, the matter seemed settled. Neuroscience had made considerable advances over the preceding decades. Nobel laureates like Francis Crick (1994) announced the 'Astonishing Hypothesis' that consciousness may be the effect of certain sets of neural activity, the neural correlates of consciousness (NCCs). Yet, even then, he acknowledged that NCCs cannot explain the qualitative or subjective experience of consciousness. He thus failed to meet John Searle's (2000) challenge that 'the most important aspects of consciousness that must be accounted for in any explanation are: unified qualitative subjectivity'.

Consider a person observing a woman and her dog out on a walk (as in Koch, 2004). In the scene, light is reflected off the pair and enters the observer's eyes, where it activates the cones and rods located in the retina, sending a set of tiny electrical pulses down the optic nerve. This signal forms a flash of neural connectivity in the visual processing areas of the brain. It is processed by the brain through electrical activity – a flash of charged ions jumping between neurons. So why do we experience such electrical activity as a picture? Where in the brain does image exist? The same question can be raised for other types of sensory experiences. Why does electrical activity in my brain stimulated by movements within my ear produce qualities of sounds in speech or melody? Why do other electrical impulses feel like 'Oww'? The brain runs on chemical electricity, but we experience life as felt qualities of imagery, sounds, sensations, tastes, smells, pains, pleasures and so on.

We call these felt sensory qualities of our conscious experience by a special term, *qualia*, to distinguish them from the purely physical properties of the external world. These internal and subjective qualities of our mental perception (qualia) are considered highly problematic for a neural interpretation of consciousness. If everything that occurs within the biological processes of our body and brain can be attributed to our understanding of physics – specifically quantum field theory – then why is it that the specific properties of physics cannot yet account for the properties of our phenomenal experience (such as the qualia of forms and colours)? Is this present-day ignorance due to be solved by subsequent discoveries? Or is it an intractable issue, because mental states are a category of functions and properties distinct from those of physics?

An additional question about this process might be, Why the need to produce such a qualitative image? To function as a stimulus/response system, the brain does not require its data to be formatted as an image. Why do we need to make sense of the image that is presented via the optical nerve? So, who are qualia for? And, who or what is the 'I' who is the subjective experiencer of these images? What gives rise to the sense of my being the observer of this image?

In addition to the initial process of the external world stimulating brain activity to create a qualitative image, we might add the question, Who is the observer? Our everyday perception involving the subjective experience of mental states and their qualities cannot be accounted for by anything we have yet discovered in neuroscience, biology or physics. In 1994, philosopher David Chalmers highlighted the challenge of qualia to a physicalist neural-based account of consciousness. He coined a term, now commonly used: the *hard problem* of consciousness. To this day, it remains hard – so much so that many researchers are forgoing neural theories of consciousness to explore more 'exotic' sources, such as quantum physics, information integration and even panpsychism.

Although the complex question of consciousness has been debated for millennia, there are three essential functions that enable us to, respectively, gather, process and experience information about the world and collectively contribute to our capacity for awareness and sense of identity:

- The biological and neural systems of our bodies and brains
- The minds that contain our thoughts and qualitative mental states which represent the world to us
- Consciousness – the capacity as the subjective 'I' experiencing those mental states

Each of us contains these discrete functions that together account for our awareness and interaction with the external world: firstly there is the body and its central processing unit, the brain, which fulfil our requirements as a functional biological organism. Within this, there is the mind, which possesses sensory information as qualia and generates our thoughts and volitional responses. And finally, both functions are distinct from the 'I', the conscious being who observes and experiences and expresses its will. To make sense of Figure 11.1, the reader could ask the following: When looking at a view or image, what does one's body/brain do, what does one's mind do and what does one's conscience do? And why is this relevant? When a child engages in a class activity, what does their body/brain do? And what of their mind and conscience? And for teachers, how far do we take into consideration these three aspects?

Manifesto 6

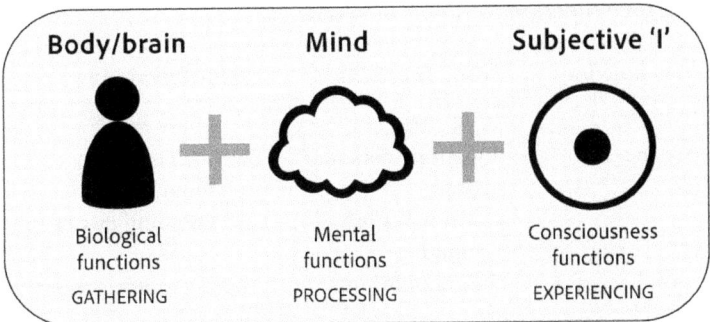

Figure 11.1 The three functions which compose human awareness and identity.

The three-function model maps onto conventional ways of referring to perception and agency. For example let us consider the functions of speech. Table 11.1 demonstrates three functions at work in speech.

The model is compatible with both physicalist and extra-physical frameworks. It is both scientifically consistent as well as theologically open. It does not adjudicate between the claim that consciousness is a product of the brain, and the claim that consciousness is a property beyond the physical. Advocates on either side may never agree, but there is opportunity to think of new ways to engage young people when both are respected and the opinions and inclinations of the other, knowing that neither has certainty on their side. This, I argue, would provide a much healthier intellectual climate for young people to determine what underpins their belief in life.

11.5 Reality beyond the Here and Now

In considering an education that is fit for the twenty-first century, and the economic, ecological and social challenges we will face, exploring the meaning of our lives within time gets us thinking about the future. Contemplating the status of consciousness *in time* raises the delicate issue of our future. Is this world all there is? Is our existence and awareness extinguished like a candle at the moment we call death? Or does some aspect of the self persist in a meaningful fashion beyond our body's physical demise? Are these questions we can ever answer? It

Table 11.1 *Three functions at work in speech*

Consciousness functions	Mind functions	Body functions
'I feel...	...a pain...	...in my arm.'
Subject experiencer undergoes	Qualitative mental state	Related to bodily stimulus
'I want...	...to focus my mind...	...on doing this task.'
Subject as wilful agent	Volitional thoughts	Bodily motor action

seems impossible for humans not to ponder these questions. They matter because our concept of *what life is* will influence our evaluation of its meaning, value and purpose. This is not an issue of morality, belief or being spiritual. My hope is that we can dissect this question – does conscious life end or continue after death – as an open philosophical proposition keeping aside religious connotations.

To do so, we must establish a neutral forum, clarifying that both the question and its possible answers are open and undecided. Nothing has been determined by any discipline to tell us categorically what consciousness is, where it comes from or what its future may be. So, at school, we should not convey a bias towards one conclusion or another. Many young people are affected by pronouncements from people like Richard Dawkins (2007) that religion is naive or sentimental, and that entertaining the idea of life after death, of God or of non-physical realms is equivalent to believing in fairies and unicorns. Such polemical oversimplifications may cause young people to hide or deny intuitions that might otherwise positively ground their perspective on life.

Though there might *seem* to be a tension between science and religion, there need not be. Even though the slightest hint that consciousness may be 'extra-physical' may be anathema to the physicalist cohort, the proposition does not contravene anything in science. Nor does it require textbooks to be rewritten. One definition of *science* is 'a system of knowledge concerned with the physical world and its phenomena' (Merriam-Webster, 2023). Science engages with the manifestation of physical reality, but it cannot address the metaphysical question of whether there is anything beyond the physical. These are not grounds to disparage science. One of its great contributions is to reveal the wonder of the world and to be inspired to think bigger. As Sir Francis Bacon (1854), credited for the experimental method, said, 'The world is not to be narrowed till it will go into the understanding ..., but the understanding (is) to be expanded and opened till it can take in the image of the world as it is in fact.' Human epistemologies (i.e. theories of knowledge), including science, do not set ontological categories (i.e. the boundaries of reality).

What does theology offer the discussion? 'Spirituality offers a worldview that suggests there is more to life than just what people experience on a sensory and physical level' (Scott, 2022). This view is not necessarily incompatible with a scientific outlook or worldview. However, I argue that both share an aspiration to elucidate the ultimate source of everything, and each, in its own way, tends to suppose that there must be a single absolute source that unites and accounts for all that is. However, since we have an unresolved conundrum regarding our own consciousness, it becomes reasonable to ask, Is that *ultimate source* sentient or non-sentient? Either answer is intellectually feasible.

If the *ultimate source* is itself sentient, it is possible we could commune with that sentient entity. Such a possibility provides a rationale for a religious worldview that could be philosophically sound and scientifically consistent. It supports various forms of spirituality including non-dual monism (which proposes that ultimate reality is one undifferentiated energy or substance) and devotional theism. It also undermines any stigma attached to those who posit the principle of divine revelation as a source of human knowledge.

Science and spirituality *mediated by philosophy* could enable young people to address foundational questions of life with greater openness and alacrity. The question is how we support children to grapple with these existential questions in the classroom. Sorting out issues of identity and selfhood are challenges that all young people face as they grow, develop and move through new social environments at home and at school, as well as online. Whatever conclusion an individual comes to, the exploration of existence might challenge and help clarify their concepts of selfhood and their relationship with the world and reality. It might also lead to other facets of meaning and purpose. For example, rather than focusing on morality and good behaviour as something defined by others, having a clearer concept of personal selfhood and its concomitant responsibilities could cause an individual to commit to values, moral behaviour and altruistic activities in keeping with that self-identity and its obligations. Thus, the impetus for morality is turned around. It becomes a self-defined effort to remain authentic to one's true moral self and what this means for one's relationships, interactions and service to others.

This project of philosophical exploration can illuminate meaning, value and purpose for the individual, and can therefore be foundational for tackling the existential emptiness that nurtures negativity, isolation, pessimism and despair.

11.6 Summary

My manifesto presents the need for philosophy at the heart of educational experience. It suggests that the silos of science and spirituality need not be so. I suggest that together, mediated by philosophical practices, they could support young people in leading choice rich lives. I end the manifesto with five reasons why this approach is needed, more so than ever.

1) Lack of Meaning Is One Underlying Factor in Mental Health Issues

Depression and mental health disorders, along with feelings of alienation, despair and a lack of purpose or vision, are major issues among schoolchildren, particularly adolescents. The pressure and expectations they face from home, school and society compound underlying vulnerabilities that may stem from feeling they cannot find meaning, purpose and value in their lives.

2) Need to Address the Questions of Existence and Reality

Such meaning and its attendant purposes arise from a clear sense of self and one's relationship with the world. Both PSHE and RE classes address this topic to a degree, but I contend that the curriculum requires an additional neutral forum of objective philosophical analysis, one that explores the foundational questions that underpin what we believe about ourselves and the greater reality of which we are a part:

- Who are we?
- What is life?
- Where did the world come from?
- Is there anything beyond?
- Is death the end?

3) *The Nature of Existence Remains an Open Question*

The wonder of being alive and the worry of our demise is fundamental to human thought. Throughout history, it has fascinated humans engaged in religion, philosophy and science. But, to date, the nature and source of our own existence and awareness of existence remain without certain explanation. A philosophical analysis of the evidence regarding subjective awareness reveals a chasm referred to as the hard problem of consciousness. Science cannot confidently pronounce that human consciousness is a product of physical nature, and religion cannot claim with certainty that it is something transcendent. The question persists open and undetermined. Hence, the messaging, presentations and discussions within education regarding the nature of consciousness, life and reality should be unbiased, neutral and balanced.

4) *Employ Objective Philosophical Thinking and Discourse*

One role of education should be to explore questions and issues of existence, consciousness and life, on a level playing field. If we have advanced in knowledge in the twenty-first century, let it manifest in our ability to say 'We do not know.'

5) *Exploration and Clarification*

Because the nature of existence is unresolved, each of us must clarify what we believe in order to determine our choices, goals and aspirations in life. We must enable pupils to think about the issues for themselves, to grasp the foundational issues and to hear and consider a variety of opinions. Hopefully, whatever their conclusion, the exercise itself will help them discover what matters to them and what defines their selfhood, personal and social identities, responsibilities, relationships and life's purpose. Through all this, may they find what we would all wish for them: meaningful happiness, purpose, belonging and the ability to share love.

References

Bacon, F. (1854) The great instauration (excerpts). In Montague, B. (ed. and trans.) *The works*. Philadelphia: Parry and MacMillan, pp. 3:333–342.

Crick, F. (1994) *The astonishing hypothesis: the scientific search for the soul*. New York: Scribner's.

Dawkins, R. (2007) *The God delusion*. Reading: Black Swan.

Frankl, V.E. (1966) *Man's search for meaning: an introduction to logotherapy*. London: Rider.

Hill, P.L. et al. (2010) 'Collegiate purpose orientations and well-being in early and middle adulthood', *Journal of Applied Developmental Psychology*, 31(2), 173–179. https://doi.org/10.1016/j.appdev.2009.12.001.

Jung, C. (1962) *Memories, dreams, reflections*. New York: Pantheon.

Koch, C. (2004) *The quest for consciousness: a neurobiological approach*. Denver: Roberts.

Längle, A. (1999) 'The search for meaning in life and the existential fundamental motivations', *Existential Analysis*, 16(1), 2–14.

Lyubomirsky, S. and Layous, K. (2013) 'How do simple positive activities increase well-being?' *Current Directions in Psychological Science*, 22(1), 57–62. https://doi.org/10.1177/0963721412469809.

Merriam-Webster (2023) *Science*. Available at: www.merriam-webster.com/dictionary/science.

Morgan, J. and Farsides, T. (2009) 'Measuring meaning in life', *Journal of Happiness Studies*, 10(2), 197–214. https://doi.org/10.1007/s10902-007-9075-0.

Peytrignet, S. et al. (2022) *Children and young people's mental health: COVID-19 and the road ahead*. Health Foundation, 8 February. Available at: www.health.org.uk/news-and-comment/charts-and-infographics/children-and-young-people-s-mental-health.

Scott, E. (2022) *What is spirituality: how spirituality can benefit your health and well-being*. Available at: www.verywellmind.com/how-spirituality-can-benefit-mental-and-physical-health-3144807.

Searle, J. (2000) 'Consciousness', *Annual Review of Neuroscience*, 23, 557–578. https://doi.org/10.1146/annurev.neuro.23.1.557.

12 | *Practitioner's Response to Manifesto 6*

Integrating Philosophical Thinking and Practices in Education

ANNABEL SHARMAN

12.1 Introduction

This chapter responds to the vision for a more holistic and open-minded approach to thinking about science and its relationship with spirituality. There is an urgent need to create safe spaces for children to explore and grapple with the deeper questions in life – those that go beyond the existing curriculum. Where is home? What is eternity? Is forgiveness always possible? Why am I alive?

Annabel, an experienced primary class teacher and religious education expert, with expertise in developing philosophical thinking and practices in primary schools, shares her reflections and considers how we might develop more wholesome, open-ended responses to the big philosophical questions – both scientific and spiritual.

12.2 Practitioner Wisdom from Cambridge, UK

Although not top of typical teacher's job description, one of the greatest joys and privileges of being an educator is to hold a space for children to wrestle with life's big questions – questions that sit at the heart of every person. Teaching our children numeracy and literacy is essential; yet if we do not create room for them to grow their 'inner worlds', we do them a disservice. Providing children with these spaces for exploration may also have benefits beyond the school walls. I fully agree with Karl Hanson (2015, p. 427), who says children are 'capable of making productive contributions towards increasing our understanding not only of their own lifeworlds but also of society as a whole'. With these things in mind, is it not imperative that we carve out time and space in our overcrowded curricula?

I believe philosophy is an appropriate vehicle for this exploration. As outlined in Chapter 11, philosophy is able to combine the rigour and logic of science with profound aspects of spirituality, thus building a bridge between these two areas of study. 'Inclusive in nature, providing opportunities for children's authentic voices' (Cassidy, Conrad and de Figueiroa-Rego, 2019, p. 2) – philosophical discourse can break down barriers and open up thoughtful conversation. It allows children a safe space to ask questions, to think deeply, to respectfully challenge and to be challenged in turn. By promoting critical thinking and reasoning, philosophy can help us navigate the complex relationship between science and spirituality. Through philosophy, we can ask questions about the nature of existence, consciousness and the link between our actions and ethics.

Philosophy with children is practical rather than academic, requiring teachers to act as facilitators of a structured and collaborative dialogue that is philosophical in nature. There is a lot of research about the impact of philosophy in the classroom. For example the Education Endowment Foundation (2014) found that children taking part in the Philosophy for Children (P4C) approach made approximately two months' accelerated progress in reading and maths, while children from disadvantaged backgrounds made almost double that progress. Regularly taking part in philosophy sessions was also found to positively affect pupils' confidence, communication and listening skills, as well as their self-esteem and behaviour. Philosophy within the classroom seems a worthwhile endeavour on many fronts.

In the case study that follows, I focus on how my school has sought to enable philosophical discourse in the classroom. This builds on some of the principles in the manifesto chapter, making them tangible and applicable for practitioners.

12.3 Case Study: Enabling Philosophical Discourse in the Classroom

Context

At the University of Cambridge Primary School, we have extended our initial curriculum from religious education (RE) to philosophy, religion and ethics (PRE). Our school aims to nurture compassionate citizens through exemplary teaching and learning. The continued development of our PRE curriculum is one way we seek to achieve this.

Aims and Objectives

The primary aim of extending the RE curriculum to include philosophy and ethics was to provide a dedicated space and opportunity for philosophical discourse to take place in classrooms, allowing children to explore and consider the deep questions of life. We also wanted to ensure that these vital questions were closely connected to the rest of the curriculum. This has been achieved in two ways: firstly, by using philosophy lessons to launch units of learning across the year and across the curriculum; and secondly, by making PRE a 'spotlight' subject for one half term in the year with a special emphasis on philosophy.

Launching Units of Learning through Philosophy

In all schools, a significant challenge is timetabling, namely how to fit philosophy lessons into an already crowded curriculum. One of our solutions has been to use philosophy lessons as a starting point for different units of learning. RE provides the most obvious opportunity for this, but it can work just as well at the start of any unit of learning in any subject, assuming a key theme can be identified. For example, if the children are due to learn about a world war in history, we might consider an overarching theme within this subject – for example power – and base the philosophy session on this theme to launch the unit of learning. If we are about to read a text in English, we might consider the overarching theme of the book – for example freedom. If the children are about to learn about the Muslim pilgrimage of Hajj, the theme might be 'journeys'. A unit of learning about Christian belief in the afterlife might have an overarching theme of 'eternity'. For most units of learning, a key theme can be identified.

Once the theme has been identified, the class then creates an initial 'enquiry question' in response to the theme. You'll see an example of this later in the chapter. We then find a hook or stimulus to provoke thinking around this area. This could be anything: a short story or a film, a game, a piece of music, a quote, an object, a scenario or a provocative image. The aim of this stimulus is to generate interest in the theme and provoke dialogue, which carries on beyond the initial session into the rest of the unit of learning. We have found that children are much more likely to engage in subsequent learning if they begin with an interesting, and often more open, philosophical starting point.

Philosophy for Children (P4C)

Once the theme and stimulus have been decided, we follow the ten-step P4C enquiry structure. This approach, founded in the 1970s by Professor Matthew Lipman, was created in reaction to the perceived lack of reasoning skills in his undergraduate students (see e.g. Lipman, 1976). We have found it to be a highly effective way to bring philosophy into the classroom. The ten stages of the P4C enquiry are as follows:

1) *Get set.* Children begin by sitting in a circle. The ground rules for discussion are established.
2) *Stimulus.* Children are shown the stimulus.
3) *Thinking time.* Children are given time to independently and quietly reflect on the stimulus.
4) *Question making.* Children in small groups create questions they have about the stimulus. This could be done in three stages:
    - My first question is ...
    - Which leads me to think ...
    - Which makes me wonder ...

    By staging the questions like this, children's third question is often deeper and broader and will lead to richer discussion.

5) *Question airing.* Children share their best question with the class, laying them down on the floor so the other children can see them.
6) *Question choosing.* Children vote for their favourite question and the one that they would like to discuss the most.
7) *First thoughts.* Children from the group whose question was chosen begin the discussion, sharing the rationale behind their question and their initial thoughts.
8) *Building thoughts.* Children from other groups engage in discussion. Stem sentences can be displayed during this part:
    - I agree because ...
    - I disagree because ...
    - While I agree with you on this part, I believe ...
    - Building on what ——— said, ...
    - I'd like to challenge what ——— said.

Throughout, teachers act as unbiased facilitators, summarising the discussion where necessary.

9) *Last thoughts*. This is a chance for pupils to offer their thoughts on what has been discussed.
10) *Review*. Reflections on the discussion: what went well and what could have been better. Reference to the ground rules might be made. Suggestions for further lines of enquiry are also invited.

Although at first glance the P4C structure may seem onerous, in practice it flows logically, and after a few enquiries, children become used to the structure and anticipate the flow of the discussion.

Philosophy as a Spotlight Subject
As well as using philosophy lessons to launch units of learning, in the final half term of summer, we turn PRE into a spotlight subject, creating additional lessons for each PRE unit – with a particular focus on philosophy and ethics – to raise the subject's profile. Each year group has an overarching ethical or philosophical question for the half term. For example, in Year 6, children explore the question, Can we be certain of anything? In Year 4, children consider, What does it mean to live a good life? Towards the end of the unit, children are given extended time to creatively and collaboratively respond to their cohort's overarching question.

As an example of a spotlight unit plan, here is a brief outline for Year 3, based on the Hindu belief of karma:

Lesson 1: P4C session based on a theme of choices and consequences and exploration of the question
- What is the link between choices and consequences?

Lesson 2: Further philosophical discussion related to the question
- Children explore various moral dilemmas and their responses

Lessons 3–5: Connecting the question to the main teaching content from the PRE curriculum
- Children learn about the Hindu beliefs of karma and relate this back to the question.

Lesson 6: Assessment
- Children share their learning about Hindu beliefs on the afterlife.

- They consider their own personal views on life after death and evaluate the link between choices and consequences.

Lessons 7–10: Creative outcome as a response to learning
- Children design and create their own high-quality board game inspired by snakes and ladders – a game inspired by the Hindu belief of karma, showcasing their learning from the unit

The Philosophy Corner

To generate further interest in PRE, both at school and at home, we also launched the 'Philosophy Corner'. Each week during the final half term of the school year, a member of our school community (teacher, teaching assistant, child, governor) filmed a short video from a part of the world that inspired them to ask a big question. For example one of our Year 6 children created a video standing by a big oak tree in the corner of their neighbourhood. Commenting on how long the tree must have stood there, she asked the question, 'Which things never change?' Our executive headteacher filmed a video sitting by a piano, asking, 'Can we really live without music?' Our Forest School lead, sitting in the corner of a beautiful forest, asked, 'Are the best things in life free?' These videos were sent out to teachers each week during the half term, as well as to parents in newsletters. In doing so, all children from nursery to Year 6 were able to discuss the same question each week at home and at school.

Observed Impact

Feedback from teachers and pupils about philosophy in school has been overwhelmingly positive. Children enjoy having time to think and discuss interesting topics together. Staff have noted how philosophical discourse has impacted the development of children's oracy and dialogue skills, as they have learned to agree, disagree and build on each other's ideas. A couple of teachers commented that children who wouldn't normally contribute to class discussion felt comfortable offering their views during philosophy discussions. Two of our Year 1 children were so inspired by the Philosophy Corner that they came up with their own big question, requesting that it be discussed within school: 'Would you rather play with someone you don't like or have no friends at all?' – a powerful question for our children to settle in their own hearts and minds (Figure 12.1).

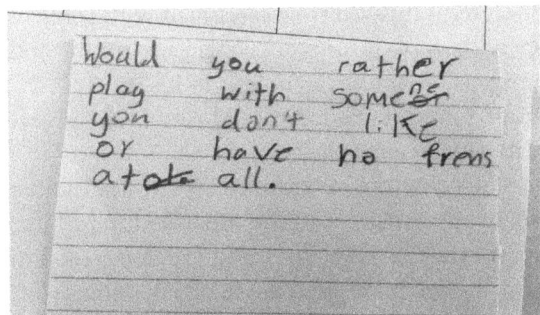

Figure 12.1 Question from two of our children in Year 1.

Final Reflections

Creating time for philosophy in school has had incredible benefits. It has opened up a space for children to wrestle with some of the deeper questions in life. It has allowed them to develop their oracy and dialogue skills, to think for themselves and to think deeply about issues important to them. Children who often struggle to speak out have found their voices within these sessions, and teachers have appreciated having the time and space necessary to hear about the issues close to the children's hearts. Philosophy has enriched our curriculum, in science and spirituality and beyond, and we are all the better for it. I fully expect that these subjective benefits, *felt* throughout our school community, to ultimately influence the objective progress data (test results, Ofsted reports) in the coming years.

Over to You

In the manifesto, the driver is to connect different ways of knowing, bridging these in a way not dissimilar to the transdisciplinary manifesto written by Pamela Burnard (Chapter 7). How do we know what we know? How do we come to know? Is there a hierarchy of knowledge? Or of ways of knowing? For example it is common for teachers in the UK to talk of the science of learning – and yet science develops and evolves, so what we know now about cognitive load theory, for example, may be a thing of the past in the future! A number of ideas and questions arise, which we share for the reader to consider:

- If you haven't been persuaded about the power of incorporating philosophy into the curriculum, can I offer a final thought:

why not take just one half term this year to experiment with some of these ideas? Come up with a plan for your own classroom, and watch and see what happens. What have you got to lose?

- Begin by looking at your school curriculum and, for each subject area, consider your units of learning.
- Can you discuss what really matters in learning? What are the big themes in life? Can an overarching theme be identified (e.g. love, loss, power, friendship, journeys)? If so, try using the first lesson in that unit as a philosophy lesson. Next, find an engaging stimulus. It should relate to your theme in some way and ought to be thought-provoking and interesting enough to generate class discussion. The Philosophy Foundation (2024) provides an array of excellent stimuli for nursery to secondary school, with links across the curriculum. Once the theme has been identified and the stimulus found, you can simply follow the ten-step P4C structure within your lessons. Children quickly get used to the structure and move through each part of the enquiry with ease. Including philosophy like this as a launch pad into units of learning is an easy and effective way to weave philosophical discussion into the fabric of your curriculum.
- How do you create space for dialogue? Creating space for philosophical discussion in the classroom needs intention and thought, but it does not need to be onerous or time intensive. By carving out short pockets of time, we hold a much-needed space for our children to grapple with the big questions in life. We do this in a safe, open forum, developing and deepening the themes that are already being explored in science, RE and other areas of the curriculum. In doing so, we nurture thoughtful, compassionate and ethically aware individuals. We build their confidence, allowing them to explore, critique and defend different perspectives. We empower them to think deeply, ask questions, use critical reasoning and stay open-hearted – vital skills that will serve to enrich them and the world around them, both now and in the years to come.

References

Cassidy, C., Conrad, S.-J. and de Figueiroa-Rego, M.J. (2019) 'Research with children: a philosophical, rights-based approach', *International*

Journal of Research and Method in Education, 43(1), 38–52. https://doi.org/10.1080/1743727x.2018.1563063.

Education Endowment Foundation (2014) *Philosophy for children*. Available at: https://educationendowmentfoundation.org.uk/projects-and-evaluation/projects/philosophy-for-children/.

Hanson, K. (2015) 'International legal procedures and children's conceptual autonomy', *Childhood*, 22(4), 427–431. https://doi.org/10.1177/0907568215609209.

Lipman, M. (1976) 'Philosophy for children', *Metaphilosophy*, 7(1), 17–33. https://doi.org/10.1111/j.1467-9973.1976.tb00616.x.

Philosophy Foundation (2024) *The Philosophy Foundation*. Available at: www.philosophy-foundation.org.

13 Manifesto 7

A Two-Way Education for Climate Justice

BENARD ISIKO, ANNA BARFORD, MOLLEN NYIRANEZA, ANTHONY MUGEERE AND PAUL MAGIMBI

13.1 Introduction

Information and education are central to climate justice. The people who are likely to be worst affected by climate change must have a good understanding of its causes and consequences. In this manifesto we also argue it is important that the knowledge and experiences of people at the sharp end of climate change be fully incorporated into the international understanding of this global challenge. In other words, climate justice requires a two-way education.

In 2020–2022, we conducted researched into how young people in Uganda are impacted by, and respond to, climate change in a collaboration between the youth NGO Restless Development, Makerere University and the University of Cambridge. To tackle these questions, we first needed to consider how climate change is perceived, understood and explained. We conducted this research just as young people's demands for a stronger and more sincere response to climate change were hitting the headlines, in Uganda and internationally. Young Europeans' critical voices cut through in the media (even if they were not always acted upon). Yet despite the swell of youth climate action in some of the world's most climate-affected places, in many instances young people at the sharp end of climate change were, quite literally, cut out – Ugandan climate activist Vanessa Nakate was cropped out of

This work was supported by a British Academy Youth Futures grant and an ESRC Social Science Impact Award. We received supportive oversight from Dame Barbara Stocking and Professor Andrew Ellias State.

a photograph of young climate activists at the World Economic Forum in Davos in January 2020. As Nakate observed, 'When it comes to the African continent, it is, of course, on the frontlines of the climate crisis. But it's not on the front pages of the world's newspapers' (Lakhani, 2022).

Many young African environmentalists, including Hilda Nakabuye and Vanessa Nakate from Uganda and Elizabeth Wathuti from neighbouring Kenya, are outspoken on climate change. Shoulder to shoulder with others in East Africa and beyond, they campaign and take practical actions on a plethora of climate change–related issues, including tree planting schemes, tackling plastic pollution and critiquing the new East African Crude Oil Pipeline. They have taken the campaign to tackle environmental damage and its social impacts to the streets, spoken at major international conferences, developed active social media campaigns and written books (Nakabuye, Nirere and Oladosu, 2020; Nakate, 2021). Between 2019 and 2020, more than 20,000 students demanded urgent climate action (Nakabuye, Nirere and Oladosu, 2020). Not only do these young women understand climate change but they also seek to raise awareness about how climate change is playing out in their own countries, while proactively working to respond.

Although many young people today are well informed about climate change, some people still haven't even heard of climate change – despite experiencing it first hand. Furthermore, some are aware of climate change but are unsure of its causes or how to respond. This was a key finding from our British Academy research on 'Peak Youth, Climate Change and the Role of Young People in Seizing Their Future' (Barford *et al*., 2021). Having identified this lack of knowledge and awareness about climate change, our team proposed a Social Science Impact Award project to the UK's Economic and Social Research Council, entitled 'Taking Climate Change to School'. Here we draw upon our learnings from both projects and discuss the implications for the design of educational offerings.

We first turn to the nature of climate change in Uganda – what young people are facing now and what they will face in the future. We then discuss young people's knowledge and understanding of climate change. Next, we set out a series of primary school–focused activities that could be used to engage young people with climate change in an informative and hopefully empowering way. Finally, we discuss the need for a global sharing of knowledge, understanding and experiences.

13.2 Climate Change in Uganda

Back in the days, the season for rainfall was being estimated but as of now, people don't know when rainfall will start or even end. So, people today are unaware compared to the past when people used to know when to start planting and when to harvest and wait for another season ahead.

Young interviewee, Jinja, Uganda[1]

Climate change is being acutely felt in Africa, even though historically and today, African countries contribute minimally to global warming. In Uganda, for example, recent years have seen hundreds of thousands of people newly displaced by weather-related events (Figure 13.1). These events include rapid-onset events such as lake and river flooding and landslides following heavy rains. Landslides are particularly problematic in mountainous areas, such as Bududa district, located in eastern Uganda on the slopes of Mount Elgon, and Kisoro district in south-western Uganda, on the Virunga Massif. Triggered by heavy rain swelling clay soils, landslides often destroy homes and agricultural land, kill people and animals and of course displace many others (Barford *et al.*, 2021; Mugeere, Barford and Magimbi, 2021). Yet flooding is not confined to Uganda's more remote volcanic mountains, with frequent inundations impacting towns and cities, including the capital, Kampala.

Slower-onset events are also destructive. Droughts destroy crops and reduce food supply, which leads to food price rises. Extreme heat increases the likelihood of disease in livestock, meaning farmers spend more on medicines for their animals. While agriculture is especially exposed to the immediate impacts of a more extreme and less predictable climate, there are also impacts elsewhere in the Ugandan economy. One interviewee told us, 'Carpentry has also been affected,

---

[1] All the quotes shared in this manifesto are sourced from the research project 'Peak Youth, Climate Change and the Role of Young People in Seizing Their Future' (2020–2022). The research was conducted using a youth co-research approach (Barford *et al.*, 2023; Proefke and Barford, 2023). The project partners were Makerere University, Restless Development Uganda and the University of Cambridge.

Manifesto 7

Figure 13.1 Recent climate change–related disruptions in Uganda. Note that the map also highlights the subregions of Karamoja and Busoga, where we did our data collection (Barford *et al.*, 2021). Illustration: Georgia King Design.

because when there is severe drought, plants wither out so there is less timber.' Another interviewee explained, 'Activities like brewing gets to a standstill because the major input for making it [beer] is sorghum and maize, in which prices automatically hike if the harvest is poor, thus rendering us unemployed.' Climate change–related events are already having serious consequences for people's lives and livelihoods in Uganda. And the disruption and devastation are only likely to worsen.

Africa is especially susceptible to the impacts of climate change because the continent is dependent on rain-fed agriculture (where no rain means no water for plants to grow), has high levels of poverty and relies on infrastructure that is readily damaged by extreme weather. The situation is made worse still by limited access to climate change information in schools and for the general public. Right now, people's lives are being disrupted by often unexplained changes, making it harder to know how to respond and how to prepare for the future. And this high exposure to the effects of climate change is affecting the continent's economic development and exacerbating poverty.

In our own research with young people, we asked about the changes they had observed. There was general agreement that temperatures had increased. One respondent explained, 'For the past few years, there have been several environmental changes in my community. These include more dry and less wet seasons. The rainfall is very unreliable, with high temperatures and frequent drought. This is majorly brought about by increased cutting down of trees for firewood and charcoal burning.' There was also agreement that rainfall had generally decreased, and rainfall patterns had become less predictable (Figure 13.2). Less rain and less predictability impact farming as most agriculture is rain fed. One interviewee reflected: 'We cannot predict seasons these days like rainfall but I can see even if I didn't study agriculture. But back in the day people could predict that this month it would rain and farmers were planting crops, but these days it's impossible and seasons change. The

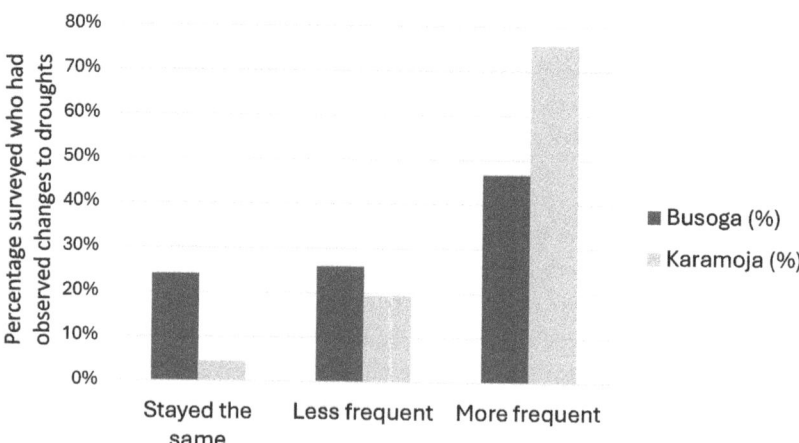

Figure 13.2 Young people's observations of changes to droughts during the past five years, by region.

seasons are no longer stable.' This experience varies between regions, most (76 per cent) of young people in the semi-arid region of Karamoja noticed increases in droughts, compared to roughly half (47 per cent) in the lusher Busoga region in the Lake Victoria basin. Overall, young people described new weather patterns in terms of strong and dusty winds, prolonged droughts, flash-floods and changeability.

Alongside extreme weather events, changing seasonality was one of the biggest problems described. In the past, most of Uganda had two predictable planting seasons, one during March to May and the other September to December (Orlove *et al.*, 2009), with specific crops planted each season. One of the young rural respondents recalled, 'There has been a change in seasons due to these climate changes [such that] these days, people [are only able to] plant in one season. Back in the past, people knew that there were two seasons in a year, but [now], it's one season in a year.' In previous generations – before the invention of modern weather forecasts – indigenous knowledge was used to predict seasons. Farmers expected two planting seasons each year, knowing which crops to plant when and whether there might be a drought that year. Typically, fast-growing crops were planted in the March to May season to catch the first rainy period, and slower-growing plants would be planted for the September to December rains (Orlove *et al.*, 2009). Before sophisticated technology to gauge rainfall, farmers would scrape soil away, or dig with hoes, to examine soil moisture to determine when it was sufficient for planting.

13.3 Young People's Understandings of Climate Change

There is no [little] teaching about climate change in schools. This makes it hard for people to understand climate change. ... However, despite the ignorance, everyone is familiar with the effects of climate change because they affect each and every one of us in various ways.

H. F. Nakabuye, S. Nirere and A. T. Oladosu, 'The Fridays for Future Movement in Uganda and Nigeria'

The environmental teaching in Uganda's primary schools usually separates questions about the local environment from discussions of the global challenges. For instance, children study waste management as a local issue, while discussions of greenhouse gases and global warming tend to focus *elsewhere* in the world – for example the melting of Arctic ice. This approach is reminiscent of neo-colonial education, whereby geography classes neither resonate with the immediate local, social, physical, economic or environmental context, nor build relevant knowledge to help them survive and thrive as climate change worsens. Strikingly, the global dimension of this education does not highlight the international causes of climate change, overlooking the stark socio-political injustice of climate change.

One of our team, a former science teacher in Uganda, first learned about the causes and consequences of climate change when he started teaching twelve years ago. He taught his pupils about the greenhouse effect, caused by gases trapping heat within the Earth's atmosphere; causing the oceans, land and air to warm up. Yet this learning was global, lacking the indigenous examples which can help pupils apply a broader lesson to a local context. Instead, local changes have been rationalised as punishments from God, or the result of local activities such as people encroaching upon the forests, cutting down trees for charcoal production, mineral mining, building in the wetlands and Ugandan industrial pollution. In our research, we found that as education levels increase, so young people's understanding of the drivers of climate change strengthens (Figure 13.3). Even so, the main cause of climate change is still identified as local deforestation, and only a tiny proportion of respondents saw global pollution as the leading cause. At

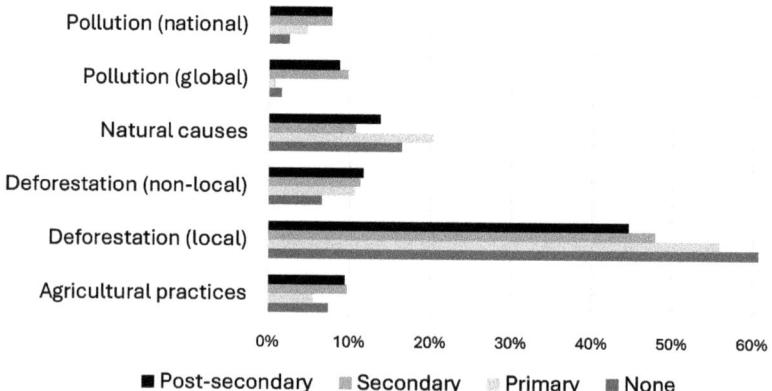

Figure 13.3 Perceptions of the main causes of environmental change, by highest level of education. Responses ($n = 1,205$) to the question, Among the causes that we have just discussed, what do you think has been the main cause of the environmental changes that you have seen in your community?

primary school level and beyond, the puzzle of how climate-disrupted daily life in Africa is linked to global pollution is clearly not addressed.

Education prepares people for climate change–related disasters, reduces negative impacts and supports faster recovery from climate shocks (Muttarak and Lutz, 2014). Many studies have shown how education can boost the ability to receive, decode, and understand information (e.g. Maponya, Mpandeli and Oduniyi, 2013, p. 278). Combined with specific knowledge about climate change, education equips people for an informed response. As contemporary climate change is anthropogenic, people need to be aware of their role in changing the environment for better or worse, as well as how to respond. Greater knowledge and understanding will support the roll out of adaptation and mitigation strategies. Molthan-Hill and colleagues (2019, p. 2) state, 'Educated people are more aware of the risks climate change poses and are better equipped to make informed decisions about responses at local, national and international scales.'

Young people with less education are also less likely to think climate change will worsen in the future. We found that among those who did not finish primary school, 72 per cent expect more environmental changes in the coming five years; rising to 92 per cent for those who completed post-secondary education. We also found that young people with more education are more likely to report being involved in mitigating and adapting to climate change. For example 17 per cent of those who did not complete primary education were involved in action to mitigate climate change, increasing to 47 per cent of those with post-secondary education. In terms of adaptation activities, there was a smaller range – 18 per cent of those without a full primary school education reporting involvement in adaptation activities, rising to 37 per cent of those with post-secondary education.

Alongside formal education, a plethora of information other sources about climate change are important – not least for those young people who leave education. We found that radios, followed by community leaders, were the most trusted sources of climate change information (Figure 13.4). For those with higher levels of education (likely a proxy for relative wealth and income), television and social media were important information sources. In addition to general information about the causes and consequences of climate change, it is important to have access to immediate and practical information about weather patterns and how best to respond to them. Among young people

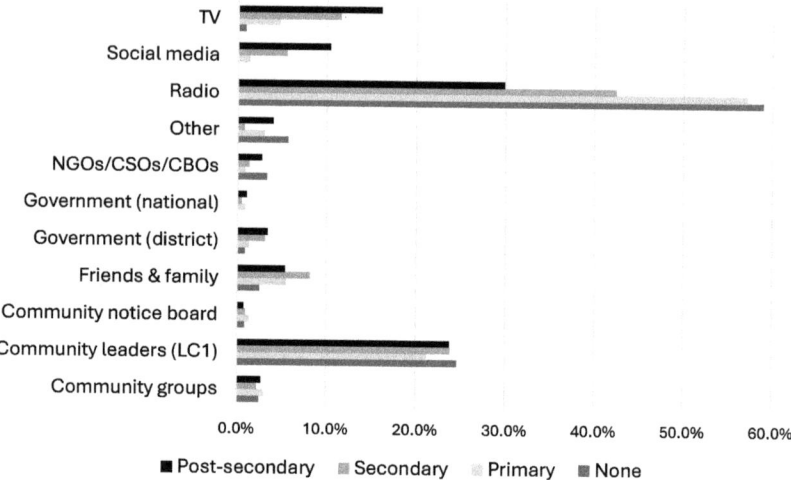

Figure 13.4 Most trusted information source, by highest level of education. These are survey responses to the research question (with reference to climate change), In general, which source do you trust most when it comes to getting information about your community?

without primary education, 78.7 per cent did not know how to access information about weather patterns, compared to 52.3 per cent of respondents with post-secondary education.

13.4 Taking Climate Change to School

Who is going to help me as an African child to understand how someone polluting over there will affect me here in Uganda?

In Uganda, schools offer education about the environment, as part of the National Curriculum. However, climate change has received little attention in Ugandan classrooms to date, in part because it has not been formalised in the curriculum. However, on 14 August 2021, President Yoweri Museveni passed the National Climate Change Act, stipulating that 'the ministry responsible for education shall ensure that climate change education and research are integrated into the national curriculum' (Republic of Uganda, 2021, Sec. 29). Thus, the learning landscape in Uganda should soon shift to systematically include climate change. Our own project was an effort to begin this engagement.

We chose to work in primary schools and teacher training colleges for several reasons. The Uganda Bureau of Statistics (2016) reports that 51 per cent of young people leave school early[2] (and girls are more likely to leave early than boys), and although children tend to leave school in order to start working, the School-to-Work Transition Survey found 71 per cent of the young people in work are undereducated for their roles. School-leaving data, combined with our own findings on climate change awareness, point to the importance of communicating climate information early in pupils' education. Although young people tend to be better educated than their parents – as access to education has improved – since these data were collected, Ugandan children have faced new barriers to education, including the almost two-year-long closure of state schools due to COVID-19. This was one of the longest COVID-19 closures in the world, after which many pupils did not return to school. And many teachers left the profession as salaries were paused, turning instead to farming.

Our multi-partner research team responded by planning a six-month pilot project to 'take climate change to school'. Our aims – which drew directly on the youth-led research we conducted in Busoga and Karamoja – were to design and share practical learning tools for primary-level climate change education, while also catalysing student interest in climate change and how to respond. Furthermore, our learnings were to be shared with experts developing climate change education for the National Curriculum for primary schools (Isiko, 2022). Our project focused on four primary schools and a teacher training college in the Busoga region. We planned extended, ongoing engagement with the schools during the six-month project, to make the lessons more meaningful and achieve deeper engagement. This began with introductory meetings followed by sensitisation meetings with the classes. Then came a series of tree planting sessions, several inter-school debates and the donation of climate change posters and 'talking compounds' to schools.

A talking compound is a sign with a message painted on it, which is displayed within the school grounds. In Uganda, talking compounds

---

[2] This is defined as 'Early school leavers are those young people who left school without completing all the grades at that given education level' (Uganda Bureau of Statistics, 2016, p. 17).

Figure 13.5 Pupils with a 'talking compound'. These painted metal signs are a popular means of communicating key health and environmental messages in Ugandan schools. Source: Benard Isiko.

are widely used to communicate information to students on a range of topics (Figure 13.5). The messages are clear, concise and understandable to students. In our project, we used talking compounds to communicate environmental awareness messages to students, focusing environmental cleanliness, tree conservation and avoiding plastic pollution. For the schools we visited, these were the first climate change specific talking compounds they had seen.

Within the Busoga subregion, the project engaged 520 pupils from four primary schools – two rural and two urban. To have a longer-term impact on other schools, we also engaged sixty trainee teachers. These campaigns made students aware of the causes and consequences of climate change and encouraged young people to restore tree cover in their schools and communities to facilitate climate change mitigation (Figure 13.6). Pupils planted trees, and school environment clubs were responsible for the growth of the new saplings. Overall, more than 1,500 trees were planted, including fruit trees, eucalyptus and avocado – based on the preferences of the schools. Fruit trees were of particular interest, as they provide snacks for the children during the school day, and their usefulness means they are less likely to be cut down. Following these exercises, pupils are taking their newly acquired knowledge and skills home, to share with others. As a result, new environmental clubs have been established; elsewhere, existing clubs have been revived.

Manifesto 7

Figure 13.6 Climate change lesson at a teacher training college, led by Benard Isiko. The session with the trainee teachers focused on what climate change is, its causes and effects and the role of teachers in the college and in their communities. Source: Mollen Nyiraneza.

13.5 Conclusion

I have seen low or no rainfall due to serious deforestation or over cutting of trees, which delays rainfall formation, thus prolongs drought. ... I am an eyewitness to some of these changes.

> Young interviewee, Uganda, date unknown

Young people in Uganda are facing the disruptions of climate change now. At the extreme, they are being displaced from their homes and fields and pushed to search for new livelihoods. Others find themselves facing unpredictable and rising costs; for some, their work is increasingly economically unviable. In short, young people in Uganda have immediate knowledge of what climate change means for their lives. Our data show that knowledge of climate change is heavily weighted towards direct experiences, especially for those with lower levels of education. This leaves young people only partially prepared for a future of worsening climate change induced disruptions.

Information and education are central to climate justice. We argue that two elements are particularly important for educators to consider:

1) *Providing an understanding of climatic changes and why they are occurring.* The people who experience the most climate disruption have a right to a true understanding of what is happening to their lives, and why. The *why* is extremely important given that the regions worst impacted by climate change tend not to be the places where most greenhouse gases were emitted.

2) *Implementing a two-way, humanised climate education.* Learning must be multidirectional, such that the knowledge and experiences of people at the sharp end of climate change are incorporated into the wider body of international understanding of this global challenge. This coheres with Paulo Friere's concept of 'conscientisation' – whereby scientific evidence is integrated with lived experiences to humanise and globalise our understandings of climate change in a holistic way (Dorling and Barford, 2006). Education 'encourage[s] people to change their attitudes and behaviour and helps them to make informed decisions' (United Nations, 2022). So, this learning needs to be an integral part of educational offerings in Uganda and the UK alike, and indeed everywhere.

There is an urgent need to bring climate change into classrooms. In the meantime, 'inaction at large is putting everything at risk' (Nakabuye, Nirere and Oladosu, 2020).

References

Barford, A. *et al.* (2021) *Living in the climate crisis: young people in Uganda.* Cambridge: University of Cambridge. https://doi.org/10.17863/CAM.75235.

Barford, A. *et al.* (2023) 'Young people "making it work" in a changing climate', *Journal of the British Academy,* 11(s3), 173–197. https://doi.org/10.5871/jba/011s3.173.

Dorling, D. and Barford, A. (2006) Humanising geography. *Geography,* 91(3), 187–197.

Isiko, B. (2022) 'Tackling the climate crisis should start at school', *Restless Development* (blog). Available at: https://wearerestless.org/2022/11/03/tackling-the-climate-crisis-should-start-at-school/.

Lakhani, N. (2022) '"Africa is on the frontlines but not the front pages": Vanessa Nakate on her climate fight', *The Guardian*, 17 September. Available at: www.theguardian.com/environment/2022/sep/17/vanessa-nakate-climate-activist-africa-cop27.

Maponya, P., Mpandeli, S. and Oduniyi, S. (2013) Climate change awareness in Mpumalanga province, South Africa. *Journal of Agricultural Science*, 5(10), 273–282.

Molthan-Hill, P. *et al.* (2019) 'Climate change education for universities: a conceptual framework from an international study', *Journal of Cleaner Production*, 226, 1092–1101. https://doi.org/10.1016/j.jclepro.2019.04.053.

Mugeere, A., Barford, A. and Magimbi, P. (2021) 'Climate change and young people in Uganda: a literature review', *Journal of Environment and Development*, 30(4), 344–368. https://doi.org/10.1177/10704965211047159.

Muttarak, R. and Lutz, W. (2014) 'Is education a key to reducing vulnerability to natural disasters and hence unavoidable climate change?', *Ecology and Society*, 19(1), 42.

Nakabuye, H.F., Nirere, S. and Oladosu, A.T. (2020) 'The Fridays for Future movement in Uganda and Nigeria', in Henry, C., Rockström, J. and Stern, N. (eds.) *Standing Up for a Sustainable World*. XXXX: Edward Elgar, pp. 212–218. https://doi.org/10.4337/9781800371781.00036.

Nakate, V. (2021) *A bigger picture: my fight to bring a new African voice to the climate crisis*. London: Pan Macmillan.

Orlove, B. *et al.* (2009) 'Indigenous climate knowledge in southern Uganda: the multiple components of a dynamic regional system', *Climatic Change*, 100(2), 243–265. https://doi.org/10.1007/s10584-009-9586-2.

Proefke, R. and Barford, A. (2023) 'Creating spaces for co-research', *Journal of the British Academy*, 11(s3), 19–42. https://doi.org/10.5871/jba/011s3.019.

Republic of Uganda (2021) *The National Climate Change Act, 2021, part VII, section 29*. Available at: https://ulii.org/akn/ug/act/2021/nn/eng@2021-12-31.

Uganda Bureau of Statistics (2016) *Labour market transition of young people in Uganda: highlights of the School-to-Work Transition Survey 2015*. Geneva: International Labour Office. Available at: www.ilo.org/wcmsp5/groups/public/-ed_emp/documents/publication/wcms_493731.pdf.

United Nations (2022) *Education is key to addressing climate change*. New York: United Nations. Available at: www.un.org/en/climatechange/climate-solutions/education-key-addressing-climate-change.

14 Practitioner's Response to Manifesto 7

Educating Differently about Sustainability

LUKE ROLLS

14.1 Introduction

The preceding manifesto has three aspects. First, it is about bringing climate change discussions into classrooms (and particularly in Ugandan classrooms). Second, it is about bringing Ugandan experiences of climate education into classrooms. And third, it is about helping children and communities make sense of climate change in their lives and futures. Climate change is often understood through the prism of personal experience – blinding us to the connections between our actions, or the issues affecting us, and life in other parts of the world. 'Think global and act local' is an overused phrase. But it remains an important concept given our increasing interconnectedness; solutions cannot be found in one country – we must raise global awareness and stoke both local and global action. In this practitioner's response, Luke reflects on his personal experiences of living in Japan and explains the thinking behind the development of a sustainable curriculum he co-developed as a school leader in the UK.

14.2 Practitioner Wisdom from Japan, Looking Back to Cambridge, UK

When I moved from the UK to Japan, I had to reaccustom myself with the country's carefully observed protocols regarding how, when and where to dispose of different types of recycling. Across Japan, on collection days, paper and cardboard boxes are meticulously folded,

Practitioner's Response to Manifesto 7

tied and arranged in designated places. However, one small rural town in Shikoku has gone above and beyond in its efforts to deal with waste and live sustainably. In only a few years, the small community of Kamikatsu has become known across the world as a model 'zero waste' town. Residents have attracted attention for their dedication to separating their waste into no less than forty-five different categories. Beyond this headline, many other local sustainability initiatives thrive – with businesses, restaurants and factories all producing new products from collected waste.

What struck me about Kamikatsu's transformation was the journey that residents were asked to go on to change their daily habits. Akira Sakano (pers. comm.), founder of Zero Waste Japan, recalls, 'We were burning our waste in the open air, in a big hole, which was obviously hurting our environment, our air and potentially our health.' Several inhabitants, who later became strong advocates of the town's approach, were initially resistant to the proposed changes to recycling, perplexed about the number of ways they had to separate their rubbish. However, the process of changing norms led to shared realisations around their use of resources, reducing unnecessary waste and rethinking what could be reused. As one resident reflected, 'For me, Zero Waste is a way to understand myself. When you live in Kamikatsu, you will not only know about waste, but also about the time you have, what you spend your effort on, how you spend your money and how waste is produced as a result' (Ding, 2021).

What educational lessons can we learn from these examples of environmentally conscious living? The insights and forms of participation cultivated in Kamikatsu resonate with Cross' (2022) conception of citizenship 'not as a status, but as something that people continuously do: citizenship as practice'. Cross cites Kerr's claim that most citizenship curricula have only managed 'to reinscribe a passive, dutiful version of citizenship that fails to inspire or convince'. An alternative is the Japanese educational concept of 'Tokkatsu' (Tsuneyoshi, 2020) – school activities and cultures that work to develop holistic education, positive personal habits and social and ethical responsibility. In Japanese schools, such 'special activities' include children cleaning their classrooms, planting rice with a local farmer or having a classroom meeting about effecting change in their community (Bloomberg Quicktake, 2020). Unfortunately, such experiential knowledge, or, as

Bertrand Russell (1910) put it, 'knowledge by acquaintance', is given less emphasis in many other education systems

What follows are three cases from the UK, India and Nepal. They all focus on the development of curricula that position sustainability as central to children's learning. The first concerns the design of a school curriculum, drawing from local research and expertise. This is the most detailed case study, shining a light on the considerations that shape curriculum development from start to finish. The second and third cases are shorter and set out final curricula decisions. The second describes a set of co-created of curricula resources, again drawn from a range of contextually specific expertise. The third sketches how a commitment to living sustainably can be situated at the core of the learning experiences embedded in a curriculum.

Case Study 1: Designing a Curriculum for Sustainability

The University of Cambridge Primary School (UCPS) is situated in a new University residential development, and sustainability is central to its design. As well as working closely with the Faculty of Education, the school teams up with other organisations at the University, such as Cambridge Zero, a solution-focused initiative harnessing research and expertise to respond innovatively to the climate crisis that is led by Professor Emily Shuckburgh.

There are various sustainability initiatives in contemporary educational practice. At the UCPS, we were interested in looking broadly at how a curriculum for teaching sustainability could be introduced for children from ages three to eleven and beyond. What would a curriculum for developing sustainability competences look like? What knowledge, behaviours and competencies do our children need to flourish? How might these intersect with other types of pedagogy? The curriculum design model in Figure 14.1 attempts to illustrate how the aim of nurturing compassionate citizens relates to school culture and ethos, and how both interact with particular forms of knowledge. We distinguished between three different forms of knowledge (Table 14.1).

While domain-specific and to a lesser extent interdisciplinary knowledges are commonly taught in schools, the third category, transdisciplinary knowledge (Arnold, 2020), is less common. However, we thought it might hold significant potential for binding different subject areas together in meaningful ways. To decide what these transdisciplinary

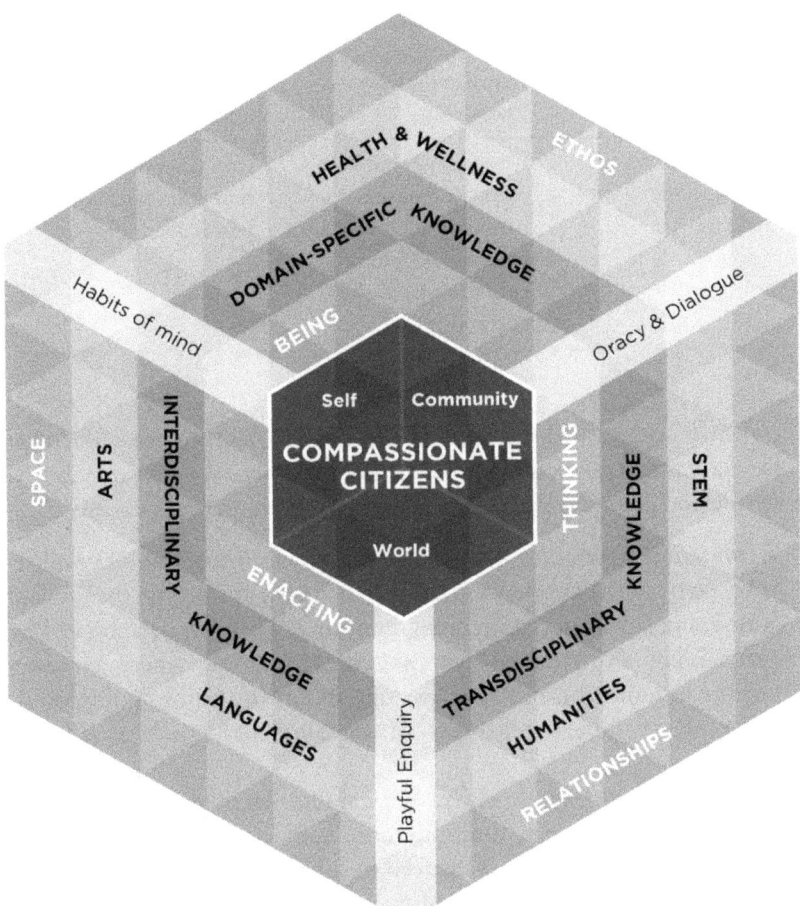

Figure 14.1 Curriculum design model.

knowledge categories would be, we conducted a consultation, asking our broader school community – academics, parents, children and teachers – what they thought. After several iterations, five themes became apparent:

1) Health and spirit
2) Sustainability
3) Diversity and relationships
4) Power and systems
5) Technology

Table 14.1 *Definitions of three forms of curriculum knowledge.*

Domain-specific knowledge	Interdisciplinary knowledge	Transdisciplinary knowledge
Specialised forms of subject-specific knowledge	Knowledge that arises through making meaningful connections between different subjects across the curriculum	Concepts or 'big ideas' that transcend subject boundaries

We then worked out how each of these areas mapped onto different subject areas and curriculum projects. For the category of Sustainability, several principles emerged in considering curriculum progression:

- *Experiencing the value of nature.* Education on sustainability must start early, with experiences that help children appreciate the joy and well-being associated with being in nature. This can be achieved by timetabling experiences such as Forest School, where children engage in hands-on outdoor learning in nature, before going on to learn about different aspects of sustainability, such as climate change.
- *Sequencing content carefully.* We created curriculum progression maps for each subject, outlining core substantive and disciplinary knowledge and vocabulary, as well as subject-specific concepts, such as 'place and space' in geography.
- *Starting local.* Before engaging children in big global environmental challenges, we start with local issues and the changes and practices children can make in their own school community and lives.
- *Identifying anchoring subject areas.* We avoided creating an extra subject or lesson out of sustainability. Rather, we used existing subject disciplines as lenses through which to understand the world and what it means to live sustainability. We drew on geography, science, Forest School, art and personal, social, health and citizenship education as the drivers of sustainability learning in the curriculum.

Together, these principles give rise to a rigorous curriculum that develops 'powerful knowledge' (Lambert, 2017), alongside wider, longer-term aims of nurturing children's 'learning autonomy' (James *et al.*, 2007). However, in practice, such principles are not easy to realise and require educators to draw on different 'pedagogical repertoires' (Alexander, 2000). These repertoires might include aspects of experiential learning and personal reflection, alongside important substantive and disciplinary knowledge. For example, in learning about deforestation and reduced biodiversity in Brazilian rainforests, children might reflect on their own consumer behaviours and any changes they are able to make. Classes may discuss how the school sources its own food and whether it is sustainable. Small examples like this demonstrate how subject learning (in this case, in geography) can lead to new understandings about our lives, while generating questions about the changes necessary in our communities.

When teaching issues relating to sustainability, we were conscious not to give children self-directed projects about complex areas like climate change before they were familiar with the concepts necessary to have a deep understanding of the ideas involved. As such, we spent time considering curriculum sequencing. For example, in geography, we knew that children would need to some understanding of weather and biomes to grapple with concepts like climate and climate zones. In science, children would need a basic grounding in the ideas of 'living things' and 'habitats' before exploring questions of biodiversity. Without careful mapping of subject progressions, it is also difficult to understand interdisciplinary connections. By contrast, by mapping subject progressions, students could see that energy and electricity (learned about in science) connected with learning about populations, the planet and globalisation. Similarly, learning about migration helped their understanding of the impact of climate change on the lives of environmental migrants.

The UCPS curriculum strives to find a balance between important subject knowledge and bigger transdisciplinary concepts. By treating sustainability as a core curriculum theme through both formal teaching and practical experiences, children are invited to engage with bigger human conversations (Wegerif, 2019) about how they can live in a symbiotic way with the planet – within their own lives, their local communities and the wider world.

Case Study 2: Pani Pahar – the Water Curriculum

Water is a precious resource. As industrialisation and migration increase, the question of fair water distribution will become more critical. How can we develop curricula in these contexts? This case study offers an example of innovative, transdisciplinary thinking about curricula design.

From 2017 to 2023, work to develop knowledge and understanding about water and its management was developed with the University of Cambridge and the Hearth Advisors, a division of Canta Consultants LLP. 'Pani Pahar – Waters of the Himalayas' grew out of a collaborative research project between the University of Cambridge, the Centre for Ecology Development and Research in India and the South Asia Institute for Advanced Studies in Nepal. The project explores the changing landscapes and escalating water crises of the Indian Himalayas. It combines academic research led by Cambridge pro-vice-chancellor for education Professor Bhaskar Vira and Dr Eszter Kovacs, then at Cambridge's Department of Geography (now at University College London), with imagery by photojournalist Toby Smith, since exhibited in the UK and India. Professor Vira explains the purpose of the curriculum and resource materials:

> These school materials are designed to allow young people, who are highly mobilised through the school strikes for climate, to develop a critical engagement with these issues, with learning resources and educational materials that are targeted at different stages of the secondary school curriculum. We wanted to show the links between our research on water scarcity and broader concerns about environmental change and crises. (University of Cambridge and Hearth Advisors, n.d.)

Designed for students between the ages of nine and fifteen, the Pani Pahar curriculum has been freely available to teachers and schools since 2020. The aim of the curriculum is to engage students in experiential learning and to instil a sense of responsibility for water conservation and environmental sustainability. The curriculum preparation and instructional design was led by the Hearth Advisors, based on research conducted at the University of Cambridge.

The curriculum aims to help students understand water resources and sustainability and how they are impacted by climate change. The detailed lesson plans encourage reflection and research on the human causes of water scarcity, and some of the effects of environmental change on humans and our shared resources. It also helps students understand the meaning of activism, recognise some of the challenges associated with activism, and begin to associate activism with the needs and issues of their school.

Each curriculum includes the following:

- Introduction to the curriculum
- Curriculum rationale
- Curriculum outline
- Guide on how to use the lesson plans
- Lesson plans (with resources/learning material)

The lesson plans included in this water curriculum are as in Table 14.2.

Table 14.2 *Lesson plan structure.*

Junior	Middle	Senior
JLP01 Sources of freshwater	MLP01 Introduction	SLP01 Introduction
JLP02 Rivers	MLP02 Presentations	SLP02 Case Study Foundations
JLP03 River Processes	MLP03 Weather Forecasting	SLP03 Investigating Further
JLPO4 Water Cycle	MLPO4 Water Paragraph	SLPO4 Climate Change and Activism
JLP05 Photo Analysis	MLP05 Water Audit	SLP05 Research Design
JLP06 Water Conservation	MLP06 Climate Activism	SLP06 Data Collection
JLP07 Water footprint	MLP07 Policy or Campaign	SLP07 Data Analysis
JLP08 Waterborne Diseases	MLP08 Pollution of the Ganga	SLP08 Research Paper Presentation
JLP09 Weather	MLP09 Survey Data and Action	SLP09 Debate
JLP10 Climate Change and Water	MLP10 Photo Stories	SLP10 Photo Stories
JLP11 Water Vocabulary	MLP11 Water Pledge	
JLP12 Ganga (The Ganges)		
JLP13 Top Trumps Game (Rivers of the World)		
JLP14 My Water Diary		

The full curriculum can be downloaded as a free resource and has potential to be adapted to different localities and contexts: https://thehearthadvisors.com/our-work/pani-pahar-the-water-curriculum/.

Case Study 3: Harmony

The Harmony Project aims to transform education to ensure it prepares young people for life in the twenty-first century, not just to pass exams. The Harmony Project envisions a way of learning to live that is based on a deep understanding of – and connection to – the natural world. The project works with teachers and other educators in the UK to reframe teaching and learning around nature and the idea of the world as an interconnected whole. This approach can help young people better understand the world and develop the skills they need to act within it. In doing so, they will learn how to live more sustainably.

The Harmony Project is led by Richard Dunne. In his thirty-year career in education, Richard has developed a school curriculum based on nature's principles of *harmony*. These principles guide and inform the way a 'Harmony curriculum' is structured, providing a coherent and meaningful framework through which National Curriculum learning objectives can be delivered. They include the following:

- *The principle of Interdependence*, revealing that elements within natural systems are interconnected; each element has a value and a role to play
- *The principle of the Cycle*, illustrating that Nature's regenerative, cyclical systems are models of sustainability, reusing resources and eliminating waste
- *The principle of Diversity*, expressed in natural systems which are healthy and resilient and better able to adapt to change
- *The principle of Adaptation*, showing that living things are always adapting to their place and to the ecosystems they are part of, which ensures each species is able to survive and thrive
- *The principle of Health*, demonstrating that the balance and well-being of natural systems is maintained by the dynamic relationships that exist within them
- *The principle of Geometry*, revealing that the patterns we see in Nature, in micro and macro form, also exist in us – far from being separate from Nature, we are Nature

- *The principle of Oneness*, uniting all the foregoing principles, revealing their interconnectedness and helping us to understand that – like all life on Earth – we are part of something greater than ourselves

For an in-depth understanding of ways to develop a Harmony approach to education, see www.theharmonyproject.org.uk.

Over to You

Given that a generation of children have now grown up in the context of a global climate crisis, the case for making sustainability central to school curricula is overwhelming. When considering curriculum aims and purpose, we should refer to Kamikatsu town's injunction to think 'about the future of the living environment … as one's own responsibility and foster people who can take action' (Kamikatsu, 2021). Such a perspective could help educators create learning experiences that go beyond simply informing students, towards mobilising our future citizens to think and act in new ways.

This chapter asks us how we might bring this about. And now, at the end, we are left with a series of questions designed to open up conversations in your own educational context:

- What are the aims of a curriculum, and how coherent is the focus given to sustainability?
- How does progression in individual subjects contribute to providing unique lenses to help children to understand issues in sustainability? What meaningful connections can be brought out between the learning in these subjects?
- Rather than indoctrinating children in a 'correct' way of thinking about sustainability, what pedagogies can be employed to draw children into a wider dialogue about the issues facing the planet?
- How are children given opportunities to practically live out what they have learned about sustainability?
- What opportunities for pupil voice, school and community change are designed into children's curriculum experiences?

References

Alexander, R. (2000) *Culture and pedagogy: international comparisons in primary education*. Oxford: Blackwell.

Arnold, M. (2020) *Transdisciplinary research (transdisciplinarity)*. Berlin: Springer, pp. 2332–2340. https://doi.org/10.1007/978-3-319-15347-6_337.

Bloomberg Quicktake (2020) *Kamikatsu: inside the zero waste town*. Available at: www.youtube.com/watch?v=OTW7fxPpF0g.

Cross, B. (2022) 'Citizenship practices in school spaces: comparative discourse analysis of children's group decision making', *Pedagogy, Culture and Society*, 32(2), 322–340. https://doi.org/10.1080/14681366.2022.2037689.

Ding, L. (2021) *Kamikatsu: Japan's first zero waste village*. Outdoor Japan. Available at: www.outdoorjapan.com/activities/travel/eco-tourism-in-japan/kamikatsu-japans-first-zero-waste-village/amp/.

James, M. et al. (2007) *Improving Learning how to learn: classrooms, schools and networks*. New York: Routledge/CRC Press.

Kamikatsu (2021) *Zero waste town*. Available at: https://zwtk.jp/en/.

Lambert, D.M. (2017) *Powerful disciplinary knowledge and curriculum futures*. Available at: https://discovery.ucl.ac.uk/id/eprint/10057994/.

Russell, B. (1910) 'Knowledge by acquaintance and knowledge by description', *Proceedings of the Aristotelian Society*, 11, 108–128. www.jstor.org/stable/4543805.

Tsuneyoshi, R. (2020) *The Tokkatsu framework: the Japanese model of holistic education*. Singapore: World Scientific.

University of Cambridge and Hearth Advisors (n.d.) *Pani, Pahar – the water curriculum*. Available at: https://thehearthadvisors.com/our-work/pani-pahar-the-water-curriculum/.

Wegerif, R. (2019) 'Dialogic education', in *Oxford research encyclopedia of education*. Oxford: Oxford University Press. https://doi.org/10.1093/acrefore/9780190264093.013.396.

Afterword

Empowering Education for a Changing World

JAMES BIDDULPH, HARRY PEARSE AND EMILY SHUCKBURGH

This collection of manifestos and practitioner responses presents a compelling and multifaceted vision for the future of education. We hope that readers will engage critically with the ideas contained in them, adopting or adapting them to create their own visions for education, or rejecting them to clear new space for dialogue.

Our aim has been to present chapters that grapple with complex and interconnected issues, highlighting the need for a fundamental shift in how we educate children and young people in a world struggling with unprecedented social, political, environmental and technological change. What would it look like if you were to accept and explore the complexity of interconnected fields of learning? How might you exploit these interconnections to better prepare children for their future lives – both their challenges and their opportunities? We encourage educators to stop and reconsider what they do, and how and why they're doing it. If a common practice isn't working, perhaps there are alternatives that would be more effective.

Three key claims or messages flow throughout the book: (1) educational practices can and should be changed to better reflect the changing world and existential uncertainties children inhabit – regarding climate, but also mental health issues and much else; (2) we must do more to respect and empower children's voices and agency, not only to support active citizenry but to ensure educational experiences are rooted in values; and (3) there is much to be gained by forging connections across disciplinary boundaries – to think in transdisciplinary ways and suspend arguments about what used to work to consider bigger, bolder questions. Pursued together, these claims have the potential to define a powerful new narrative for education that is commensurate with the challenges facing humanity in the twenty-first century.

15.1 A World in Flux

The authors offer a sobering assessment of the world that today's children are inheriting, particularly the existential threats posed by climate change and environmental degradation. As Chapter 1 warns, there is a 'rapidly closing window of opportunity to secure a liveable and sustainable future for all'. Not only are young people increasingly aware of, and anxious about, the climate crisis but they also experience the stark inequalities underlying and being expressed by climate breakdown, despite not being responsible for them. By a similar token, over the past century, wealthy overconsumption, primarily in the Global North, has had a disproportionate impact – in climate terms – on the Global South, and particularly the poor, who have contributed least to the problem. These intergenerational and distributional injustices demand a reassessment of our values, as well as, perhaps relatedly, a review of the remit and purpose of education – geared more towards the cultivation of sustainability.

Related technological shifts, such as the transition to clean energy, and social shifts, such as increasing urbanisation, are also transforming the world and placing new demands on education. For many people, digital literacy is increasingly central to what it means to be educated. Though some chapters in this collection nod to these developments, clearly they would benefit from further exploration, and the publication of any further manifestos will centre on technology, virtual worlds and developments in digital tool and services.

15.2 Empowering Agents of Change

As noted throughout the volume, the need to empower children's voices must go beyond tokenistic consultation; beyond 'short-term initiatives' that, in failing to engage large enough numbers of children or young people, deepens marginalisation, cynicism or disaffection. Nurturing authentic pupil voices requires sustained effort, consistently applied inclusive practices and a genuine commitment to considering children's perspectives.

James visited a school in the East of England and spoke with a thirteen-year-old boy who felt that the current structure of democracy in his school was not working. He had thoughtful suggestions for how to ensure a system involving school councils and prefects does not become a popularity contest, and instead makes sure that aspiring leaders 'get a fair chance based on our skills and ideas, not on who can stand up and smile and crack jokes'. This serves as a reminder that democracy – either in schools or in society – is more than voting or the electoral process. In a truly democratic culture, there are multiple outlets to express one's perspectives, and different ways to be heard and to contribute to discussion.

We must let children speak in the ways they want, and we must listen in ways that enable them to be heard – only then will children develop a strong sense of self, of self-ownership, and feel empowered to act positively for themselves, their communities and their world. At the same time, education needs to support the development of oracy and dialogue skills to enable children to express views and ideas clearly and effectively. Dialogic practices also engender tolerance and a capacity to sensitively probe alternative points of view. A number of the practitioner chapters highlighted the foundational role of discourse in educational curricula.

Each chapter in this collection endorses the promise of children's agency – either by proposing ways to liberate children's voices or by describing children's rights or capacity to act. All of them, therefore, subscribe to a form of children's empowerment and, if only implicitly, a claim about children's political status. One manifesto sees this thought, asking, if we think children's voices are important – if we think they are consequential and should be listened to – shouldn't we set up political and legal frameworks that truly empower them? However, most of the chapters argue that the best way to support children's agency is through value-led education and the cultivation of practical wisdom – offering the tools necessary to make critical judgements and contribute solutions to shared problems.

This collection is committed to both the democratisation of education and the better integration (in whatever form) of children into democracy. Involving children in decision-making – either in schools or through formal political infrastructure – is no guarantee that the issues pertinent to their future, such as climate change, will be taken more seriously. Democracy is unpredictable – that's the whole point of it. However, affording children a greater role, or more rights, will likely breathe life into these processes – shifting and expanding our conversations and outlook, and possibly the tone in which decision-making (or politics) is conducted. At the very least, it will make it *harder* (though not impossible) for children's concerns and priorities – about climate, or how their schools are run, or anything else – to be dismissed or overlooked.

15.3 Reimagining Knowledge and Learning

A siloed disciplinary structure is at the heart of traditional educational offerings. Yet the complex, interconnected challenges facing society today clearly require a holistic, systems-based response. It is unsurprising, therefore, that the importance of transdisciplinarity is a recurring theme across these chapters. If we want education to embolden children to shape a new and better future – and not simply prepare them for a known or predicted one – we need to orchestrate broader and deeper collaborations between the sciences and arts and ensure curricula are shaped by a range of voices – including children's and families'. Many chapters emphasise the central role that schools play within communities, and several highlight opportunities to include these communities more fully in the educational process itself.

As well as breaking down disciplinary boundaries, curricula ought to broaden their horizons by addressing core human needs and concerns. As several chapters note, this might include the provision of emotional health education or time spent in philosophical exploration, helping young people to address existential questions and find meaning and purpose in their lives. The chapters also describe a wealth of creative ways to incorporate experiential learning and local issues into the curriculum, from direct engagement with nature in gardens and laboratories to learning emotional regulation through yoga poses, from computing coding of traditional knitting patterns in Norway to message boards with talking compounds such as 'Forests Are the Lungs of the World' in Uganda.

If children are to thrive in the future, education needs to foster creativity, problem-solving skills and the ability to engage in thoughtful deliberation, both individually and collectively. It must also unlock ethical considerations and explore our capacity to apply abstract principles to complex, real-world situations. These affordances cannot be bestowed by single disciplines; rather, they are the result of disciplinary collaboration.

15.4 Looking Ahead towards a More Humane and Compassionate Future

Together, these manifestos and practitioner responses are a clarion call for more humane and compassionate approaches to education. To thrive on planet Earth, we must nurture humanity's capacity for empathy, kindness and curiosity and re-establish a mutually supportive, sustainable relationship with the natural world.

In a world increasingly dominated by digital technology, including, especially, the rise of artificial intelligence, we hope to have shown the importance of cultivating human connection, while also appreciating nature and the environmental systems upon which we depend. To do this, we need learning environments where collaboration, dialogue and social interaction are valued; in which the critical thinking skills necessary to navigate ever-expanding digital landscapes are fostered; and which understand the world, and the pedagogic disciplines used to explore it, as holistic.

Ultimately, the vision of education encapsulated in these chapters is about more than transmitting knowledge; it is about empowering individuals to live meaningful and fulfilling lives, contribute to a better world and create a future where humanity can flourish. The true impact of these ideas (and the ideas that might evolve from them) will depend on the willingness of educators, policymakers, families and communities to embrace the challenge, engage in critical dialogue and work together to transform education for the benefit of all.

Finally, though perhaps missing from the foregoing reflection and analysis, it is *essential* to remember that learning and school should be enjoyable, enriching, engaging and fun. Within and alongside the seriousness of these manifestos – and the issues at hand *are* serious – there is also the importance of play, a vital quality in children's childhood experiences. As Biddulph (2025, p. 187) explains,

> Play is not only for children. It is also for the adults who educate them. In modelling the capacity to occupy 'spaces of uncertainty', to face challenges, to consider new ways of engaging in the world, to ask bigger, better questions, to suspend what we believe to think about what might be, is to engage the social imagination. Play is for schools because schools are highly intense social places – and schools that are playful could nurture more healthy, balanced, mentally robust people who can together face the challenges of an uncertain world.

To thrive on planet Earth, we argue that the time *is* for playfulness: in how we respond to the challenges we face and which our children and grandchildren and their grandchildren will have to solve, in the way we come together for a common good and in the ways we articulate an equitable and socially just future.

Reference

Biddulph, J. (2025) 'Play is for children not for school', in Durning, A., Baker, S. and Ramchandani, P. (eds.) *Unlocking research: empowering play in primary education.* Abingdon: Routledge, pp. 185–187.

Index

active citizenship, 7, 11, 12, 34, 36, 38, 41, 49, 88, 199, 209
activism, 31, 205
Argarwal, Anil, 29, 31
agency, 7, 8, 13, 15, 36, 49, 50, 51, 53, 62, 63, 68, 70, 97, 142, 169, 209, 211
AI. *See* artificial intelligence
artificial intelligence, 2, 15, 17, 19, 35, 60, 69, 90, 98, 101, 102, 104, 106, 107, 111, 112, 115, 116, 121, 123, 124, 127, 143, 145, 152, 212, 213
air pollution, 22, 28
Anthropocene, 23

biodiversity, 26, 28, 29, 42, 104, 203
bir Sethi, Kiran, 49

Cambridge Climate Quest, 31
Cambridge Primary Review, 14, 19, 50, 53
Cambridge Zero, 1, 6, 7, 20, 200
Centre for the Future of Democracy, 2, 87, 97
Chartered College of Teaching, 13, 56
Children's Commissioner, 4
children's voices, 2, 10, 15, 19, 31, 34, 48, 49, 50, 51, 53, 57, 62, 63, 63, 66, 67, 68, 70, 71, 84, 88, 90, 99, 176, 181, 209, 210, 211, 212
Citizens Assembly, 31
Cixous, Helene, 18, 19
Class Congress, 64
climate anxiety, 1
climate change, 1, 2, 4, 5, 7, 8, 10, 12, 14, 15, 17, 19, 22, 23, 25, 26, 27, 28, 31, 32, 39, 40, 42, 71, 85, 90, 99, 104, 112, 123, 184, 185, 186, 187, 189, 190, 191, 192, 193, 194, 195, 196, 197, 198, 202, 203, 204, 210, 211

climate justice, 6, 184, 196
Colwell, Mary, 6
community, 4, 5, 7, 9, 13, 15, 19, 39, 42, 45, 57, 68, 81, 84, 95, 109, 115, 137, 141, 140, 142, 143, 147, 152, 180, 181, 191, 199, 202, 207
compassion, 35, 36, 41, 43, 54, 132, 134, 139, 140, 140, 147, 150, 151, 159
conservation, 5, 166, 167, 168, 169, 170, 171, 173, 174, 176, 194, 204
COVID-19 pandemic, 12, 50, 107, 127, 142, 193
creativities thinking, 17
creativity, 7, 15, 16, 17, 36, 41, 42, 65, 69, 70, 101, 104, 105, 106, 107, 109, 112, 115, 122, 124, 140, 156, 163, 212
curriculum design, 13, 14, 31, 38, 39, 43, 47, 53, 54, 64, 65, 67, 68, 70, 91, 93, 93, 94, 100, 111, 114, 123, 142, 140, 141, 145, 147, 148, 153, 155, 157, 158, 172, 175, 176, 177, 179, 181, 181, 182, 192, 198, 200, 202, 203, 204, 205, 206, 207, 212

Dasgupta Review. *See* Dasgupta, Partha
deforestation, 21, 23, 33, 40, 190, 195, 203
democracy, 2, 3, 8, 9, 10, 11, 15, 19, 35, 49, 73, 74, 75, 77, 81, 88, 89, 95, 94, 97, 211
Dewey, John, 62
Dhun School for Now, 67

Ecological Committee, 42
ecological crisis, 25
ecosystem services, 27
extinction, 5, 21, 25, 26

215

food production, 26
Forest School, 141, 180, 202
Fraser, Rod, 54

Gathercole, Sue, 14
geography, 35, 40, 190, 196, 202, 203
Goswami, Usha, 14
grandchildren, 12, 214
Green School (Bali), 39
Greene, Maxine, 17, 53
greenhouse gases, 28, 189, 196
Guterres, António, 21

Harmony Project, 39, 206
health, 6, 21, 24, 28, 82, 90, 97, 126, 131, 132, 134, 135, 136, 139, 140, 142, 143, 145, 147, 151, 155, 159, 161, 164, 172, 174, 194, 199, 202, 209, 212

imagination, 12, 15, 17, 35, 101, 107, 156, 213
India, 24, 28, 30, 31, 62, 64, 67, 68, 200, 204
inequality, 2, 5, 22, 29, 30, 82, 83, 136, 142, 210
innovation, 15, 31, 33, 74, 112
intercultural spaces, 12
Intergovernmental Panel on Climate Change, 5, 20, 23
Intergovernmental Science-Policy Platform on Biodiversity and Ecosystem Services, 26
IPCC. *See* Intergovernmental Panel on Climate Change

Japan, 30, 198
Jubilee Centre for Character and Virtues, 51

Lancet Countdown on Health and Climate, 22
life expectancy, 21, 22
local action, 36, 41, 45, 198

Makerere University, 184, 186
Mexico City, 38, 40, 41
migration, 12, 25, 28, 152, 203, 204

Nakabuye, Hilda, 185
Nakate, Vanessa, 184, 185
Narain, Sunita, 29, 31
nature, 25

oracy, 14, 65, 67, 93, 94, 94, 180, 181, 211

Pahar, Pani, 31, 32, 204
philosophy, 43, 86, 87, 143, 176, 177, 178, 179, 180, 180, 182, 183
phronēsis. *See* practical wisdom
pollution, 5, 21, 26, 44, 185, 190, 194
possibilities thinking, 15, 17, 18, 53, 58, 71, 101, 121
post-human, 15
practical wisdom, 48, 49, 50, 51, 52, 53, 55, 57, 58, 62, 88, 95, 110, 145, 152, 175, 198, 211
professional development, 14, 141
purpose of education, 1, 2, 110, 155, 160, 210
purpose of life, 2, 160

research schools, 12
research-informed teaching, 1, 12, 13, 56, 147
resilience, 25, 35, 41, 42
Round Square, 54
Rudduck, Jean, 48, 62

Satterthwaite, David, 29
science, 1, 15, 21, 46, 47, 99, 102, 106, 109, 112, 113, 114, 115, 124, 127, 137, 138, 148, 166, 170, 171, 172, 173, 174, 175, 176, 181, 181, 182, 190, 202, 203
spirituality, 160, 164, 170, 171, 174, 175
stress, 2, 75, 126, 127, 128, 131, 132, 133, 134, 135, 137, 139, 139, 141, 145, 146, 147, 148, 149, 150, 151, 152, 154, 157, 158, 161
sustainability, 1, 5, 6, 7, 8, 14, 15, 16, 31, 33, 35, 38, 40, 42, 43, 47, 53, 54, 121, 198, 199, 200, 202, 203, 204, 206, 207, 210
Sustainable Development Goals, 27
systems thinking, 35, 41, 44

Index

talking compounds, 193, 212
Thunberg, Greta, 8, 48, 63
tipping points, 24
transdisciplinarity, 1, 6, 15, 17, 98, 99, 100, 101, 102, 103, 104, 105, 106, 107, 108, 110, 111, 112, 113, 115, 116, 117, 121, 122, 123, 181, 200, 200, 203, 204, 209, 212

UCPS. *See* University of Cambridge Primary School
Uganda, 184, 185, 186, 187, 189, 190, 192, 193, 195, 196, 212
UN Convention on the Rights of the Child, 49, 89
UN Sustainable Development Goals, 6, 40, 45

University of Cambridge Primary School, 1, 9, 13, 14, 18, 64, 64, 74, 88, 110, 112, 113, 145, 146, 176, 200
University Training School, 19
Urdd Gobaith Cymru, 58

values, 6, 34, 50, 51, 53, 65, 93, 102, 136, 149, 162, 164, 172, 209, 210

water, 22, 24, 27, 28, 31, 32, 40, 41, 42, 43, 100, 102, 188, 204, 205
Wathuti, Elizabeth, 185
WWF Living Planet Index, 26

Zero Waste Japan, 199

For EU product safety concerns, contact us at Calle de José Abascal, 56–1°, 28003 Madrid, Spain or eugpsr@cambridge.org.

www.ingramcontent.com/pod-product-compliance
Ingram Content Group UK Ltd.
Pitfield, Milton Keynes, MK11 3LW, UK
UKHW021918080226
467821UK00019B/507